THE UNITED STATES 1929-1945

Years of Crisis and Change

THE UNITED STATES 1929-1945

Years of Crisis and Change

Richard S. Kirkendall

Indiana University

McGraw-Hill Book Company

New York   St. Louis   San Francisco   Düsseldorf
Johannesburg   Kuala Lumpur   London   Mexico
Montreal   New Delhi   Panama   Rio de Janeiro
Singapore   Sydney   Toronto

THE
UNITED STATES
1929–1945
Years of Crisis
and Change

1 2 3 4 5 6 7 8 9 0 K P K P 7 9 8 7 6 5 4 3

This book was set in Times Roman by Black Dot, Inc. The editors
were Robert P. Rainier and Sally Barhydt Mobley; the designer was
Joseph Gillians; and the production supervisor was Thomas J. LoPinto.
The photo editor was Juanita James.
The printer and binder was Kingsport Press, Inc.

Library of Congress Cataloging in Publication Data

Kirkendall, Richard Stewart, date
    The United States 1929–1945.

    (Modern America series)
    1. United States—History—1933–1945. 2. United
States—History–1919–1933. 3. United States—Economic
conditions—1918–1945. 4. United States—Foreign re-
lations—1933–1945. I. Title.
E806.K57 1974   973.917   73-16207
ISBN 0-07-034806-5
ISBN 0-07-034805-7 (pbk.)

TO MERLE CURTI

CONTENTS

PREFACE

Change is one of the basic facts of life, and change in human affairs is the historian's basic concern. Thus, American historians have been and will continue to be very interested in the years from 1929 to 1945. During those years, some very significant changes took place, and some others that seemed possible at the time, at least to some people, did not occur. Thus, the period poses some very intriguing, very difficult, and very controversial problems for students of American history.

This volume attempts to grapple with those problems. It does not try to discuss everything that happened in those action-packed years. Attention is limited to the developments that seem most important. I am concerned with the description, measurement, and explanation of the major changes in American life in a very significant period of American history.

This book was written for the college students in American history, especially those in courses that can devote a substantial block of time to the years of the Great Depression and the Second World War. The book seeks to supply students with a fresh interpretation of the period based upon the truly impressive work on it by the American historical profession during the past generation. The work has been impressive in both quantity and quality, and I have tried to benefit from it and to bring to bear upon it my own conceptions of the historian's tasks and the historical process.

In the suggestions for additional reading, I have tried to acknowledge, at least implicitly, my most obvious debts. I am grateful for the opportunities that I have had to read some excellent work and to join in discussions of the period with many of the historians who have written about it. I value highly my membership in the historical profession and in that part of it that is concerned with what one member has called the "Age of Roosevelt."

The editor of this series on Modern America, Dewey Grantham, is one of the historians who has helped and encouraged me during the past decade. At this point, I wish especially to thank him for giving me the opportunity to write this book and for supplying good advice and words of encouragement as I worked on it. I am also grateful to Robert P. Rainier, Sally Mobley, and others at McGraw-Hill for their patience as well as their encouragement and help.

As with several other things that I have done, this book is a product of a very valuable teaching opportunity from 1958 to 1973. It was supplied by the University of Missouri, Columbia, and I am grateful to members of the administration who supported my efforts and to my colleagues and students who stimulated and assisted them in many ways.

The book was written at home and required the cooperation of my wife and sons. I am grateful to them for this and for the many joys of life with them.

I welcome this opportunity to dedicate a book to Merle Curti. I have known him well for more than twenty years and have long regarded my close association with him as one of my greatest privileges. I am grateful for his teaching and for his friendship.

Richard S. Kirkendall

THE UNITED STATES 1929-1945

Years of Crisis and Change

Introduction

For the American people, the years from 1929 to 1945 were packed with action. The nation was hit by two crises: first the Depression and then the war. And these crises generated powerful pressures for changes in the nation's economic system and its role in the world.

In this situation, two major developments took place. A system of collective capitalism was established, and the United States became a major power in world affairs. Collective capitalism and America's large role in the world were, however, not simply responses to the Great Depression and Fascist aggression; they had been taking shape for many years before the 1930s. They merely evolved further, though very significantly, from 1929 to 1945. Furthermore, these features of modern American life had not ceased to be matters of debate by 1945; their future at the end of the period remained uncertain.

Nevertheless, looking back on the period, we can now see that these aspects of American life became quite firmly established during those years. One feature of collective capitalism that had taken shape long before—big business—though seriously criticized in the period, survived and in fact was strengthened in many ways, although its power was reduced. The other major features—government and labor—grew at an accelerated pace and became much stronger so that they could justifiably be labeled "big" by the end of the period. Although people could still talk of destroying them, chances of doing so were slight. In other words, the building of the structure of collective capitalism that had been going on since the late nineteenth century was essentially completed during the "Age of Roosevelt". In addition, the country, still fearful of a large role in the world at the beginning of the period, seemed to most Americans incapable of escaping such a role by 1945. The chief uncertainties concerned the way in which the nation would play its role and the size of demands that it would make upon the American people.

Part One

The Great Depression and the New Deal

Chapter 1

The Coming of the Great Depression

Late in 1929, the economy, which had seemed so strong to its many admirers, collapsed disastrously, producing widespread and intense suffering. The American economic system experienced a very big change in a very short period of time, a change from prosperity to depression, and the crisis was a severe one. All groups in American society felt the tremendous impact of the Depression, and most Americans suffered from it. The crisis resulted from fundamental weaknesses in the economy. The great men of power—the men who were capable of making and enforcing the big decisions concerning its operations—did not know how to operate the system successfully. The American people in the 1930s were forced to pay a heavy price.

One of the basic difficulties was the distribution of income. At the beginning of the 1920s, the top 5 percent of the people had had 24 percent of the disposable income; by 1929, their percentage had increased to 35. In the same period the top 1 percent moved from 12 to 20 percent of the disposable income and 31 to 36 percent of the wealth. At the same time better than 60 percent of the population lived below the poverty line.

This situation resulted from the unequal distribution of power in the economy, the decisions of business leaders, and the bias of the national administration. Business decisions during the 1920s stressed increasing output per worker, holding the line on wages and on the prices of raw materials, maintaining consumer prices at a high level, and inflating profits. Government policies were based on great confidence in the wisdom of business leaders. Thus, the central government refused to attack business policies, did not help labor develop the power needed to force increases in the worker's income, and made little effort to raise farm prices.

In this situation, most wage earners and farmers did not prosper. While output per worker in manufacturing increased by nearly 40 percent, the real income of industrial workers rose only 11 percent. Unemployment during the twenties rose as high as 5 million, was never lower than 1 million, and usually ranged from 1.5 to 3 million. In other words, most of the time, 4 to 7 percent of the labor force was unemployed.

Agriculture experienced a drop of nearly 45 percent in its share of the national income. The price break of 1920 had dropped farm income from nearly $17 billion in 1919 to less than $9 billion in 1921. Throughout the 1920s, it never reached $12 billion, and in 1929, the purchasing power of farm goods was only 91 percent of the prewar level. Increased use of fertilizer and machinery had resulted in a great increase in farm production at the same time that demand for farm products had dropped.

Dividends and corporate profits, on the other hand, were high during most of the twenties and increased by more than 60 percent during the decade.

The economy of the 1920s, in short, did not produce the mass purchasing power needed in a mass production economy. Looking back, a banker, Frank Vanderlip, suggested that "capital kept too much and labor did not have enough to buy its share of things." And a historian, Arthur M. Schleslinger, Jr., agreed: "The mass of the population simply lacked the increase in purchasing power to enable them to absorb the increase in goods." As a consequence, the home building and the automobile industries, two that had expanded productive capacity tremendously during the early years of the decade, cut production well before it came to an end and forced industries that were dependent on them to make cuts. These industries were not able to sell all the things they were capable of producing even though millions of people wanted their products. Those people did not have the dollars needed to buy homes and cars. By the summer of 1929, many industries found their productive capacity ahead of effective demand and felt compelled to cut back.

With the masses unable to function as vigorous consumers, the economy by the late 1920s was heavily dependent on the willingness of the upper-income groups to buy luxury items and invest in job-producing enterprises.

Another weakness in the economy was the nation's failure to adjust to its postwar status as a creditor nation, owed money rather than owing it to other nations. As a debtor, before the war, the United States had been able to export goods, for those exports had served as a means of paying debts. During the war, however, Europeans had been forced to use their investments here to buy goods, and they had also been forced to borrow money in order to purchase more of the things they needed. During the 1920s, the nation returned to the high protective tariff system of the past, refused to import more than was exported, and thus made it impossible for Europeans to get out of debt. In this situation, Americans made new foreign loans, thereby supplying Europeans with dollars needed to pay debts and buy American goods.

Thus, the continuation of American sales abroad at high levels as well as the repayment of loans depended upon the continued willingness of Americans to make foreign loans.

In this economic situation, the stock market crash of October 1929 played a highly significant role. The crash was preceded by a stock market boom that moved the Dow-Jones industrial average from 99 in October 1925 to 381 in September 1929. The tax-cutting and easy-money policies of the federal government and the Federal Reserve banks facilitated the boom, providing investors with funds that they poured into the market. The boom depended upon a steady supply of new customers for stocks who were willing to buy at ever-higher prices because of confidence that stock prices would go even higher.

Confidence that stocks would continue to rise evaporated in the fall of 1929. The decisive influence, apparently, was the decline in production that had been underway for several months. The decline suggested that some industries had developed greater capacity than the economy could use. Also, the stock market boom itself must have generated concerns about the future. With these influences at work, the market began to tumble in October 1929. By July 1932, the Dow-Jones had dropped to 41. Nearly 80 percent of the total value of stocks had been wiped out. Even the "blue chips", the stocks that seemingly one could always rely upon, had fallen sharply. American Telephone and Telegraph had dropped from 304 to 72; United States Steel had plummeted from 262 to 22; General Motors from 73 to 8; Montgomery Ward from 138 to 4.

The crash hit and shattered the confidence of the men who had been buying the luxury items, making the investments and the foreign loans, managing the leading firms, buying the raw materials, and employing the workers. It damaged economically and psychologically the very men upon whom the economy had become so very dependent.

Thus, business confidence declined after 1929, and the key men in the economy stopped playing their essential roles. Business leaders cut wages, prices, production, and employment and refused to invest and loan. The profit picture was profoundly discouraging. Industrial profits after taxes dropped from $8.3 billion in 1929 to a minus $3.4 billion in 1932. Many businessmen concluded that investment had been too heavy in the 1920s and that the economy now had greater capacity than it needed, and private investment in the American economy dropped from $16 billion in 1929 to $900 million in 1932.

And the federal government did not move in vigorously to fill the void created by the retreat of the businessmen. The leaders in Washington had great confidence in the business system, and they did not believe that government was obligated to fill the investment gap.

Thus, the economy spiraled downward, and as it did, millions of Americans were hurt. The influence of the Depression spread into every part of the land and affected every group in society. Millions of people sustained serious economic losses, but loss characterized other aspects of life as well. Many people suffered psychologically as well as economically. Some lost confidence in themselves; others lost confidence in the system and/or its leaders.

Even business leaders suffered. They experienced economic losses as the share of disposable income for the top 1 percent dropped from 20 to 13 percent and for the top 5 percent from 35 to 30 percent, and the share of the nation's wealth held by the richest 1 percent of the population dropped from 36 percent in 1929 to 28 percent in 1933.

Business leaders also suffered psychologically. They had had great confidence in themselves, their policies, and their ability to control the system. Now, they could not come up with a solution, and they offered much foolish advice. Some suggested reductions in spending by government and consumers; others called for a nationwide agreement to restrict production and raise prices.

The prestige of business leaders dropped sharply. It had been at an unusually high point, but now many Americans concluded that these men were incompetent and immoral. Never before had the American people had such a low opinion of the major figures from industry and finance.

The farmers were also hit very hard. By 1933, national income had dropped about 40 percent since 1929, but farm income had dropped 60 percent, reaching $5 billion. The price of cotton, which had averaged 12.5 cents per pound from 1909 to 1914, was only 5.5 cents in February 1933; the price of wheat dropped from 88.4 to 32.3 cents per bushel in the same period; but the farmer's tax burden doubled from 1914 to 1933; his debt load was heavy in the early 1930s; and the prices of goods he needed to buy did not drop nearly as far as farm prices. While agricultural prices dropped nearly 63 percent from 1929 to 1933, industrial prices dropped only 15 percent. Industrialists could control production more effectively so that agricultural production declined only 6 percent while industrial production dropped 42 percent. Thus, by February 1933, farm commodities could purchase only half as much as they could before the war. Many once-prosperous farmers had been impoverished by the Depression.

Thousands of farmers lost their farms and became tenants of insurance companies and other institutions that had made loans to farmers. Such changes took place even in areas that had enjoyed prosperity, including Iowa's excellent farming regions. Prominent land-owning families whose farms had been a continuous source of income now lost their fortunes, not, one Iowa lawyer noted, "as a result of extravagance or carlessness, but because of conditions beyond their control, and which were not envisaged by the most farsighted."

Lower on the social ladder, thousands of tenants were forced off the land as the landowners no longer needed them, providing themes of suffering, displacement, and migration for John Steinbeck, Woodie Guthrie, and other talented observers of depressed America. Entire families were set in motion. "The roads of the West and Southwest teem with hungry hitchhikers," one Oklahoman reported in 1932. A woman, wearing a ragged coat and hugging a dead chicken that she had found on the road, commented to him: "They promised me a chicken in the pot, and now I got mine."

In the cities and towns, wage earners experienced a drop in income of nearly 40 percent from 1929 to 1933. Even those fortunate enough to hold on to jobs experienced hardships, for their wages and hours were cut sharply as work-sharing schemes were adopted by many companies. The workweek in manufacturing dropped from more than 44 hours in 1929 to 40.5 two years later, while weekly earnings in manufacturing moved from $28.63 to $22.23 and then continued to fall into 1933. Unemployment reached 4 million by January 1930; 8 million a year later; 11.5 million by the beginning of 1932; 14.5 million a year after that and more than 15 million by March 1933. Unemployment was not spread evenly over the work force. It was unusually high among blacks and among workers in heavy industries, groups that had been paid very low wages. For many, the period of unemployment was long and included the frustrations involved in being turned down repeatedly when looking for a new job. And the unemployed did not have the unemployment insurance that was available in other Western countries.

The unemployed turned in many directions in search of help.

Interest in jury duty increased, as did the number of shoeshine and newspaper "boys"; street corners in the business districts were occupied by people selling apples or begging for money. "Brother, can you spare a dime?" Al Jolson asked in a pop tune of the time. Many people lived in shanties, flophouses, caves, pipes, and parks; some even welcomed a chance to go to jail.

Many of the unemployed of all ages and both sexes moved about the country in a desperate, futile search for jobs or in an aimless effort to escape intolerable conditions at home. A railroad reported that it had discovered nearly 200,000 people trying to ride on its boxcars in 1931. (Less than 14,000 had been discovered in 1929.) By early 1933, the nation had an estimated 1 million transients. Americans had always been highly mobile, but their mobility in the past had had direction to it. Now, many drifted about aimlessly while established patterns, such as migration from Europe to America and from farm to city, were disrupted by the Depression.

Suffering was especially severe for the children of the unemployed. Many did not have adequate clothing or shelter. Many did not have an adequate diet during crucial years of physical development.

In the past, many Americans of the comfortable classes had comforted themselves with the theory that only the immoral were poor. Now, it was hard to hold on to that theory. The unemployed were not "a good-for-nothing lot . . . out of work because of their own fault," a social worker testified. ". . . They had had good job records and are active, earnest human beings. All they want is a job." Failing to find one, a study concluded, the "once resourceful worker becomes pauperized, loses faith in himself and society."

The urban middle classes also suffered. They were hit by the stock market crash as they had purchased stocks; they were hurt by the epidemic of bank failures for they had put money in savings accounts and could not recover it after their banks failed. They were hurt by the loss of customers if they owned their own businesses and by the slashing of salaries if they worked for someone else. They were hurt by the reduction in the number of jobs for managers, engineers, chemists, architects, advertising men, and schoolteachers as companies cut their work forces on all levels and governments and school boards were forced by the decline in tax revenues to cut their budgets. Some experienced a loss of status as they were compelled to take off their white collar and don a blue one when the only job to be found was a wage-earning job.

These experiences challenged the beliefs of middle-class Americans. They had behaved as they had been taught they should if they wished to succeed. They had obtained an education, worked hard, saved

Figure 1   A Bread Line *(Wide World Photos)*

some money, and invested some. But now they were experiencing failure rather than success. Surely they were not to blame! Could the system be at fault? Their newspapers and magazines told them of respected members of their communities, such as highly regarded bankers, who had betrayed their positions of trust, even looting their banks and businesses. The experiences suggested to the middle-class American that his personal qualities alone could not guarantee success. He depended heavily upon the quality of the system.

That system was in trouble. It was not nearly as strong nor as skillfully directed as it had appeared to be. It was not as far ahead of other countries as Americans had long believed. In fact, industrial production dropped much farther in the U.S. than it did in France, the United

Kingdom, and Japan. For Americans, these were confidence-shattering developments.

American history had developed a crisis of serious proportions. The American people were caught in the type of situation that produces change. The question in the early 1930s was not "Would change take place?" Instead, the questions were "How much change would there be?" "What kinds of changes would be made?"

SUGGESTIONS FOR ADDITIONAL READING

The major surveys of the period include efforts to explain the coming of the Depression. Important examples are William E. Leuchtenburg, *The Perils of Prosperity 1914–1932*, The University of Chicago Press, Chicago, 1958; John D. Hicks, *Republican Ascendancy, 1921–1933*, Harper, New York, 1960; and Arthur M. Schlesinger, Jr., *The Age of Roosevelt: The Crisis of the Old Order, 1919–1933*, Houghton Mifflin, Boston, 1957. Perhaps the most interesting and stimulating account is John Kenneth Galbraith's *The Great Crash, 1929*, Houghton Mifflin, Boston, 1961. See also Robert Aaron Gordon, *Business Fluctuations,* 2d. ed., Harper & Row, New York, 1961. Leuchtenburg's splendid essay in C. Vann Woodward, ed., *The Comparative Approach to American History*, Basic Books, New York and London, 1968, puts the American experience in international perspective.

For the impact of the Depression, David A. Shannon's collection of contemporary accounts, *The Great Depression*, Prentice-Hall, Englewood Cliffs, N. J., 1960, provides a good place to begin. On the farmer, Van L. Perkins, *Crisis in Agriculture: The Agricultural Adjustment Administration and the New Deal, 1933*, University of California Press, Berkeley and Los Angeles, 1969, is excellent. And Irving Bernstein, *The Lean Years: A History of American Workers 1920–1933*, Houghton Mifflin, Boston, 1960, is the best book on the worker in the period. Also see Bernard Sternsher, ed., *Hitting Home: The Great Depression in Town and Country,* Quadrangle, Chicago, 1970. On the businessman, see Thomas C. Cochran, *The American Business System: A Historical Perspective 1900–1955*, Harvard, Cambridge, Mass., 1957, and "The History of a Business Society," *Journal of American History*, vol. 54, pp. 5–18, 1967.

Chapter 2

President Hoover
and the Great Crisis
of American Capitalism

The man who presided over the collapse of the American economy and had the initial responsibility for dealing with the crisis was Herbert Hoover, the thirty-first President. Although he did not attempt to use government funds to fill the investment gap created by the retreat of the businessman, he did not endorse the do-nothing philosophy for government and attempt to rely only on the military and police forces to suppress any agitation and violence that the Depression might produce. Instead, he enlarged the role of government in economic affairs in an effort to protect the system and promote its recovery. In a cautious fashion, inhibited by his conservative philosophy, he promoted change, enlarging the operations of government while trying to rely chiefly on business leaders, and he opened doors to greater changes.

Hoover brought to the White House and to the Depression crisis that emerged soon after his arrival there a point of view that included great confidence in the business system and a willingness to use government to help businessmen, especially to help them cooperate, seeing this as an effective way of promoting the general welfare. He also believed that the federal government should encourage others to cooperate with it and with one another. His belief in voluntary cooperation had appeared in his activities during World War I. As Secretary of Commerce, he had promoted trade associations, and as President prior to the crash, he had developed a farm program, enacted by the Agricultural Marketing Act of 1929 and administered by the Federal Farm Board, that encouraged commercial farmers to form cooperatives.

The crash and the Depression did not alter Hoover's point of view. At first, he blamed the latter on speculation. Then, as the Depression worsened, he blamed it on fundamental weaknesses abroad that were hurting the American economy. Foreign systems were to blame. Thus he rejected advice from those who said that fundamental changes were needed in the American system, and he placed heavy emphasis upon the restoration of confidence, giving frequent pep talks and assuring the people that their economic institutions were sound and the Depression would soon end, as had all downturns since the 1890s. But he also rejected the advice of those who argued that he should behave as earlier presidents had when faced with a depression, not "interfere" with the operations of the economy and permit "natural forces" to produce recovery. "This is no time for rash experiments in men or measures," ex-President Coolidge advised in the fall of 1930. Hoover, however, feared the social and political consequences of a hands off policy, and he tried to attack the economic problems as he understood them and pushed forward with confidence that government and business, working together, could control the business cycle.

In the early stages of the Depression, Hoover employed his policy of "voluntary cooperation." He attempted to use the powers of the presidency, which he regarded as rather narrowly limited, to influence the behavior of private and public groups and institutions in American society. Soon after the crash, he held a series of conferences, chiefly with business leaders but also with labor leaders and state and local officials. The conferences produced agreements about maintaining production, employment, and wages and expanding construction and led to the formation of a National Business Survey Conference of business leaders to promote these goals by persuasion and reassurance. The program had only a limited role for the President. He functioned largely as adviser and cheerleader. Congress had no role, for Hoover believed that no legislation was needed. He did encourage governments to maintain and expand their construction programs and thus did at least call upon Congress to appropriate the funds needed to accelerate development of projects already under way. Yet, he rejected proposals during 1930 and 1931 for costly new federal or federally financed programs created in response to the crisis, even though earlier he had maintained that an increase in spending for public works could reduce unemployment in a depression.

Voluntary cooperation was also applied to the farm problem. Agricultural officials formed stabilization corporations that made loans on wheat and cotton, holding portions of the output of each off the market until prices improved. The officials also called upon the producers of these commodities to cut back on production. The administration relied upon persuasion, rejected stronger methods of control, and assumed that the chief role of the federal government in agricultural production was to supply advice so that farmers could devise sound plans as industrial corporations did.

In October 1930, with unemployment mounting, Hoover formed a President's Emergency Committee for Employment, another experiment in voluntary cooperation. To provide relief, he had been relying chiefly upon existing social welfare agencies, private and public, plus private individuals, and now he attempted to coordinate and stimulate the work of these agencies. He believed that this was the "American way," which indeed it was as the plight of the unemployed had traditionally been the responsibility of private individuals and groups, and many people at first were reluctant to turn even to city governments for relief. He was confident that the local agencies could succeed with only a small amount of help from the federal government.

Reluctant to rely on state agencies, Hoover strongly opposed a large role for the federal government. He insisted that relief was an obligation of others. It was chiefly an obligation of neighbors and local communities. They were obliged to help the underprivileged people in their midst. He feared the destruction of the American character by federal action. Federal relief for the needy would harm those who received help from the government. It would also weaken the character of those who had traditionally been responsible for assisting the unfortunate. They must not be permitted to shift that burden to Washington.

Hoover also feared that a large federal relief program would destroy business confidence. He continued to believe that the restoration of confidence was the basic need, and he believed that it was necessary to avoid large budgeting deficits in order to promote business confidence. Businessmen, he was convinced, believed that government must balance its budget. If it failed to do so, businessmen would have serious doubts about the future. A vast program of relief for the unemployed would, of course, create a large budget deficit.

Hoover's philosophy involved a social theory as well as economic and political theories. He stressed society's dependence upon upper-income groups. The poor depended upon them for charity and relief; everyone depended on them for job-creating and product-creating investment. His philosophy did not involve a crucial role for the masses. He did not emphasize the economic significance of the consuming public.

In October 1931, Presidential action led to still another experiment in voluntary cooperation. This step followed a record-breaking rate of bank failures and the increasing reluctance of banks to make loans as bank loans could not be repaid and bankers lacked the funds needed to meet escalating demands from their depositors for their savings. Bank failures had been numerous in the 1920s, owing to fundamental weaknesses in the banking system, including too many small, inadequately supervised banks, and to other weaknesses in the economy, such as low farm prices, but now failures jumped from 651 in 1929 to nearly 2,300 in 1931, a new high in the nation's history. Hoover put pressure on the banking leaders to establish a National Credit Corporation that would enable the strong banks to save weak ones. Those capable of contributing were expected to establish a credit reserve fund that could provide banks with the money needed to avoid closing down. The banking leaders regarded the proposal as foolish, but he assumed that the new corporation would restore public confidence in the banks, thereby enabling them to avoid demands for money from depositors who feared their banks would soon close. He also assumed that the program would encourage bankers to make loans. Furthermore, the program attracted him because it did not require congressional action.

The policy of voluntary cooperation assumed that the entire country would benefit from cooperation between government and business. Production and employment would expand; prices would rise. The nation would move out of the Depression.

Unfortunately the policy failed. It failed to improve farm prices. They continued to fall sharply while agricultural production dropped only slightly, and the warehouses of the stabilization corporations became filled with commodities that could not be sold.

The policy failed also to produce the desired behavior by business leaders. The nation's giants, as well as many other firms, cut construction, employment, and wages. Faced with deflationary pressures, business leaders were convinced that they could not live up to the agreements and also make a profit. These men were not, after all, running charitable institutions.

In addition, business leaders were not faced with a strong labor movement capable of enforcing agreements to maintain wages. In fact, the unions lost members as unemployment grew, dropping from nearly 3.5 million in 1929 to less than 3 million four years later. Labor's chief weapon, the strike, lost much of its effectiveness. With job and profit opportunities in decline, the strike was used much less frequently, and when used, it was most often designed to prevent wage cuts and usually failed. Neither management nor the administration paid much attention to the feeble demands of labor.

The policy of voluntarism failed to provide adequate relief for the unemployed. As unemployment grew, the welfare agencies were swamped with requests for help. By the fall of 1931, the relief programs in nearly every city were bankrupt, and Hoover's theory of local responsibility had been discredited. The local agencies simply did not have the means to deal with a national problem of gigantic size. And the experience forced many Americans to surrender their traditional beliefs about the ways in which relief should be provided and to turn to state and national governments.

The banking policy also failed. The leading bankers did not cooperate adequately, fearing that cooperation would weaken their institutions, and a new wave of bank failures hit the nation at the end of 1931. Furthermore, the banks were not called upon for large amounts of money that could be poured into productive enterprises. With prospects dim and confidence low, businessmen had little or no interest in enlarging their operations and moving into new ventures.

The failure of Hoover's policy had two major consequences. First of all, it contributed to the decline in the prestige of the business leaders and bankers. They seemed to have supplied additional evidence of their incompetence. In addition, the failure increased pressure for more government action.

The economic collapse of Europe in 1931 was one source of Hoover's difficulties. It accelerated the downward course of the American economy. The United States had added to Europe's troubles by raising tariffs still higher in 1930. He had accepted that move, but now he devoted some of his energies to efforts to strengthen foreign economies, obtaining congressional approval for a moratorium on the payment of debts owed to the United States by European powers. He also pressed for an international economic conference to find solutions to international economic problems.

Early in 1932, the economic activities of the federal government were enlarged significantly. In January, Congress passed Hoover's proposal of December for the establishment of a Reconstruction Finance Corporation. This constituted a pragmatic and reluctant departure from his ideals in response to his recognition that voluntary cooperation had not been enough. The bankers, who did not share his belief in it, demanded more help from the federal government, and Congress passed this major piece of legislation. It cooperated with Hoover even though the Democrats, as a result of the congressional elections of 1930, now controlled the House and nearly controlled the Senate.

The RFC provided direct federal relief to business. The new government institution, which was supplied with capital of $500 million and authority to borrow additional funds, made loans to banks and other economic institutions. As it pumped money into the economy, the number of bank failures dropped sharply. The agency aided men, including prominent bankers of large firms, who opposed government aid to nonbusiness groups, and it was criticized as a "millionaire's dole." Hoover, however, defended the RFC with arguments about the great importance of the financial institutions to the entire economy. The government was not, he insisted, trying to save only the men who owned these institutions. The main purpose was to save the millions of people who depended on them for their savings and their jobs.

RFC policies did protect important institutions, but the policies, even when supplemented by antidepression policies of the Federal Reserve System, did not result in the expansion of bank loans. Continued doubts about the future discouraged banks from lending and business from borrowing.

At the same time that RFC was getting into operation, Hoover resisted pressure for the further enlargement of government. For example, he turned down a farm relief scheme called the Voluntary Domestic Allotment Plan. It was devised by social scientists, chiefly M. L. Wilson, an agricultural economist from Montana State College who had firsthand knowledge of the critically depressed conditions of Montana's wheat farmers. He proposed that the government should do more than talk to farmers. It should employ its taxing and spending powers to reduce output. His plan involved a tax on farm commodities to be paid by the processors when they handled these products and to be used to finance a system of payments to farmers who agreed to adjust production. Each farmer could refuse to participate but would be encouraged to do so not merely by the promise of high prices in the market but by payments to him from the government. This, however, was more government action than Hoover could accept. To him, voluntary cooperation was the only way to make farming profitable while maintaining freedom for farmers.

Hoover also resisted pressure for the expansion of federal expenditures for public works and relief. People close to the unemployment problem, including the social workers who staffed the welfare agencies and the mayors of big cities, concluded that the local communities could not manage it and insisted that the federal government must send either relief or troops. Progressives in the Senate, led by Edward Costigan of

Colorado, Robert La Follette, Jr., of Wisconsin, and Robert Wagner of New York, took up the call for federal action. Wagner, an immigrant raised in a working-class family in New York City and a Tammany Democrat, had been an advocate of social welfare legislation since the Progressive era, and now he, La Follette, Costigan, and several others insisted that the Congress must become more active and the government must attack the problem of unemployment directly and restore purchasing power in order to bring the country out of the Depression.

As 1932 moved forward, opposition to federal action declined. Early in the year, opposition from conservative congressmen, business spokesmen, and the White House remained very effective, and progress was hampered also by conflict among the advocates of federal action over the question of federal grants to the states versus federal loans to them. But as the Depression worsened, the inability of existing programs to deal with the problem of unemployment became increasingly obvious, and support for federal action of some sort grew rapidly. Thus, with John Nance Garner, the Speaker of the House, as well as Wagner playing leading roles, Congress in July authorized a $2.1 billion program of federal loans to the states and federal public works.

Hoover, however, vetoed the measure. He did so even though it included the loan principle that he favored. He was opposed to additional federal public works, favoring only revenue-producing, self-liquidating public works by the states, and he was opposed to the cost of the program, even though the bill called for a much smaller program than Wagner, La Follette, and Costigan desired.

Hoover remained very much concerned about the condition of the federal budget. "The course of unbalanced budgets is the road to ruin," he had warned in May. His budget had become unbalanced, for federal expenditures had moved from $2.6 billion in 1929 to $4.2 billion two years later while receipts fell from $3.8 billion to $2 billion. The deficit had troubled him so much that late in 1931 he had proposed a large increase in taxes. "Our first step toward recovery is to reestablish confidence and thus restore the flow of credit which is the very basis of our economic life," he announced in explanation of his proposal. "The first requirement of confidence and of economic recovery is financial stability of the United States Government." When the decision was made, confidence was at a very low level, as the banking crisis indicated.

Most members of Congress shared this belief in the importance of balancing the budget. The proposal, which was worked out in cooperation with the congressional leadership, included a sales tax, a form that most businessmen preferred to the income tax. Most of the leading Democratic congressmen, heavily influenced by Bernard Baruch, a large contributor to their campaigns and a strong advocate of a balanced budget, endorsed the proposal. A coalition of Democrats and progressive Republicans from the South, the Middle West, and the Far West, however, successfully rebelled against the leaders, not on the issue of a tax increase, but on the sales tax, arguing that it imposed an undesirable burden on lower income groups and interfered with the tax programs of the states. Only Wagner, La Follette, and a few others dissented from the belief in a balanced budget, and thus taxes were increased in the Revenue Act of 1932, which Hoover signed in June. It raised income and estate taxes and imposed excise taxes on many products, and it did increase federal receipts. It failed, however, to balance the budget.

A new federal program contributed to Hoover's failure to balance the budget. After his veto of the relief bill, Congress passed an Emergency Relief and Reconstruction Act that authorized the RFC to make loans to the states for relief and productive, self-liquidating public works and authorized the federal government to spend $300 million on public works. Hoover accepted this measure in July 1932.

Hoover had departed from his principles in accepting this small program of federal relief. It was the first measure of its kind. He had delayed the move, had successfully insisted upon loans rather than grants to the states and upon projects that would eventually pay for themselves rather than merely provide jobs, and had held spending below the level desired by the strongest advocates of federal relief, but he accepted this departure from the past. The program, however, was administered very cautiously, and pressure for enlargement and other changes mounted during Hoover's last months in office.

The President contributed nothing but his signature to the major labor law of the period. This was the Norris-La Guardia Act of 1932. It successfully attacked two important antiunion weapons; the yellow-dog contract and the use of injunctions in labor disputes. Two progressive Republicans, George Norris of Nebraska and Fiorello La Guardia of New York City, were chiefly responsible for the measure.

Although restrained by his philosophy, Hoover was a highly significant president. He did expand the economic role of government. In fact, to some, he seemed a dangerous centralizer. Ultraconservative James Beck, a Republican congressman from Pennsylvania, complained in 1932: "Few states are more socialistic than the U.S. Russia is no more bureaucratic than America." And Democratic Senator Carter Glass of Virginia believed that Hoover's recommendations in 1932 were "tainted with State socialism."

Hoover was not attempting to create something new. He was attempting only to promote the recovery of the business system of the

1920s. He regarded it as fundamentally sound and the embodiment of the finest ideals. The system did not need to be discarded. It did not even need to be changed significantly.

The President's approach to the Depression involved elements of both tradition and novelty. Americans had long believed that the government had significant economic responsibilities. Hoover agreed. They had not believed that the government was responsible for recovery from a depression. He did believe that. Thus, he took an old idea and applied it to a situation to which it had not been applied before. Furthermore, he was influenced by a relatively new assumption. He assumed that men could control the business cycle.

The President made changes that opened the door to additional and greater changes. By trying but failing to control the business cycle, he helped, in spite of his own intentions, to lead people to the conclusion that they should not rely as heavily upon business leaders as he had and that they should accept a much greater expansion of government than he could accept.

Thus, Hoover and the experiences of the Congress while he served in the White House were very important parts of the background to the New Deal. Before he left office, pressure was mounting for a larger role for the federal government in many areas, and Congress was becoming willing to attack the crisis more actively.

SUGGESTIONS FOR ADDITIONAL READING

Historians have long recognized that Hoover promoted as well as resisted change. Broadus Mitchell in *Depression Decade: From New Era through New Deal 1929–1941*, Rinehart, New York, 1947, was one of the first to develop the theme. Harris Gaylord Warren, *Herbert Hoover and the Great Depression*, Macmillan, New York, 1959, and Albert U. Romasco, *The Poverty of Abundance: Hoover, the Nation, the Depression*, Oxford, New York, 1965, developed it much more fully. See also Carl Degler, "The Ordeal of Herbert Hoover," *Yale Review*, vol. 52, pp. 565–583, 1963. For especially critical interpretations, consult Richard Hofstadter, "Herbert Hoover and the Crisis of American Individualism," in *The American Political Tradition and the Men Who Made It*, Knopf, New York, 1948, and Arthur M. Schlesinger's *Crisis of the Old Order*. Hoover defended his record in his memoirs, published by Macmillan in 1952.

Scholarship on the period is now moving quite rapidly, and specialized works are appearing. One of the most important is Herbert Stein, *The Fiscal Revolution in America*, The University of Chicago Press, Chicago, 1969. On unemployment and relief, consult Bernstein's *Lean Years* and Sternsher's *Hitting Home*. Susan Estabrook Kennedy's *The Banking Crisis of 1933*, University Press of Kentucky, Lexington, 1973, provides an unusually revealing picture of the political economy in 1932–1933. See also Gerald D. Nash, "Herbert Hoover and the Origins of the Reconstruction Finance Corporation," *Mississippi Valley Historical Review*, vol. 46, pp. 455–468, 1959. Jordan A. Schwarz, *The Interregnum of Despair: Hoover, Congress, and the Depression*, The University of Illinois Press, Urbana, 1970, and J. Joseph Huthmacher, *Robert A. Wagner and the Rise of Urban Liberalism*, Atheneum, New York, 1968, are very valuable on Congress in the period, while William D. Rowley, *M. L. Wilson and the Campaign for the Domestic Allotment Plan,* University of Nebraska Press, Lincoln, 1970, should be consulted on efforts to solve the farm problem.

Chapter 3

The Swing to the Democrats

By 1932, pressures for change were on the rise. They pointed most clearly to the removal of Herbert Hoover from power, but beyond that the direction was unclear. Some men hoped and others feared that a revolution would take place. But the political developments of 1932 were not quite so spectacular. The main theme was a big swing to the Democratic party and the election to the presidency of a progressive Democrat who shared Hoover's commitment to capitalism and his determination to preserve it but had a stronger interest in producing changes in the system.

Hoover's great reputation had been destroyed by events since 1929. Bitter criticism of him had become commonplace. An often-told though apochryphal tale captured the change that had taken place in his prestige. The story involved a conversation between the President and his Secretary of the Treasury. They were walking in Lafayette Square across from the White House, and Hoover asked for the loan of a nickel in order to call a friend. "Here's a dime," Mellon replied. "Call all of your friends."

And when Babe Ruth demanded $80,000 from the Yankees and was criticized for asking for more money than the President received, the slugger replied: "I had a better season than he did."

If unfair, the collapse of Hoover's reputation was understandable. In part, it was a consequence of the contrast between expectations and results. Expectations had been very high when he became president. He was the "great engineer," the first representative of "the modern techni- cal mind" to serve at the head of a government. And Hoover's own words had contributed to the rise of those expectations. "Given a chance to go forward with the policies of the last eight years," he had promised in 1928, "we shall soon, with the help of God, be in the sight of the day when poverty shall be banished from the nation." He had been given that chance, but prosperity had been displaced by depression, and poverty was increasing rapidly. People were now disillusioned and even felt betrayed, and, just as he once had given Republican policies credit for prosperity, he was now blamed for the Depression.

An apparent contradiction in his policies also contributed to Hoo- ver's decline. He seemed so eager to supply government aid to business and so reluctant to extend it to the unemployed. To many, this suggested a probusiness bias and even encouraged them to maintain that he was actually doing nothing to bring the nation out of the Depression.

Hoover added to his woes by following the advice of the advocates of suppression in the summer of 1932. An "army" of more than 20,000 unemployed and discouraged veterans of World War I moved into Washington to press for full and immediate payment of the bonus that Congress in 1924 had approved for payment in 1945. They assumed that the nation owed this to them and that payment now would stimulate recovery. Hoover opposed payment for budgetary reasons and because he doubted that most veterans needed help from their government, and, while the House said yes, the Senate defeated the proposal on June 17. Within the next month, several thousand veterans left Washington but most remained, hoping their government would reconsider. The adminis- tration urged these petitioners to leave; several small skirmishes took place; the President on July 28 sent the United States Army, under the command of the Chief of Staff, General Douglas MacArthur, into operation against the Bonus Army, and the soldiers quickly drove the veterans out of the nation's capital. The President had been persuaded that the group was filled with a revolutionary spirit and was led by Communists. "Subversive influences," he explained, "obtained control . . . ," and MacArthur regarded the group as "a mob . . . animated by the essence of revolution." Actually, the Communists had tried to gain control of the movement but had failed.

Figure 2   The Bonus Army *(Copyright by Harris & Ewing)*

There were revolutionaries, including Communists, in the nation in
1932. A revolutionary spirit did not grip all who were in distress. For some
people, the Depression was a profoundly discouraging experience.
"Years ago," an old man recalled, "Horace Greeley made a statement,
'Young man, go West and grow up with the country.' Were he living
today, he would make the statement, 'Go West, young man, and drown
yourself in the Pacific Ocean. . . . '" Many of the unemployed felt
unneeded; some felt defeated; some even felt guilty. "Have you anybody
you can send around to tell my wife you have no job to give me?" a
husband asked a social worker. "Certainly I lost my love for him," a wife
reported. "How can you love a husband who causes you so much

suffering?" More than a few who were out of work committed suicide.

Not everyone was demoralized by events, however. Some were stimulated by the sudden collapse of capitalism. The situation seemed to provide opportunities for fundamental, radical changes. As the economy spiraled downward and the prestige of business and established political leaders declined, the left took on new life and hope. The day of victory seemed to be fast approaching. Radicals had long predicted that since capitalism was unworkable, it would produce a major crisis and then the suffering masses would overthrow the system and introduce a new one.

Protest and radicalism took various forms. A "proletarian literature" emerged that treated art as a weapon, glorified mass action, and sought to stimulate readers to act. The Social Gospel movement in the Protestant churches revived and moved left. "The people," the Northern Baptist Convention declared in 1932, "have the natural right to hold, and can safely be entrusted with, the power of democratic control over their economic life." The most prominent of the radical clerics was Reinhold Niebuhr, who combined Marxism and Christianity and advocated socialism. At Columbia University, a movement labeled "Technocracy" took shape and recommended that the nation should substitute the engineer for the businessman, for the former would serve collective efficiency while the latter was motivated by private acquisitiveness. In the new society, everyone would enjoy an economy of abundance.

The Communist party was another active participant in the politics of the early 1930s. It worked to gain support from the unemployed, the blacks, students, the unorganized and unskilled workers, farmers, and intellectuals. In search of followers, Communists moved into trouble spots, like Harlan County, Kentucky, where coal mine operators and state officials combined to suppress striking miners. Communists worked throughout the South in a quest for black support that involved protests against disenfranchisement, lynching, and discrimination in the administration of justice and demands for self-determination for Negroes, and Communists also participated in protests in the rural Middle West. Everywhere, the party worked to organize the unemployed for revolution, and in many cities, party members provided leadership in demonstrations by the jobless.

In October 1932, a group of prominent intellectuals endorsed the Communist party. The list included Theodore Dreiser, Sherwood Anderson, John Dos Passos, Erskine Caldwell, Waldo Frank, Granville Hicks, Sidney Hook, Lincoln Steffens, and Matthew Josephson. Only the Communist party, they announced, proposed the real solution: the overthrow of capitalism. "It is capitalism which is destructive of all culture," they insisted, "and Communism which desires to save civilization and its cultural heritage from the abyss to which the world crisis is driving it."

For many who joined, the Communist party satisfied deep needs and desires. "I was on the side of history where I could look across and view with sincere pity the floundering liberals and the obstructing capitalists," one former party member recalled, looking back on this period. He had assumed that "history would crush them like a juggernaut." According to the historians of the party, "The new converts . . . came rushing in quest of a system . . . ; they wanted to feel that at the very moment the world was being shattered, they had found a key to its meaning."

The largest organization on the left was the Socialist party. Nominating Norman Thomas for the second time in 1932, the party offered the nation a very broad platform. It contained a large-scale program for the emergency that included a federal appropriation of $5 billion for immediate relief to supplement state and local appropriations and another $5 billion for federal public works. In addition, the platform called for numerous long-run reforms: a thirty-hour workweek without a reduction in wages, a comprehensive system of unemployment compensation with adequate benefits based on contributions by government and employers, old-age pensions for people sixty and over, health insurance, the abolition of child labor, and adequate minimum wage laws.

The party shared an interest in these proposals with various types of reformers, but the final feature of the platform set the Socialists apart from those who hoped only to reform capitalism. It was a call for a revolution, although not a violent one. The party proposed the public ownership and democratic control of the basic industries.

Loud and at times violent protests also erupted in rural America. Many corn-hog farmers in the Middle West, who had known prosperity but were now faced with falling income and threatened with the loss of property, joined the Farmers' Holiday Association and participated in what the historian of the association called "the most agressive agrarian upheaval of the twentieth century." The association organized a farm strike that began in August and ran into November 1932, and the participants, while usually peaceful, did employ violence on several occasions in their efforts to keep farm products off the market. In addition, there were many protest marches and meetings during the fall and winter of 1932–1933 that demanded immediate action to halt debt payments, evictions, and property seizures, raise prices, distribute food to the needy, and cut the profits of middlemen. Furthermore, farmers took direct action to halt the great wave of foreclosures and sales for tax delinquency that was turning landowners into tenants or farm laborers or placing them on relief rolls.

With discontent growing and many radicals seeking to give direction to it, predictions of revolution were made repeatedly, often by farm and business leaders. While some Americans hoped for revolution, others feared it. The American right had long feared that the masses, when provoked by economic problems, would behave irrationally, follow wild leaders, and overthrow the capitalist system. Now the time of troubles seemed to be at hand, and calls for suppression of agitation and disorder were frequently heard. As many believed that radicals were responsible for protest and violence, a special committee was established in the House of Representatives to investigate "un-American activities." Special antiriot training was provided for military and police units so that they would be able to defend the system. These forces were used to disrupt meetings, break strikes, and suppress demonstrations of the unemployed and the depressed farmers. Leaders were jailed, and blood was shed. Unlike police and military forces in nations where revolutions have succeeded, these forces in the United States in the early 1930s remained loyal to established institutions.

Billy Minsky had a more peaceful solution to the problem of revolutionary agitation. He increased the hours that his burlesque shows were available. "No man plots or even thinks when he attends my shows," Minsky assured the worriers.

The American voters, however, chose Roosevelt, not revolution, and he was no more than a progressive Democrat. Born in the family's comfortable Hudson River estate at Hyde Park, New York, in 1882 and educated at Groton and Harvard, he had developed his point of view largely through participation in the politics of the Progressive period as a state senator in New York and Assistant Secretary of the Navy in Wilson's administration.

By the time he left the Navy Department in 1920, Roosevelt had learned a great deal. His participation in politics had supplied him with conceptions of both the desirable and the possible. His theory of the desirable involved the use of government to reform economic and social conditions. His theory of the possible stressed the need to operate the political machinery with great skill, work with a variety of groups, and carefully appraise shifts in the political situation.

In 1921, Roosevelt was changed still more by a severe bout with polio, although this crippling disease did not alter his basic ideas or ambitions. Prior to this, he was already a progressive, and he was already eager to become president. He had, in fact, run unsuccessfully for the vice-presidency in 1920. But polio did leave him unable to walk. It also made him a more attractive political figure, more serious, more sympathetic with the suffering of other people, and also more optimistic about man's capacity to triumph over adversity. Furthermore, it enabled him to avoid running for office in bad years for Democrats. Yet, polio did not prevent him from working hard at politics during the 1920s. He corresponded systematically with politicians throughout the nation, supported Al Smith, became better acquainted with Southern Democrats, and tried to unite the sharply divided urban and rural Democrats and to give the party a clearly defined progressive orientation. His wife Eleanor also helped, serving as his stand-in with the Democrats, keeping his name before the public, and bringing people to see him.

In 1928, party leaders pressured Roosevelt into running for governor of New York. He did not want to run, for he felt the year was not a good one for Democrats and he wanted more time to try to recover his ability to walk. Nevertheless, he ran and won, carrying the state while Smith failed there as well as in the nation.

Under the pressure of the Depression, Roosevelt's progressivism developed still more. He continued to support old progressive measures, such as conservation, and he endorsed proposals, such as public power, farm relief, unemployment insurance, and old-age pensions, that had become important parts of the progressive agenda in the 1920s. But he also championed depression programs that were in line with the progressive emphasis upon the ability of government to tackle social and economic problems but reflected the specific needs of the situation after 1929. For example, in August 1931, he became the first governor to call for state aid for the unemployed, a step that clearly denied that responsibility in this area rested solely upon the individual and the local community. The result was the establishment of the Temporary Emergency Relief Administration, with a social worker, Harry Hopkins, in charge. Furthermore, Roosevelt demoted the divisive issue of prohibition, advocating repeal of the Eighteenth Amendment and state or local option. He emphasized economic questions.

Roosevelts's development from 1929 to 1933 was influenced by the fact that he was running for the presidency. His desire to reach the White House forced him to try to top Al Smith's record as governor and to associate himself with developments among progressives elsewhere. Much of his early and significant support for the presidency came from progressive Democrats of the South and West, such as Senators Burton K. Wheeler of Montana and Cordell Hull of Tennessee. He also obtained support from some progressive Republicans, including George Norris of Nebraska and Robert La Follette of Wisconsin.

Roosevelt succeeded in gaining the Democratic nomination in 1932 chiefly because of the support that he gained from Democrats in the South, Midwest, and Far West who feared domination of the party by

Smith. Much of Roosevelt's opposition came from conservative Eastern Democrats, such as John J. Raskob, the former chairman of the board of General Motors and the chairman of the Democratic National Committee. They preferred Smith and hoped to make repeal of prohibition *the* issue and to enlarge business support for the Democratic party, but Smith's bid for a second nomination was weakened by anti-Eastern and anticonservative sentiment in the party. Many conservative to moderate Democrats outside the East favored Garner of Texas, but he was hurt by his role in the battle over the sales tax. When the Garner forces swung to Roosevelt on the fourth ballot at the Chicago convention in July, Roosevelt obtained the nomination, and Garner was rewarded with second place on the ticket.

In making his bid for the presidency, Roosevelt relied upon a large group of advisers. He paid some attention to advocates of substantial change, such as Rexford Guy Tugwell, an economist from Columbia who wanted the candidate to emphasize recovery, propose deficit spending as a means of achieving it, and call for a form of collectivism involving coordination of business and government and centralized management and planning. As time passed, FDR paid even more attention to others, including Louis Brandeis, who called for government efforts to restore competition, and Bernard Baruch, a financier who spoke for many business leaders and conservative Democrats in recommending efforts to restore business confidence by cutting back on government spending and balancing the budget.

The pattern of advice reflected the complexity of the Democratic party at the time, and Roosevelt's campaign drew upon all of his advisers. In addition to harsh criticism of Republican policies, insistence that the Depression had domestic, not foreign origins, and a promise of strong Presidential leadership, he called for the expansion of purchasing power and for planning. He placed heavier emphasis upon the proposals for government regulation of business that came from those progressives who were hostile to large business organizations. He also advocated the development of public facilities for the production of electrical power, social welfare legislation, unemployment relief, public works, and government efforts to raise farm prices. At the same time, he called for a reduction in government spending and a balanced budget. This reflected his personal views and also the advice of most progressives, as well as the pressure from conservatives, for at the time only a few people believed in large-scale government spending and deficit financing.

To a person as ambitious as Tugwell, Roosevelt's campaign was rather discouraging. The campaigner paid too much attention to the opponents of substantial change. Focusing his attention on political

Figure 3 Roosevelt Campaigning—1932 *(Wide World Photos)*

victory, Roosevelt did not believe that he could draw chiefly on Tugwell's advice. Political realities seemed to demand that he pay more attention to others.

If Roosevelt seemed too timid to Tugwell, he seemed dangerous to many conservatives, including Hoover. Nominated without significant opposition, Hoover ran on a conservative platform that included a promise "to stand steadfastly by the principle of a balanced budget" and warned that his foe was a radical. The fundamental issue, Hoover insisted, "is whether we shall go on in fidelity to the American traditions or whether we shall turn to innovations, the spirit of which is disclosed to us by many sinister revelations and veiled promises." The proposed New Deal would "destroy the American system of life."

To genuine radicals, like Norman Thomas, FDR seemed as hopelessly committed to capitalism as Hoover was. The radicals were correct in their assumption that Roosevelt was committed to capitalism, but Hoover was correct in suggesting that Roosevelt was interested in change.

Although his campaign had the normal lack of clarity, Roosevelt had, by November 1932, developed a proposed New Deal that amounted essentially to an extension of the progressives' assumption concerning the importance of government action. He had less confidence in the business system than Hoover and less confidence in government than Thomas. He accepted capitalism but called for changes in the relations between government and business in order to change business behavior and promote the general welfare.

Roosevelt's philosophy was the philosophy of the "middle way." He rejected what Arthur Schlesinger has called the "unconscious Platonism" of the ideological conservatives and radicals of the period who insisted that a nation could have either "capitalism" or "socialism," and he sought to demonstrate that there was a middle way superior to almost exclusive reliance on either business or government. His basic principle, Schlesinger suggests, "was not to sacrifice human beings to logic."

Roosevelt's philosophy also involved a belief in the conservative function of reform. He believed that capitalism and democracy were seriously threatened in the world of the early 1930s; he was determined to preserve them, and he was convinced that the way to do so was to come to grips with the social and economic problems that threatened them. Opposed to revolution, he believed that democratic statesmen must reform capitalism in ways that would convince Americans that they had no need to turn to other economic and political systems.

Most voters chose Roosevelt's middle way. He received 57 percent of the popular vote; Hoover received 40 percent; the other candidates, including Thomas and William Z. Foster, the candidate of the Communist party, divided the remainder, Thomas receiving less than 900,000 and Foster only slightly more than 100,000. The Democrats also gained thirteen seats in the Senate and ninety in the House, displacing many conservative Republicans and gaining the largest majority the party had had in the Senate since before the Civil War and the largest it had had in the House since 1890.

Roosevelt gained the support of every part of the nation. He carried all but six of the states and earned 472 electoral votes to 59 for Hoover. The race was very close in the East; all the states he lost were there. His victory margin was substantially larger in the Middle West and the Far West and especially large in the traditionally Democratic South.

To grasp the significance of the election, it must be compared with earlier ones. The "third party" vote had increased by a small amount

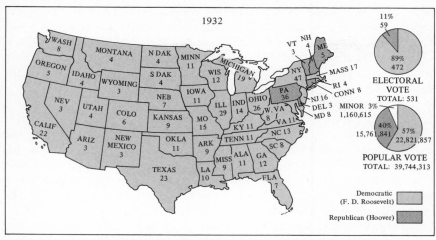

Figure 4 Election Results—1932 *(National Atlas, U.S. Geological Survey, Washington, 1970. Used by permission.)*

since 1928—from 1 percent of the total to 3 percent. A much larger change had taken place in the relations between the two major parties. The Republican presidential vote had dropped from 58 percent, while the Democratic vote had moved up from 41 percent. Never before in American history had such a large swing from one party to another taken place in four years. Obviously, many voters had given thought to politics in 1932. They had not merely relied upon their party traditions in making their voting decisions. Had they done so, Hoover would have won, for his party had been the majority party since the 1890s. Many people, such as Jewish voters in the big cities and Iowa farmers, rejected those traditions and switched from the GOP to the Democrats, and many others chose a party for the first time, some because they had recently reached voting age or become citizens and others because politics now seemed significant to them. Many of the new young voters rejected the party tradition of their families. Also obvious, the voters had confidence that the established political system could produce solutions to their social and economic problems.

The vote of the urban working classes was especially significant. This was the group upon which the left had counted most heavily for the support that would usher in the new system. But workers voted for Roosevelt, giving him even more support than they had given Smith in 1928. And they voted for FDR in spite of the fact that he had displaced Smith and had devoted most of his campaign to efforts to capture the

West and the South. And the working classes voted for Roosevelt even though most labor leaders did not endorse him. Many workers who voted for him had voted for Smith in 1928; many others had voted for Hoover, and many had not voted for anyone. The workers were unhappy with joblessness and Hoover's policies, but they were willing to give the established system another chance.

Perhaps inadequate leadership was the explanation for the left's failure, but the competition from Roosevelt may have been too tough for any leader. He may have understood the American people better and known how to communicate with them more effectively than any actual or potential leader of the left. He agreed with the left that there was revolutionary potential in the United States, but he did not see it as a force with as much strength as the left assumed that it had. While he assumed that Americans preferred to behave in nonradical ways, the left was very optimistic about the revolutionary potential of several groups.

Several factors, however, restrained these people. Many of them had not lost confidence in the system and its ability to supply them with satisfactory incomes. Also most of them were influenced by religious and nationalistic beliefs that made them hostile to revolutionary philosophies. And many were apathetic and demoralized as a result of the severity of their suffering and could not be aroused and organized for revolutionary activity—or political action of any type.

Nonvoting was one of the major political characteristics of the American poor. Voter turnout had fallen sharply after the 1890s, dropping from nearly 80 percent in 1896 to less than 50 percent in the early 1920s, and the left, as well as other parties, was unable to reverse the trend in a large way in the early 1930s. Thus, more than 40 percent of the adults did not vote in 1932. Many of the nonvoters, perhaps 20 percent of them, could not vote because they were black. Most Negroes still lived in the South, and there effective restrictions on the franchise kept all but a very small number of blacks off the polling lists. Most nonvoters were white and poor, and they apparently were not convinced that voting was worthwhile. It seems reasonable to suggest that many of these people were alienated, not contented. The left professed to speak for such people, but it failed to mobilize them for political action. Voter turnout, which had jumped above 57 percent in 1928, increased by less than 1 percent in 1932, and those who moved from nonvoter to voter status tended to vote for Roosevelt.

The others upon whom the left was counting moved in the same direction. Midwestern farmers, most of whom had voted Republican in the past, now gave most of their votes to Roosevelt. They wanted higher prices, just as workers wanted relief and jobs. Some Northern Negroes deserted the Republican party in 1932 but moved to the Democrats, not one of the parties of the left, giving the Democrats more votes than they had received from Negroes in the past. Some black leaders, such as Robert Lee Vann, the publisher of the *Pittsburgh Courier*, argued that the Republicans no longer served Negro interests and that Hoover's record in race relations was especially bad. Most black voters, however, maintained their allegiance to the Republican party, the party of emancipation, and their distrust of the Democrats, the party of white supremacy. Few showed any interest in the Communist or Socialist party.

The left and the right failed while the center succeeded. Roosevelt's strong support in both urban and rural America was especially impressive, given the history of the party in the 1920s. Then, it had been torn apart and rendered quite ineffective by a clash between the well-established rural wing and the growing urban wing. The latter had reached a new high in 1928, when Smith broke the hold that the Republicans had had upon the big cities since the 1890s and demonstrated especially great appeal to immigrants and their children, converting some Republicans and bringing many people to the polls who had not voted earlier. The Depression helped to submerge prohibition and other divisive noneconomic issues and to bring the urban and rural groups together in opposition to Hoover's economic policies, and Roosevelt's ability to work fairly well with representatives of both factions also helped to unite them. He both benefited from the gains that Smith had made for the party in the cities and overcame the problems that he had produced in the South.

The Democrats under Roosevelt did not merely put together two blocs that had joined the party earlier. The two blocs also grew in size under the impact of the Depression and the promise of a New Deal. The party regained and added to its strength in rural areas and maintained and increased its strength in the cities. The South became solid once again; farmers in the Far West and Middle West shifted to the Democrats; recent immigrants and their children in the cities continued to support the Democrats and did so in larger numbers than before; and urban workers supplied more Democratic votes than they had in 1928. Carrying thirty-two of the thirty-six largest cities, Roosevelt received over 17 percent more votes in them that Smith had in 1928. In other words, a significant change had taken place in the depressed economic situation. The election was a major part of "a realigning electoral era" or "a critical period of voting change." Many voters were changing their basic partisan commitments, and a new party balance was taking shape. Such shifts have been rare in our history.

The American voters were eager for change in 1932 but not for revolutionary change. They wanted more change than Herbert Hoover could provide but not as much as Norman Thomas proposed. Rather than switch from a Republican to a Socialist or a Communist, they switched only to a Democrat. Rather than move from a conservative to a radical, they moved only to a progressive. The man who won the presidential election of 1932 shared Hoover's commitment to capitalism but was more willing to employ the powers of government. Many who voted for him did so because they could not conceive of voting for anyone other than a Democrat or anyone outside the two major parties. And millions of other people maintained their ties with the Republican party. The two-party tradition revealed that it still had strength, and the American people revealed that they were not as flexible as revoluntionaries expected. Many people, however, voted for Roosevelt because they had confidence in the reform tradition that he represented. They believed that the political system could rescue the economic system and make it function successfully. They saw no need to turn to a new system.

SUGGESTIONS FOR ADDITIONAL READING

There is a rich literature on the rise of Franklin Roosevelt and the Democratic party. On Roosevelt's development, the place to begin is Frank Freidel's superb biography, published by Little, Brown from 1952 to 1956. It devotes three volumes to FDR's life before he became president. Also important are Bernard Bellush, *Franklin D. Roosevelt as Governor of New York*, Columbia University Press, New York, 1955, and Daniel R. Fusfeld, *The Economic Thought of Franklin D. Roosevelt and the Origins of the New Deal*, also published by Columbia in 1956. Essentially favorable interpretations, their point of view is shared by Thomas Greer, *What Roosevelt Thought: The Social and Political Ideas of Franklin D. Roosevelt*, The Michigan State University Press, East Lansing, 1958, but not by Richard Hofstadter, "Franklin D. Roosevelt: The Patrician as Opportunist," in *The American Political Tradition and the Men Who Made It;* Edgar Eugene Robinson, *The Roosevelt Leadership, 1933–1945*, Lippincott, Philadelphia, 1955; and James MacGregor Burns, *Roosevelt: The Lion and the Fox*, Harcourt, Brace, New York, 1956. On the Roosevelt literature, see Richard A. Watson, Jr., "Franklin D. Roosevelt in Historical Writing, 1950–1957," *South Atlantic Quarterly*, vol. 57, pp. 104–126, 1958; Clarke A. Chambers, "FDR: Pragmatist—Idealist," *Pacific Northwest Quarterly*, vol. 52, pp. 50–55, 1961; and William E. Leuchtenburg, ed., *Franklin D. Roosevelt: A Profile*, Hill and Wang, New York, 1967. See also the writings of his advisers, especially Rexford Guy Tugwell, *The Brains Trust*, Viking, New York, 1968, and Raymond Moley, *After Seven Years*, Harper, New York, 1939, and *The First New Deal*, Harcourt, Brace & World, New York, 1967. Alfred B. Rollins, Jr., *Roosevelt and Howe,* Knopf, New York, 1962, discusses Roosevelt's relations with a top political adviser; Richard S. Kirkendall, "Franklin D. Roosevelt and the Service Intellectual," *Mississippi Valley Historical Review*, vol. 49, pp. 456–471, 1962, discusses a different type of adviser, and Joseph Lash, in *Eleanor and Franklin,* Norton, New York, 1971, discusses his relations with his wife.

David Burner's *The Politics of Provincialism: The Democratic Party in Transition, 1918–1932,* Knopf, New York, 1968, deals with the rise of the Democrats on the national scene while the subject is examined impressively on the state and local levels by J. Joseph Huthmacher, *Massachusetts People and Politics 1919–1933,* Harvard, Cambridge, Mass., 1959; Franklin D. Mitchell, *Embattled Democracy: Missouri Democratic Politics, 1919–1932,* University of Missouri Press, Columbia, 1968; and John M. Allswang, *A House for All Peoples: Ethnic Politics in Chicago 1890–1936,* University Press of Kentucky, Lexington, 1971. Both Mitchell and Allswang consider the behavior of black voters, a subject that is also examined in essays by James H. Brewer, Allswang, and Ernest M. Collins in Bernard Sternsher, ed., *The Negro in Depression and War: Prelude to Revolution, 1930–1945,* Quadrangle, Chicago, 1969. On voting behavior in general see the excellent anthology compiled by Jerome Clubb and Howard Allen, *Electoral Change and Stability in American Political History,* Free Press, New York, 1971. It contains major essays by Samuel Lubell, Angus Campbell, Carl Degler, Charles Sellers, Gerald Pomper, John Shover, and the editors that relate the election to earlier and later ones. On turnout see Robert E. Lane, *Political Life: Why and How People Get Involved in Politics,* Free Press, New York, 1959, and Walter Dean Burnham, "The Changing Shape of the American Political Universe," *American Political Science Review,* vol. 59, pp. 7–28, 1965. Freidel has supplied a useful survey in Arthur M. Schlesinger, Jr., ed., *History of American Presidential Elections 1789–1968,* Chelsea House Publishers, New York, 1971.

The literature on the left and its failure is large and rich. See especially Sternsher's outstanding effort to solve the problem of the left's failure in his introduction to *Hitting Home.* This anthology and the one on the Negroes also contain important essays on the Communists in the period. The basic book on them is Irving Howe and Lewis Coser, *The American Communist Party: A Critical History,* Praeger, New York, 1962, while David A. Shannon's *The Socialist Party of America: A History,* Macmillan, New York, 1955, is the basic book on its subject. It should be compared with Murray B. Seidler, *Norman Thomas: Respectable Rebel,* Syracuse University Press, Syracuse, N. Y., 1961, and Bernard K. Johnpoll, *Pacifist's Progress: Norman Thomas and the Decline of American Socialism,* Quadrangle, Chicago, 1970. Also very useful are Paul A. Carter, *The Decline and Revival of the Social Gospel: Social and Political Liberalism in American Protestant Churches, 1920–1940,* Cornell University Press, Ithaca, N. Y., 1956, and John Shover, *Cornbelt Rebellion: The Farmers' Holiday Association,* The University of Illinois Press, Urbana, 1965. Schlesinger's *Crisis of the Old Order* and Bernstein's *Lean Years* range widely over the politics of the early 1930s and contain important discussions of the election and of the left and its failure.

Chapter 4

Establishing the New Deal

In power Roosevelt established a New Deal. Its most obvious feature was a greater role for the national government in American economic life. This was not a revolution. The American economy remained capitalistic. The New Deal deliberately and actively promoted the survival and recovery of the capitalistic system. The change from Hoover to Roosevelt was significant, however. The New Deal did not merely prop up the system that had collapsed after 1929. Alterations were made in hope that capitalism could function successfully, and efforts were made to serve the interests of many groups.

The capitalistic orientation of the New Deal was very obvious in its banking program. Here, the administration sacrificed an opportunity to nationalize a major form of economic power, a step that Norman Thomas would surely have taken had he been president and one that would have been supported by many people, for they had lost confidence in the bankers as a consequence of widespread losses and of congressional disclosures of malpractices. In spite of RFC, bank failures had escalated once again after the election. The cause was fear of Roosevelt's policies, Hoover insisted, as he tried to get Roosevelt to commit himself to the continuation of Hoover's policies and to abandon plans for a New Deal. Others blamed Hoover's policies and loss of confidence in bankers. By the time Roosevelt took office, almost all the banks that had not collapsed had been closed or restricted in their operations by state officials eager to prevent total collapse. FDR quickly closed all banks. Rather than establish government ownership and operation, he called upon the bankers themselves plus several officials from the Hoover administration to work with some of his more conservative advisers in the development of a program. The result emphasized quick action as a means of restoring normal banking.

The government acted boldly for conservative purposes. An Emergency Banking Act was passed five days after Roosevelt's inauguration. It authorized the Federal Reserve System to issue currency against banking assets of banks that belonged to the system. The Reconstruction Finance Corporation was empowered to provide funds to banks by buying stock in them. And the Treasury Department was empowered to supervise the reopening of the banks, permitting the strong ones to reopen immediately, strengthening the weaker ones prior to opening, and forcing the permanent closing of those that seemed certain to fail. The government would assure the public that it could have confidence in the banks that reopened their doors. Roosevelt supported all this with his own assuring words to the American people.

The program worked! Confidence in the banks was restored by government action, although the government acted quickly and approved a very high percentage, keeping the doors closed on only about 5 percent. As banks opened their doors, money flowed back in. And to guarantee that the banks would never again be weakened by loss of confidence in their ability to honor commitments to depositors, the government in the Banking Act of June 1933 established a Federal Deposit Insurance Corporation. Bank failures and depositors, losses dropped sharply and soon ceased to be features of American life.

Given an opportunity to nationalize the banks, Roosevelt had worked to preserve and strengthen them. Although rapid, his behavior resembled Hoover's in important ways. He even relied heavily on former Hoover lieutenants and used an institution that Hoover had created, the RFC. Roosevelt, however, succeeded. The ingredients he added included his own boldness, his own enthusiasm for action, and his own optimism.

Roosevelt also quickly honored his commitment on prohibition. Just before he came to power, Congress had voted for repeal of the Eighteenth Amendment, and now, while waiting for the states to act on the

Figure 5 With the People—1933 *(United Press International Photo)*

amendment, he urged Congress to repeal the Volstead Act and legalize beer. The congressmen quickly agreed, and by April 7, the sale of beer was legal once again. This act gave the economy a small boost, especially in such great beer centers as St. Louis and Milwaukee. Before the end of the year, the amendment was repealed, and the corner saloon and the bar quickly reappeared.

A much broader program was established by the National Industrial Recovery Act of June 1933. It had debts to Theodore Roosevelt's New Nationalism, Woodrow Wilson's War Industries Board, and Hoover's promotion of trade associations. Much of the pressure for it came from business leaders eager to preserve capitalism by changing it, men such as Gerard Swope of General Electric and Henry I. Harriman of the United States Chamber of Commerce. Holding price-depressing competition responsible for the Depression, they advocated the formation of a national council of businessmen that would work through the trade associations and control production, raise prices, and benefit workers. A basic feature of their proposal was relaxation of the antitrust laws. To promote recovery, government, these businessmen assumed, should encourage businessmen to cooperate rather than force them to compete.

Important Roosevelt advisers, such as Tugwell, agreed. They believed it would be foolish to try to restore the world of small business. Instead, they advocated further progress along the collectivist path.

Others contributed to the development of the program, thereby making it very broad and far from harmonious. Senator Hugo Black of Alabama, backed by the American Federation of Labor, pressed for a law establishing a thirty-hour workweek and forced the administration to get busy on broader legislation so as to prevent enactment of this proposal, which Roosevelt regarded as undesirable. Labor leaders, including John L. Lewis of the United Mine Workers and Sidney Hillman of the Amalgamated Clothing Workers, also participated, convinced that competition encouraged exploitation of the workers. Wagner worked for a guarantee of collective bargaining and an expanded federal public works program, arguing that these proposals would contribute to recovery by expanding investment, employment, and purchasing power. Social workers, represented by Frances Perkins, worked for provisions that would end child labor, regulate wages and hours, and accomplish other objectives that they had been pursuing since the Progressive era.

Foes of big business, represented chiefly by Senator William E. Borah of Idaho, also made contributions, but only minor ones. He was eager to protect and preserve small business from the giant firms, and he pressed unsuccessfully for the addition of a provision prohibiting price fixing. All that he could obtain was a provision expressing a vague determination that the program would not create monopolies or monopolistic practices or harm small enterprise.

The participants in the development of this new program disagreed on a basic question: Where would power be located? Answers ranged from Harriman's emphasis upon business leaders to Tugwell's insistence that the national government must ultimately control the program.

In theory, the National Industrial Recovery Act exalted the federal government. Introduced into Congress by Wagner, the legislation authorized the adoption of codes of "fair competition" for all businesses by committees representing management, labor, and the public. The codes were to include acceptable provisions on wages, hours, working conditions, union membership, and collective bargaining. The code-making process was to be supervised by a federal administrator, and the code was to be examined by the President. If he approved the code, it would have the force of federal law, and businessmen who violated it would be prosecuted. Thus, while the program resembled Hoover's, it had a much larger role for government than he had been willing to accept. Cooperation would not be voluntary.

In actual operation, the program was dominated by the major

business groups. Most of the codes were first written by the trade associations, and they were dominated by the larger firms. Each code was administered by a code authority, and it was usually composed of business leaders. And the government did little to supervise the process and force changes in codes.

Several factors explain the divergence between theory and practice. One was the immense size of the task. Efforts were made to bring all of business under control in a very short period of time. Furthermore, the major government officials, the President and the top administrators of NRA, Hugh Johnson and Donald Richberg, were very eager to secure cooperation of business leaders in order to assure the success of the program. The administration was especially eager to draw the automobile industry into the experiment, for that industry seemed to be the key to recovery. Auto leaders did not share that eagerness, for they were satisfied with established modes of behavior in the industry, including the lack of collective bargaining and of vigorous price competition, but they submitted a code, largely for public relations reasons. The code was not in harmony with the law's provisions on unions, but Roosevelt signed it. An industry spokesman saw this as "the first victory of industry over organized labor under the Industrial Recovery Act."

The fundamental factor was the unequal distribution of power in American society in 1933. Although under a cloud, business leaders did control the most important instruments of production, were well organized, and knew how to work with and influence Washington officials. Consumer organizations, on the other hand, were very small and ineffective, and the labor movement had been in decline for more than a decade. Only in a few industries, such as clothing and coal mining, did labor have enough strength to exert a significant influence and gain substantial benefits for the workers. In the very important automobile industry, on the other hand, labor lost one contest after another. After the establishment of the automobile code, management continued to discriminate against union members and to resist the principle that employees should be represented by the organization chosen by the majority of workers in a plan, and the Roosevelt administration continued to take management's side because of the weakness of the American Federation of Labor and the belief that recovery depended on expansion of the auto industry. The administration also resisted the AFL's demands for revision of the labor provisions of the code, especially the denial of the majority rule principle. Critics of NRA could produce only a few changes.

Labor did make some progress under NRA. The movement was so weak when Roosevelt came to power that it was unable to get one of its own members chosen as Secretary of Labor. Roosevelt instead chose a woman and a social worker, Frances Perkins, and she, like Roosevelt himself, stressed social welfare legislation rather than government protection of labor's right to organize and bargain collectively as the solution to the problems of the workers. Nevertheless the recovery act included section 7A with its apparent guarantee of the right of collective bargaining. Labor leaders greeted this with enthusiasm and embarked immediately upon major organizing campaigns. Lewis, Hillman, and David Dubinsky, the president of the International Ladies' Garment Workers, rebuilt their unions in 1933. Growth also took place in other areas as workers demonstrated a new eagerness to join unions.

The burst of union activity was countered by strong resistance from employers. Most industrialists opposed the prounion provisions of the recovery act. With the National Association of Manufacturers supplying much of the leadership, management resisted the formation of strong, independent unions, formed company unions, fired workers who joined others, spied on workers and unions, employed force and strikebreakers against them, refused to bargain with them or to accept the majority rule principle, and denounced union organizers and leaders as "outside agitators," radicals, and racketeers.

Many of the AFL leaders also hampered the drive to establish a strong labor movement. Some were lethargic, and almost all of them opposed the formation of industrial unions, thereby limiting labor's opportunity for growth by ignoring unskilled and semiskilled workers.

None of the leaders received the help from Washington that was needed to overcome the powerful opposition of business leaders. The labor movement did have some friends in power, especially Senator Wagner, who served for a time as chairman of NRA's National Labor Board. The NLB and its successor, the National Labor Relations Board, tried to check antiunion practices and to promote collective bargaining. These agencies opposed company unions, provided protection for workers who belonged to independent unions, held elections to select representatives for workers, and tried to establish the majority rule principle. But the agencies had little power to enforce their decisions and were successful only when employers were willing to go along. Many refused. Johnson and Richberg did not back up prounion officials, and Roosevelt tended to support the NRA administrators. He shared their fears that strikes and the organizing drive were impeding recovery.

Thus the National Industrial Recovery Act had only a small impact on the structure of the economy. It did stimulate some expansion of the labor movement and enlarged the role of the federal government in economic affairs. The legislation, however, did not establish a powerful labor movement capable of dealing effectively with organized business, nor did it create a system of effective economic planning conducted by the federal government or the representatives of the major interests. Its major tendency was to strengthen business leaders and their organizations.

The experiment also made contributions in the area of social welfare, but its contribution to recovery was far from spectacular. One of the most impressive gains was a substantial reduction in child labor. Also, NRA increased jobs slightly and improved the earnings of the workers. The business leaders who dominated the program, however, stressed price increases and production control, rather than the expansion of production and sales, as the ways to maintain and enlarge profits. Their efforts did check and reverse the downward spiral of prices and profits but did not produce rapid recovery.

Unfortunately, a supplementary program also failed to give the economy a significant boost. NIRA established a two-year, $3.3 billion public works program. Wagner, La Follette, Costigan, Tugwell, Perkins, and Johnson, among others, had favored a larger program, but Roosevelt and the Bureau of the Budget had scaled it down. The President believed that the amount of useful work on which the government could spend money quickly was small, and he did not believe that the indirect benefits of such spending would be large. The new program was administered by the Public Works Administration, headed by Harold Ickes, the Secretary of the Interior. A product of the reform movement in Chicago, Ickes distrusted men, especially politicians, and thus he administered the program very cautiously, looking skeptically at proposals and examining them with great care, convinced that the forces of corruption were very strong. His attitude hampered PWA as an agency of recovery, for it pumped money into the economy more slowly than the situation demanded. In addition to being very cautious, he emphasized large projects involving large capital expenditures. In time, he would become a mighty builder of many important facilities, but during its first year, PWA supplied employment for no more than 1 million men. Hoover's RFC, which now adopted bold lending and investing policies, did more to stimulate the economy.

NIRA, however, was not the only major piece of legislation passed in 1933. Another was the Agricultural Adjustment Act. This response to the farm crisis provided further evidence of the Roosevelt administration's commitment to capitalism and of its determination to promote further evolution along collectivistic lines.

Roosevelt selected an advocate of the allotment plan as Secretary of Agriculture. His choice was Henry A. Wallace of Iowa, an agricultural journalist, scientist, and businessman. Significantly, his leading compe-

Figure 6 Two New Dealers: Wallace (seated) and Tugwell *(U.S. Department of Agriculture)*

titors included George Peek, an opponent of the plan. And Wallace selected two other advocates of it, Tugwell and Mordecai Ezekiel, as his top lieutenants. Tugwell became Assistant Secretary, and Ezekiel became the Secretary's economic adviser.

In spite of these favorable developments, the advocates of the allotment plan did not achieve a complete victory during Roosevelt's first "hundred days." The Agricultural Adjustment Act that was passed in May 1933 included Wilson's major suggestions: production control, voluntary participation encouraged by rental or benefit payments, self-financing through processing taxes, and a role for farmers in administration. But the law also included two programs with which Peek was most closely associated: the disposal of surpluses abroad at low prices and the development of agreements whereby the processors and distributors of farm products could promise the government to pay agreed upon prices to farmers. The law also empowered the President, who had already taken the country off the gold standard, to experiment with monetary policy as a means of raising prices, and a supplementary Farm Credit Act sought to protect the farmer against foreclosure on his property.

Advocates of production control, including Wilson, now moved into important positions in the new Agricultural Adjustment Administration, but Peek was appointed to the top spot. The appointment meant that the battle over farm policy would now rage inside government. While Peek was forced to accept cuts in production, he did so reluctantly, resisted pressures to make this the main feature of the program, emphasized marketing agreements as the means of raising farm prices, and continued to seek ways to sell the surplus. Wallace, however, publicly criticized Peek's agreements in the fall of 1933; Peek challenged Wallace's authority to control AAA, and Wallace and Tugwell vetoed Peek's plan to dump butter in Europe and pressed the President for a decision that would indicate clearly where authority lay. Forced at last to make a choice between representatives of different farm policies, Roosevelt in December moved Peek into a new post as special adviser to the President on foreign trade.

Wallace had crushed Peek's attempt to make AAA an independent agency, free from control by the Secretary and subordinate only to the President, and now he placed it under the direction of Chester Davis, who believed in production control. Now, under his vigorous leadership, which lasted until 1936, production control emerged clearly as the major program to raise farm prices.

Defenses of the program often emphasized its similarities to the practices of large corporations. Administration spokesmen pointed out that giant corporations used their power to control production in order to uphold prices and that the more indvidualistic farmer was at a disadvantage in such a system. He could not exercise the same control over production and thus "administer" prices. For him, in contrast with the corporation, price rather than production was the flexible factor. Furthermore, the farmer suffered from the industrialist's ability to restrict production because it led to higher industrial prices and reduced the demand for agricultural products. Factories working at less than full capacity needed fewer agricultural products, and unemployed workers had little purchasing power. Thus, the farmer needed help from the government so as to be able to imitate industrial practices. AAA served the farmer's need for the centralizing powers of government to achieve the same results industries achieved through corporate organization. If the industrialist could adjust production to demand, was it wrong, AAA's defenders asked, for government to help the farmers do the same? Had not the industrialist, by cutting back on his production and thereby reducing demand for farm products, forced the farmer to reduce output?

The argument implied that the New Deal farm program was not a radical program. Farmers were merely behaving like urban businessmen. Farmers were not trying to destory the practices of the corporate giants. Instead, rural businessmen were accepting and seeking to employ an established feature of collective capitalism.

At the same time that the farm program promoted further development of an organized type of capitalism, it protected the system by undercutting agrarian protest. Farm protest erupted once again in the fall of 1933 for relief had come more slowly than farmers expected, and the administration responded with crop loans, the distribution of farm surpluses to the unemployed, and moderate monetary inflation. As benefits began to reach the farm and prospects brightened, they sapped the strength of the protest movement. Few farmers had had revolutionary aspirations; they had protested in hope of improvements in the farm business. The New Deal had made some and had thereby robbed the radicals of support. By 1934, farm prices and farm income were rising, and farmers were receiving checks from the government for their participation in the farm program.

For many farmers who did not own land, the farm program had serious shortcomings. By the 1930s, over 45 percent of the nation's farms were operated by tenants, and most of them, especially the sharecroppers in the South, were suffering from more than the drop in farm prices and seemed to be caught in a system of permanent povery. And AAA did not rescue them. Although nearly three-fourths of the cotton farms were operated by tenants, they were not represented in the development and administration of the cotton program. Dominated by the larger landowners, it harmed rather than helped many sharecroppers. Many received only a small share or no share at all of the benefit payment from the government as the landlords kept all or most of it, and many tenants were demoted from sharecropper, the lowest form of tenancy, to day laborer or evicted from the land as the cuts in production were made. As with NRA, the explanation lay in the distribution of power.

Clearly, the New Deal involved a strong commitment to capitalism. In spite of the sharp decline in the prestige of business leaders and the many suggestions that the country should turn away from them, the administration drew heavily upon them for advice and tried to use the powers of government in ways that would enable the business system to prosper.

The administration's attitude limited the amount of change that could take place in the crisis situation, but its attitude did include a willingness to make some changes. The role of government was enlarged and employed to make alterations in the operations of the business system. The New Deal was, in other words, both maintaining and changing the capitalistic system.

The New Deal was, even in its first two years, a complex movement. Recovery was the dominant aim, but the Roosevelt administration did not seek merely the recovery of the system that had developed by 1929. That had been Hoover's aim because he had assumed the system was fundamentally sound. Roosevelt, on the other hand, assumed that the system had serious weaknesses, and he sought to reform it as well as to promote its recovery.

The New Deal in 1933–1934 included efforts to reform "Wall Street." They reflected the old populist-progressive fears of the power of the bankers and demands that big business be regulated by government, and the efforts drew upon years of experience with failure in securities regulation on the state level, the experiences of World War I, which stimulated interest in national regulation, and the failure of private institutions, such as the New York Stock Exchange, to control the selling of stocks. The efforts were influenced also by the decline in popular confidence in banking leaders that was promoted by Senate investigations as well as the crash and the Depression. The Senate Committee on Banking and Currency, encouraged by Hoover because of his unhappiness with the New York Stock Exchange's failure to reform itself and assisted by a hardworking New York lawyer, Ferdinand Pecora, explored the Street from 1932 to 1934. The testimony of leading financiers revealed failures to pay taxes, the existence of "preferred lists" composed of influential people who were able to buy stocks at bargain prices, tremendous salaries and bonuses for bank executives, and bad investments made by gullible people on the advice of seemingly well-informed and trustworthy bankers.

Two groups in the Roosevelt camp were especially eager to impose regulations on the financiers. One was the Brandeis group that was closely associated with the Supreme Court Justice and led by a professor from the Harvard Law School, Felix Frankfurter. He frequently visited with the President and helped to staff government agencies. The group included Benjamin Cohen, Thomas Corcoran, and James M. Landis. The other group advocating regulation was composed of Western and Southern progressives, including Congressman Sam Rayburn of Texas and Senator Burton Wheeler of Montana.

The first product was the Securities Act of May 1933. Drafted in large part by Landis and Cohen, it required full and complete disclosure about every issue of securities. The public had to be informed about the condition of the firm.

In June 1934, Congress passed the Securities Exchange Act. Again, the Brandeisians—Cohen, Landis, and Corcoran—made large contributions as legislative draftsmen. Two Southerners, Senator Duncan Fletcher of Florida and Rayburn, introduced the bill. The new law added to the regulatory powers of the government and created a new regulatory agency, the Securities Exchange Commission, to administer the laws concerned with the exchanges. To encourage financiers to cooperate with the SEC, Roosevelt appointed one of them, Joseph P. Kennedy, as the first chairman. ("The President has great confidence in him because he has made his pile, has invested all his money in Government securities, and knows all the tricks of the trade," Ickes complained to his diary. "Apparently he is going on the assumption that Kennedy would now like to make a name for himself for the sake of his family, but I have never known many of these cases to work out as expected.") To satisfy the critics of the Street, Roosevelt also appointed Pecora and Landis to the commission.

This series of laws amounted chiefly to an enlargement of government and an increase in its power. They forced business and financial leaders to make changes in their behavior. They had to provide more information to potential investors.

The development of this legislation amounted also to a challenge to the status of the financiers. Roosevelt believed that the "Stock Exchange crowd" could not "understand the country or the public or their obligation to their fellow men," but the president of the New York Stock Exchange, Richard Whitney, insisted, when battling against the legislation, that the exchange was a "perfect institution," the country had been "built by speculation," and the exchange should be permitted to regulate itself. As the battle raged, Will Rogers suggested that "those Wall Street boys are putting up an awful fight to keep the government from putting a cop on their corner."

While the legislation did involve significant changes, it was designed to improve and protect the workings of the capitalistic system. The legislation sought to free the system from certain practices that had harmed it in the past and to restore confidence in an important part, the selling of stock. Some members of the financial community actually welcomed the finished product, arguing that it could promote "a more professional relationship between broker and customer" and "confidence in the stock exchanges," and the SEC in the 1930s, chaired by Kennedy, then Landis, and then William O. Douglas, was dominated by a desire to perpetuate as well as discipline capitalism. The commission gained the confidence and cooperation of financiers and investors. Both regulators and the regulated shared certain interests, especially an interest in private investment as a means of producing economic recovery.

Another agency established in the first three months of the Roosevelt administration, the Tennessee Valley Authority, sought to reconstruct a region. TVA was the product of several movements, including scientific agriculture, conservation, the campaign for public power, and the rising interest in social and economic planning. The program also reflected two of Roosevelt's strongest interests: a desire for better use of natural resources and a hope to give more people a chance to live close to the land.

The TVA dealt with a vast impoverished area. Income there was less than one-half the national average, and over half the families were on relief in 1933. The land suffered from floods and erosion; the forests had been stripped by lumbermen and by fire; the people were ravaged by tuberculosis and pellagra; the public services were starved, and there was little industry or electricity.

A government corporation, the TVA developed a multipurpose program. Eventually, the agency produced and distributed electrical power, manufactured fertilizer, conserved the soil, promoted the electrification of farms, withdrew poor lands from agricultural production, grew forests, prevented floods, converted the Tennessee into a navigable river, promoted industrial development, developed recreational facilities, and improved the health of the people.

Like SEC, TVA affected the power and status of government and business. It challenged the assumption that the country could rely chiefly on business leaders for the promotion of social and economic development, rejecting the argument of Wendell Willkie, the president of Commonwealth and Southern, a giant public utility holding company, that private enterprise could supply the area's need for electricity. The TVA produced electricity and sold it to municipal systems and rural cooperatives. The private companies challenged TVA in the courts but lost, persuading Willkie and others that they should sell their properties to the government corporation.

Although TVA involved public enterprise and reduced the importance of the private power companies, it also cooperated with and stimulated other businesses. The government officials worked closely with many business groups and the commercial farmers in the region and assisted them in many ways, and the program of cheap and plentiful electricity provided a new market for the producers and distributors of electrical appliances and stimulated investment in other enterprises in the region.

At the same time that it established TVA, the new administration also supplied relief for the unemployed. This program, which Wagner sponsored in the Senate, grew out of the social welfare wing of the Progressive movement with its rejection of the theory that poverty was a consequence of the defects of the individuals who were poor. More immediately, the relief program was a product of the crisis in relief that greeted Roosevelt in 1933. More than 15 million people were unemployed on inauguration day, and one problem was to keep them going until jobs became available. The state, local, and private agencies were incapable of handling the load, and experts in this field were demanding greater federal action than Hoover had been willing to accept. The government responded with the establishment of the Federal Emergency Relief Administration in the spring of 1933 with a fund of $500 million that could be distributed in grants to the states for relief. It was passed in spite of complaints about the "dole" and damage to "business confidence."

The relief program brought to Washington one of the most remarkable and most controversial New Dealers, Harry Hopkins. He believed that his job was to restore the morale and health of millions of discouraged people and prevent them from moving in radical directions, and he emphasized the morale problem of the people forced to live by government assistance. This struck him as the crucial problem of relief. As a social worker, he was convinced that the loss of a job was usually the result of forces beyond the individual's control and that the person on relief must not be made to feel like a pauper. Hopkins would rather give a person cash that he could use as he desired than supply him with a commissary even though that would be more healthful. And Hopkins would rather give a person a job than merely hand him the money even though the latter form of relief was less costly.

As quickly as possible, Hopkins established a work relief program. In the fall of 1933, a Civil Works Administration was created under his leadership, and, funded by PWA and RFC money (about $800 million), it was soon employing over 4 million people in a wide variety of tasks, thereby enabling them to survive the winter. Unfortunately, it was criticized severely as costly, competitive with private industry, and incompatible with American individualism, and Roosevelt abolished it in the spring of 1934 in order to reduce government expenses.

Hopkins's activities involved an effort to use government to deal directly with the problems of lower-income groups. These activities rejected reliance on government programs for business and rejected the theory that the poor should depend upon the benevolence of the wealthy, and they assumed that the lower-income groups had a right to be treated adequately by their social system and that if business was not serving their needs, government must. Unfortunately, the relief programs, which cost about $2 billion in 1933–1934, were small relative to the size of the problem.

A closely related program combined relief and conservation. This was the Civilian Conservation Corps, which was established in the first month of the New Deal and moved unemployed young men out of the cities and put them to work in the forests. More than any other New Deal agency, the CCC was Roosevelt's personal creation. It reflected his Jeffersonian attitude toward the land.

The CCC was an extraordinarily popular part of the New Deal. There was criticism of low wages, high costs, the large role of the Army in the management of the program, discrimination against Negroes, the location of Negro camps, the agency's inability to solve the basic problems of the unemployed, and its inadequate educational programs. Much more significant was the widespread enthusiasm for it. It provided practical benefits to many groups, tapped the "mystique of the forest," and had cautious management. While new and experimental and a promoter of some changes in land-use practices and the physical and mental conditions of many young men, the CCC was directed by men who had only limited aspirations, a fact that was revealed most clearly in their handling of education and race relations. Also, by taking more than 2,500,000 unemployed young people out of the cities, the agency helped to stabilize American politics in the 1930s.

All these programs increased government spending in 1933 and 1934 and increased the national debt. Roosevelt inherited a $4.6 billion budget from Hoover and increased spending to $6.7 billion in fiscal 1934 and $6.5 billion the following year. Tax receipts also increased but so did deficits, moving from $1.5 billion in 1932 to $2.9 billion in 1934.

Roosevelt was not a bold advocate of deficit financing. He was willing to tolerate small deficits in the emergency, but he was convinced that unbalanced budgets were bad. He strongly opposed massive deficit spending, expected to balance the budget as soon as possible, and promised that expenditures and deficits would decline as recovery progressed.

After taking office, the President had moved quickly to honor his pledge to balance the budget. Announcing his determination to avoid "loose fiscal policy" and put the "Government's house . . . in order," he had called for cuts of half a billion dollars in payments to government workers and veterans. Within two days of his message of March 10, Congress had passed the Economy Act.

In spite of this effort, Roosevelt did not balance the budget. He satisfied himself by distinguishing between the "regular" budget, which he regarded as balanced, and the "emergency" budget, which involved expenditures on his depression programs that were financed by borrowing. The President argued that this was a sound and not a reckless way to proceed. He did not feel compelled to cut spending and raise taxes. And his policies did not so shatter business confidence as to make the Depression worse.

To at least one of his advisers, however, Roosevelt appeared to be reckless and dangerous. This was his Director of the Budget, Lewis Douglas, a man who regarded Hoover as extravagant. Douglas had advised Roosevelt to cut spending in March 1933, and seventeen months later, he resigned, distressed that he had failed to accomplish his major objective. Roosevelt, Douglas insisted, "must bring the budget into actual balance," and the President's "place in history" and "conceivably the immediate fate of civilization," the adviser suggested, depended on this.

Roosevelt increased government spending during his first two years as he enlarged the federal government and its role in American life. The changes took place in order to preserve and reform capitalism and to promote economic recovery. New Dealers assumed that capitalism was a valuable system with serious weaknesses that could be remedied by government action. Thus the federal government became larger, more important, and more active than it had been in the past, except during World War I. The federal government also became more responsive to nonbusiness groups than it had been in the 1920s and the early 1930s, but business leaders remained very powerful and influential. The commitment to capitalism, the enlargement of government, and the effort to serve the interests of many groups were the main features of the New Deal in its early years.

SUGGESTIONS FOR ADDITIONAL READING

There are several valuable surveys of the early New Deal. The most important are Arthur M. Schlesinger's *The Age of Roosevelt: The Coming of the New Deal*, Houghton Mifflin, Boston, 1959, and William E. Leuchtenburg, *Franklin Roosevelt and the New Deal*, Harper & Row, New York, 1963. Also very important is the biography of Roosevelt by Burns.

Beyond these broad works, the historical literature extends almost endlessly, for this has been one of the most active parts of American historiography during the past twenty-five years. Ellis Hawley's *The New Deal and the Problem of Monopoly*, Princeton University Press, Princeton, N.J., 1965, deals broadly and very impressively with business policies. More specialized works of very large value are Sidney Fine, *The Automobile Industry under the Blue Eagle: Labor, Management, and the Automobile Manufacturing Code*, The University of Michigan Press, Ann Arbor, 1963, and Michael Parrish, *Security Regulation and the New Deal*, Yale, New Haven, Conn., 1970. Two books cited in Chapter 2,

Kennedy's on banking and Stein's on fiscal policy, are the best on their subjects, while Preston J. Hubbard, *Origins of the TVA: The Muscle Shoals Controversy, 1920–1932*, Vanderbilt, Nashville, Tenn., 1961; Thomas K. McCraw, *TVA and the Power Fight, 1933–1939*, Lippincott, Philadelphia, 1971; and Wilmon Henry Droze, *High Dams and Slack Waters: TVA Rebuilds a River*, Louisiana State University Press, Baton Rouge, 1965, are very important on their subject. On relief, consult Searle F. Charles, *Minister of Relief: Harry Hopkins and the Depression*, Syracuse University Press, Syracuse, N.Y., 1963, and John Salmond, *The Civilian Conservation Corps, 1933–1942: A New Deal Case Study*, The Duke University Press, Durham, N.C., 1967, and on agriculture, see the very good book by Perkins cited in Chapter 1, Shover's important study of the Farmers' Holiday Association, also cited earlier, Gilbert Fite, *George Peek and the Fight for Farm Parity*, University of Oklahoma Press, Norman, 1954, and Richard S. Kirkendall, *Social Scientists and Farm Politics in the Age of Roosevelt*, University of Missouri Press, Columbia, 1966. The second volume of Bernstein's book, *Turbulent Years: A History of the American Worker 1933–1941*, Houghton Mifflin, Boston, 1969, contains the best general study of labor policies and the unions in 1933–1934, and for one of the most important individuals in the period, Senator Wagner, the reader should turn to the biography by Huthmacher.

Chapter 5

Pressures from Right and Left

The early Roosevelt years were years of conflict, not consensus. After a brief "honeymoon," criticism began to mount, and by 1935, Roosevelt faced strong pressures for change in his policies. These pressures, however, pointed in conflicting directions. From the right came demands that the administration cut back on government activities and develop a more friendly attitude toward business. On the left, various groups and individuals were insisting that FDR must expand the role of government and use it more effectively to solve the problems of lower-income Americans.

From the beginning, some businessmen had disliked the New Deal. More typical, however, was the businessman who supported the New Deal during its early months. Most businessmen welcomed it as a solution to their economic and political problems.

By the fall of 1934, however, business hostility was developing rapidly. By then, as Harold Ickes remarked, bitterness was rising from the grass roots of every country club in the land. A definite break had taken place in the relations between the Roosevelt administration and much of the business community.

Monetary policy played a large role in the break. In 1933, the administration antagonized financial leaders, and politicians and economists who shared their views on money matters, by embarking on a monetary experiment. After leaving the gold standard and rejecting a plan for an international agreement to stabilize world currencies, Roosevelt in October accepted the advice of an economist from Cornell University, George Warren, and embarked upon a gold-buying experiment involving purchases of gold at increasingly higher prices as a means of raising commodity prices. Chambers of commerce in the leading financial centers and the American Bankers Association criticized the experiment, arguing that it harmed business confidence and was developed by advisers who lacked essential experience in the business world.

Then, Roosevelt alienated another group of businessmen by bringing the experiment to an end. This group, the Committee for the Nation, was led by James Rand of Remington Rand, among others, and they had actively promoted the experiment, viewing it as a means of raising all prices, satisfying the loud clamor for farm relief, and avoiding more radical policies. Unhappy with the results of the scheme, which failed to produce the predicted price increases, Roosevelt in January 1934 stabilized the dollar at a point far below that desired by committee members.

Rather soon thereafter, Congress responded to the demands of some advocates of inflationary monetary policies with the Silver Purchase Act, which pleased at least one group, the silver mining industry, by supplying it with a large subsidy, but Roosevelt's move on gold, along with the effort to pass the Securities Exchange legislation, led to a large campaign by the Committee for the Nation. The organization tried to draw together all antiradical groups, push devaluation farther, and defeat all other New Deal measures.

In August 1934, a new anti-New Deal organization took shape. This was the Liberty League, a bipartisan organization that united conservative politicians, especially Democrats, and business leaders, including Al Smith, John J. Raskob, John W. Davis, James Beck, the Du Ponts, Alfred Sloan and William Knudsen of General Motors, J. Howard Pew of the Sun Oil Company, and Sewell Avery of Montgomery Ward. They hoped to destroy the New Deal.

According to the Liberty League and other right-wing spokesmen of the period, America was being changed radically. The New Deal was a revolution, not the continuation and implementation of the progressive tradition and not an effective antiradical force. The right compared the new America with the absolute governments of Europe before the liberal revolutions of the eighteenth and nineteenth centuries. They also saw similarities between Roosevelt's America and the totalitarian regimes in Europe in the 1930s. Identifying the American way with their brand of thought and ignoring competing American traditions, the conservatives believed that the nation was being moved in "un-American" directions. And they explained the change as a consequence of the shrewd exploitation of the economic crisis and an amiable but reckless President by a collection of impractical intellectuals allied with a group of ambitious political bosses. The many intellectuals in the administration were attacked frequently as impractical and radical, and their ideas were compared unfavorably with the ideas of people who had enjoyed experience in business.

America was being damaged severely by the New Deal. It was preventing recovery by damaging business confidence, destroying the qualities of initiative and self-reliance that had made the country great, and abolishing freedom. In the Liberty League view, government power, not business power, was the oppressive form. The greatest need was the restoration in Washington of a positive attitude toward business.

Why had so many business leaders changed their attitude toward the New Deal? Their initial attitude had been influenced by the crisis, which had shattered their confidence in their own power. They could not promote recovery, and they seemed to be seriously threatened by radicals. Then Roosevelt had come to office, rejected radicalism, shown an interest in saving the business system and in promoting recovery, and turned the economy around. Soon, however, his programs and proposals, which involved the expansion of government and unions, began to look like threats to the power and status of business leaders. The New Deal seemed, in fact, to be the greatest threat in existence in 1934 for he had much more strength than any of the radicals. Furthermore, he did not seem to be a miracle worker, for recovery slowed after the spring of 1934.

The rise of the Liberty League revealed that Americans in the 1930s had not severed all ties with the past. The Liberty Leaguers expressed an American tradition that had been used to combat challenges from radical, reform, and labor movements. Business leaders had not changed their political ideology significantly. Most of them remained opposed to a powerful government and a powerful labor movement. Furthermore, the behavior of business leaders harmonized with traditional political methods. The Liberty League was not a secret conspiracy of men of great wealth seeking a strong man to protect their property. The Liberty League was simply a well-financed pressure group that attempted to convert the American people to its point of view.

The behavior, however, took place in a new situation. Earlier, the kinds of people involved in the Liberty League had been the objects of attack by the protest movements, but now those people formed one of the nation's major protest movements. And earlier, the major promoters of change had been the builders of American business, whereas now the leading roles were being played by the builders of the national government.

From the point of view of these business leaders and their political allies, too much change was taking place. At the same time, other figures in American politics were demanding much more change. They were putting pressure on Roosevelt to increase the activities of the government, especially to deal in larger ways with the problems of lower-income groups in American life. These people were inclined to criticize business leaders, the business system, and also the New Deal.

The critics included various types of "native radicals." Some were successful politicians such as Floyd Olson, the Farmer-Labor governor of Minnesota, "Young Bob" La Follette, his brother Phil, and Thomas Amlie, three Progressives from Wisconsin who served as senator, governor, and congressman during the 1930s. Other were unsuccessful. Utopian socialist Upton Sinclair, for example, ran unsuccessfully for governor of California in 1934. Many, including Sinclair, John Dewey, Charles Beard, John T. Flynn, and Alfred Bingham, were intellectuals.

America, the native radicals maintained, was unique. They were critical of Marxism, arguing that its concepts of class and class war were not relevant to the American situation. "We Americans . . . are different from Europeans," Phil La Follette insisted. " . . . We in the North . . . skipped feudalism entirely, while Europe still has a terrible psychological hangover from it." He called upon the frontier for the explanation of the difference and insisted that "the idea of classes has no vital tradition in our American past" and that any attempt to install it would only "produce endless dissension among many who now have nothing against each other." Bingham insisted that the American revolutionary movement could not depend on the working class, for it was too small and middle class in orientation, and he maintained that success depended upon the the development of radicalism in "the technical and managerial middle classes."

Some of these "radicals" were only militant progressives who accepted capitalism, advocated a much larger role for government, and called for the destruction of monopolies and the nationalization of only a few forms of property, but most of these people advocated the estabishment of a cooperative commonwealth as a substitute for capitalism and rejected the reformer's assumption that reform could make that system work successfully. They assumed that it was not worth the expense needed to save it and called for public ownership and operation of natural resources and the basic industries and production for use rather than profit as the ways to achieve the economy of abundance for all. They also assumed that fascism was the only alternative to socialism in the 1930s. There was no middle way.

While some of these people, including Senator La Follette, enjoyed friendly, cooperative relations with FDR and expected him to promote the necessary changes, most by 1935 were hostile. The New Deal is "a fraud and a sham in spite of its humanitarianism," Bingham insisted. The New Deal was trying to make capitalism work, and since it could not be made to work for long, the New Deal was "doomed to failure." Roosevelt and the New Deal were captives of the old system; reforms could help it last a little longer by reducing the pressure for change, but it would surely fail. When it did, radicals would have their chance.

The leader of the Socialist party, Norman Thomas, was critical of the New Deal from the beginning. He insisted that it was not socialism. It was, instead, a haphazard attempt to save capitalism.

Thomas also regarded the New Deal as part of a swing toward fascism. The rise of fascism had come as a great shock to socialists, for they had assumed that the collapse of capitalism would lead inevitably to socialism, and now they suggested that fascism was a method that the crumbling capitalist order was using to preserve its dominance. Thomas did not regard Roosevelt as a fascist, but he did believe that FDR's program would set the stage for the triumph of fascism in America. "The outstanding task before all lovers of peace, liberty, and economic justice is the fight against Fascism," Thomas insisted in 1934. "The way to fight Fascism is to build Socialism."

Beyond these broad appraisals, Thomas criticized specific aspects of the New Deal. He found its relief programs much too small, and he maintained that the large employers were circumventing NRA and that it neglected the interests of consumers. He also attacked AAA, especially its treatment of tenant farmers and also its cuts in production. Farm products, he insisted, should be made available to needy people.

A Catholic priest developed a much larger following. In radio broadcasts from his suburban Detroit church, Father Charles E. Coughlin had been discussing political issues for several years, warning of the dangers of a Communist revolution, blaming business leaders and conservative politicians, and arguing that the solution was to use the state as an instrument of social justice. He was especially critical of the bankers and emphasized the nationalization of the banks and the establishment of a managed currency. He gained the largest radio audience in the world, demonstrating a capacity to appeal to both urban, working-class Catholics in the Northeast and Protestant farmers in the Middle West.

At first, the radio priest supported Roosevelt and most of the New Deal, but Coughlin became increasingly unhappy during 1934, especially with developments in monetary policy. Arguing that both of the established parties were inadequate, he formed a new political organization, the National Union for Social Justice. He became explicitly anti-Semitic, denounced "a New Deal which protects plutocrats and comforts Communists," maintained that Roosevelt was dominated by the Chamber of Commerce and the international bankers, and demanded that the New Deal both nationalize the banks and stop interfering with private industry.

Senator Huey Long was another popular critic of the New Deal. He had built a large following in Louisiana by capitalizing on the exploitation of the poor whites by the large corporations, the planters, and the political bosses and had risen rapidly in politics as a champion of political and economic change. Elected governor in 1928 at the age of thirty-four, he furnished a variety of services for those who supported him: better schools, free textbooks, school buses, and the like, and he paid for them by levying heavy taxes on corporations such as Standard Oil while reducing sharply the taxes on lower-income groups. He did not pay much attention to constitutional limits on his power. Determined to destroy his opponents, he built a powerful machine, used military force to silence his opponents, seized control of the executive and administrative agencies, employed patronage, threats, bribes, and other means to gain control of the legislature, passed laws putting local governments under state control, and obtained control of the courts. Also, he monopolized the power to count the votes in elections, a very useful form of power.

Elected to the United States Senate in 1930, Long became a national figure, and like Coughlin, he turned from support for to hostility toward Roosevelt. The Louisiana senator came to regard the President as dominated by the same clique of bankers that had dominated Hoover. Long concluded that maldistribution of wealth was the basic national problem, called for programs to redistribute it, and developed a large, national "Share Our Wealth Society" in 1934. A powerful and exciting orator, he built a following of several million, and he saw his organization as an alternative to the two major parties, which seemed to him to lack significant differences and to be exploiting the people. He predicted that his third party would soon send him to the White House, and a poll by the Democrats suggested that he would get several million votes in 1936.

There were alarming signs that Long and Coughlin were forming an alliance with one another and with a third critic of Roosevelt who had great strength in the West, Dr. Francis Townsend. He represented a unique feature of American life, the organized politics of the aged. Millions of old people who were suffering from the Depression joined

Figure 7   Huey Long (*Wide World Photos*)

Townsend clubs to support a plan calling for a tax on business transactions to finance a pension of $200 each month for every person over sixty who would retire and spend the money. The plan promised prosperity for old folks and full employment for younger members of American society.

Millions of workers added to the pressures on Roosevelt. Several cities, including Minneapolis, Toledo, and San Francisco, many textile towns in New England and the South, and the rich agricultural valleys of California experienced large, often violent, frequently crippling riots and strikes in 1934. Like 1886 and 1894, 1934 was a year of unusually bitter and extensive class conflict. Workers were bitter about NRA, convinced that economic improvement provided better opportunities than had been available for several years, and determined to develop and demonstrate their strength. Communists and Socialists participated actively in the upheaval. And the protesters encountered equally intense class feelings among employers who resisted worker demands and often received help from state and local officials. Thus, the strikers had to contend against the police, National Guard units, and private forces. Strikes were numerous, but they usually failed. The workers needed help from government but seldom got it.

Senator Wagner concluded that much more effective legislation than NRA was needed if unions were to develop. Working with members of the National Labor Board and the American Federation of Labor, he developed legislation that sought to spell out the rights of workers, place restrictions on employers, and establish a strong agency to enforce the law. Although supported by organized labor and the Socialist party, among others, Wagner's proposal encountered much opposition, especially from business groups, and did not get support from the Roosevelt administration in 1934. Thus the proposal was not enacted. Wagner promised to fight on, arguing that "we are but commencing a new deal that will in proper time be pushed forward to its ultimate conclusions." The New York senator was another pressure with which Roosevelt had to contend.

Pressures for change were building inside as well as outside the administration. The Brandeisians, including Frankfurter, Corcoran, Cohen, and Landis, were very critical of NRA, stressing its failure to promote recovery and portraying it as evidence that government and business could not cooperate successfully. These people feared bigness and believed in decentralization and competition. Private and public "socialism" were equally hostile to individual freedom and development, they insisted; centralized planning was a bigger task than man could manage and was inevitably dominated by big business. They denied that bigness was the inevitable consequence of technological development and believed that government could and should be used to restore and maintain freedom. It should be employed in an attack upon concentrations of power and should be used to impose certain restrictions upon business behavior. The goal would be a more decentralized and competitive economy. These insiders had support from outsiders, such as Senators Borah and Wheeler, and from economists who were providing evidence on the ability of big corporations to control production and prices, the great and growing importance of monopolistic conditions in the American economy, the maldistribution of wealth, and excessive savings.

Another group, the Keynesians, also disliked NRA. Of these men, Marriner Eccles was the most important. A Utah banker, he became governor of the Federal Reserve System in November 1934. Eccles had ideas that, while similar to those of John Maynard Keynes, had been derived from his own experiences, not from the writings of the British economist. The Keynesians rejected emphasis on direct controls of the NRA type and advocated indirect controls as the way to promote recovery and maintain freedom. They would rely on monetary and fiscal policies and believed that the chief responsibilities of government in a depression were to compensate for the lower level of investment by private enterprise and to place purchasing power in the hands of those who needed it and would use it. To accomplish these objectives, the government should increase spending, reduce taxes on lower-income groups while raising taxes on those who tended to save rather than spend, and run a large deficit in the budget. The Keynesians believed that government could deal with economic problems and make capitalism work successfully, and they would make government the indispensable partner of business.

Social reformers also pressed for new programs. Led by Perkins and Hopkins inside the administration and Wagner in the Congress, they emphasized government action on behalf of lower-income groups. The basic theory of the welfare state and specific welfare proposals had been developed earlier, had gained some support, and had been translated into a few state and national laws. Now the situation seemed right for large-scale application of social justice progressivism. Support seemed to be available for moves that had been prepared long before.

Several important steps were taken in 1934, including the establishment in June of a cabinet committee on Economic Security, headed by Secretary Perkins. She brought with her more than two decades of experience in the social reform movement. Pressures that had been developing for many years came to a focus in her committee, which was authorized to develop a social insurance proposal.

Inside the Department of Agriculture, some officials were working for more than higher prices and higher profits for commercial farmers. Tugwell, who became Under Secretary in 1934 in spite of the opposition to the appointment of an intellectual to such a position, and Wilson, who replaced him as Assistant Secretary, hoped that the acreage reduction plan would stimulate discussion about planning and open the way for long-range programs that would limit commercial agriculture to the most efficient farmers operating the best land, convert other lands to other uses, and move the other farmers into other occupations. After Davis became administrator of AAA, he established a Division of Program Planning, headed by Howard R. Tolley, another economist. The division became the main planning agency for a department that for the first time had authority to plan a national agricultural program and put the plan into effect, and Tolley worked to move the existing program beyond production cuts and substitute the idea of adjustment. He frequently criticized the farm program, arguing that it paid little attention to regional and individual differences, did not allow the agricultural colleges and the farmers to contribute as much as they could to planning, and seemed likely to become rigid and to freeze existing patterns of farming rather than promote conservation and shift the production of crops into the regions in which they could be grown most successfully. He also argued that the farm program must serve the interests of tenant farmers, agricultural laborers, and urban workers, not merely the interests of commercial farmers.

Another group in AAA developed an especially strong interest in the tenant farmers of the cotton South. Centered in the Legal Division, the group was headed by Jerome Frank and closely allied with Tugwell. Urban rather than rural in background, these people looked upon AAA as an opportunity for reform.

Early in 1935, the reformers made a bold move. The Southern Tenant Farmers' Union, a new, biracial group that was being developed by critics of the Southern way of life and the cotton program, was organizing tenants in the Mississippi Delta, and some planters responded by evicting tenants who had joined the union and recruiting substitutes, encouraged by an official interpretation of the contract between AAA and the planters that suggested that while the latter were obligated to keep their normal number of tenants, they were not required to keep the same people that had been on their land before 1933. In December 1934, the union took one of the landlords into court to test his right to make such changes. Informed of this episode and of the way in which the contract was being interpreted, the Legal Division issued a reinterpretation that required landlords to keep the same people, not just the same number. The ruling could help both the union and the tenants.

This was an attempt to use the farm program to provide greater security for these low-income people. The lawyers justified their efforts as needed to realize the basic purpose of the legislation. They argued that the goal was the economic welfare of all rural groups, not just the landowners, and that the alternative interpretation of the contract did not provide adequate protection for the tenants.

The congressional elections of 1934 suggested that the advocates of change rather than the champions of resistance had the support of most voters. Many conservative Republicans went down to defeat, and the Democratic party enjoyed a landslide victory in spite of the historical tendency of the party in control of the White House to lose seats in

Congress in midterm elections. In races for the House, 322 Democrats were elected and only 122 Republicans were, giving the GOP the lowest percentage there in its history. The new ratio in the Senate was 69 to 27. Neither party had ever enjoyed such a large margin in that legislative chamber. And the new Congress was dominated by a demand for action. To avid New Dealers like Wagner and Hopkins, the situation now seemed right for enactment of the measures that interested them.

The United States Supreme Court, however, was more responsive to conservative arguments. There were liberals on the Court—Louis Brandeis, Harlan Fiske Stone, and Benjamin Cardozo. They emphasized a restrained use of judicial power and were inclined to tolerate the efforts by the states and the national government to deal with social and economic problems.

The liberal justices, however, had to contend with two other groups. One was composed of Willis Van Devanter, James C. McReynolds, George Sutherland, and Pierce Butler. Their thinking was heavily influenced by a set of beliefs that supported the exercise of judicial power, especially in the area of government-business relations. They believed in the changeless character of the Constitution and the scientific nature of judicial review and maintained that "dominant opinion" and social conditions were irrelevant and the Court could and should save society from itself. "If the Constitution . . . stands in the way of desirable legislation, the blame must rest upon that instrument and not upon the Court for enforcing it according to its terms," Sutherland declared. "The meaning of the Constitution does not change with the ebb and flow of events."

The third group was composed of Chief Justice Charles Evans Hughes and Justice Owen J. Roberts. They tended more toward the conservative than the liberal position. "When an act of Congress is appropriately challenged in the Courts as not conforming to the constitutional mandate," Roberts argued, "the judicial branch of the Government has only one duty—to lay the article of the Constitution which is invoked beside the statute which is challenged and to decide whether the latter squares with the former."

One result was the invalidation of the National Industrial Recovery Act. On May 27, 1935, the Court ruled in the Schechter case that the law was unconstitutional, for it involved an unconstitutional delegation of power and an unconstitutional regulation of business operations that had only an indirect, not a direct effect on interstate commerce. The decision, which was announced and explained by Hughes, had the support of all justices, including Brandeis, although Stone and Cardozo agreed only with the argument about the delegation of power. Roosevelt complained that the result relegated the nation "to the horse-and-buggy definition of interstate commerce."

The Court, by a vote of 6 to 3, with Brandeis, Stone, and Cardozo in dissent, also invalidated the Agricultural Adjustment Act. Behind this lay a campaign against production control by the processors and distributors of farm products. These businessmen had large sums invested in facilities designed to handle farm products and depended on large sales to make profits, and the processors were hit by the tax that financed the program. Thus, they challenged the constitutionality of the law, charging that it taxed processors to pay producers, and on January 6, 1936, the Supreme Court in *United States v. Butler* declared that the processing tax and the production controls violated the Constitution. In ruling against the farm program, the justices relied upon a distinction between production and commerce and a doctrine that taxes must not operate as penalties in order to control what was otherwise beyond congressional reach.

The decisions amounted to an unusually vigorous exercise of judicial power. The justices placed severe restrictions on the government's ability to solve economic problems. Dissenting in a very strong fashion in the Butler case, Stone said the Court had come to think of itself as "the only agency of government that must be assumed to have capacity to govern."

In the mid-1930s, Roosevelt was a man in the middle, as he had been in 1932. He had changed capitalism; the changes had infuriated some people, but others demanded still more change. The voters had not endorsed the calls for the abolition of capitalism that continued to be made, but they had clearly repudiated the Liberty League's demands for a return to past relations between government and business. If Roosevelt moved with the popular pressures, however, he would surely be hit by strong criticism from businessmen and encounter effective opposition in the United States Supreme Court. His political situation was very complex, containing strong groups who were alarmed by the pace of change and others who believed that it was much too slow. The situation placed heavy demands on his ability to make choices and provide leadership.

SUGGESTIONS FOR ADDITIONAL READING

Several of the books mentioned earlier remain valuable for subjects considered in this chapter. They include the surveys by Schlesinger and Leuchtenburg, Burns's biography of Roosevelt, Shannon, Seidler, and Johnpoll on Thomas and the Socialist party, Bernstein on labor, Huthmacher on Wagner, and Kirkendall on farm politics. Schlesinger's third volume, *The Politics of Upheaval*, Houghton Mifflin, Boston, 1960, also becomes useful at this point. For a broad survey of the opposition to Roosevelt, see George Wolfskill and John A. Hudson, *All but the People: Franklin D. Roosevelt and His Critics, 1933–1939,* Macmillan, New York, 1969.

An earlier book by Wolfskill, *The Revolt of the Conservatives: A History of the Liberty League, 1934–1940,* Houghton Mifflin, Boston, 1962, is the most thorough study of that organization. The best biography of a man of the left is T. Harry Williams, *Huey Long,* Knopf, New York, 1970. Clarke A. Chambers, *Seedtime of Reform: American Social Service and Social Action 1918–1933,* The University of Minnesota Press, Minneapolis, 1963, is a major book on the origins of the welfare state. It should be compared with Richard Hofstadter, *The Age of Reform: From Bryan to FDR,* Knopf, New York, 1955; J. Joseph Huthmacher, "Urban Liberalism and the Age of Reform," *Mississippi Valley Historical Review,* vol. 49, pp. 231–241, 1962; Abraham Holtzman, *The Townsend Movement: A Political Study,* Bookman Associates, Inc., New York, 1963; and Otis L. Graham, Jr., *Encore for Reform: The Old Progressives and the New Deal,* Oxford University Press, New York, 1967. And on the New Deal and the tenant farmers, a subject that has attracted a substantial amount of attention from historians recently, one should consult and compare David E. Conrad, *The Forgotten Farmers: The Story of the Sharecroppers and the New Deal,* The University of Illinois Press, Urbana, 1965, and Donald H. Grubbs, *Cry from the Cotton: The Southern Tenant Farmers' Union and the New Deal,* The University of North Carolina Press, Chapel Hill, 1971.

Robert G. McCloskey, *The American Supreme Court,* The University of Chicago Press, Chicago, 1960, and Alpheus Thomas Mason, *The Supreme Court from Taft to Warren,* Louisiana State University Press, Baton Rouge, 1958, are useful introductions to the Court and the New Deal. Leon Friedman and Fred L. Israel, eds., *The Justices of the United States Supreme Court 1789–1969: Their Lives and Major Opinions,* 4 vols., Chelsea House Publishers, New York, 1969, supplies a biographical sketch of each of the members of the Court.

Chapter 6

Changes in the
New Deal

In 1935, Roosevelt changed the New Deal. He did not move away from capitalism; he continued to reject demands to do so; government action remained the basic feature of his program, and the New Deal continued to rest upon the assumption of the progressive tradition that the powers of government could and should be employed to attack social and economic problems. But the administration became more critical of business leaders and more actively concerned with the welfare of lower-income groups; the federal government became more powerful in economic affairs and was converted into an active promoter of the labor movement.

Faced with a multitude of conflicting demands, Roosevelt could have moved in another direction, the one the conservatives desired. As he evaluated his situation, however, that direction involved great dangers: the growth of discontent and the possibility that one of the radicals actively competing with him for leadership would rise to power. The mounting criticism from the right reached a new high in May 1935, when the United States Chamber of Commerce in its national convention replaced its pro-New Deal president, Harriman, with a critic of the New Deal and denounced the New Deal very strongly. Such criticism, coupled with the pressure from the left, strengthened FDR's doubts about the wisdom of business leaders. He had attempted to protect and cooperate with them, but they had turned against him. Their concern about the loss of power and status suggested to him that they would oppose any policies capable of convincing most Americans that their institutions could serve their interests. The businessmen seemed foolish rather than wise. They lacked the wisdom needed to save themselves.

Furthermore, a swing to the right would be undemocratic as well as dangerous. The voters had repudiated the Liberty League in the congressional elections of 1934 and demanded further government action to deal with their problems. Additional government action, on the other hand, seemed likely to lead to victory in 1936. One of Roosevelt's shrewdest political advisers, Ed Flynn, argued that the President must develop policies that had greater appeal to lower-income groups. Greater support from them would compensate for the loss of business support and could enable the Democrats to replace the Republicans as the nation's majority party.

In addition, a swing to the right would involve a repudiation of Roosevelt's own past. For more than two decades, he had been steadily expanding the list of proposals for government action that he endorsed. Additional attempts to use government to promote the recovery and reform of the system would involve a continuation of the line of development he had been following since 1910.

The economic situation also suggested that changes should be made. Recovery was now moving very slowly. National income in 1934, while well above 1933, was less than half of what it had been in 1929. Unemployment remained especially discouraging. By 1935, more than 10 million workers still did not have jobs.

In this complex situation, the administration became more critical of the power of big business and made a larger effort to reduce it. The attitude had been present earlier but had not been as influential as the philosophy that insisted government must accept big business and attempt to work with business leaders in the management of the economy. A shift in emphasis took place. The administration moved away from the NRA emphasis upon government-business cooperation.

After the Supreme Court invalidated the National Industrial Recovery Act in May 1935, the administration made little effort to reenact the probusiness features of NRA. Harriman, Swope, Johnson, Richberg, and Moley—all advocates of cooperation between government and business— advocated efforts to revive NRA in some form, and Tugwell called for a reformed NRA, dominated by government rather than business and aimed at an economy of abundance. He and a few others, mostly intellectuals in and out of government, such as John Dewey and Mordecai Ezekiel, continued to believe that overall planning by a federal government responsive to all major economic groups was both possible and desirable, even essential, given the power of business institutions, the undesirable ways in which it was used, and the folly of the antitrust approach. Such planning proposals, however, had little popular or pressure group support, and Roosevelt did not push for reestablishment of NRA in any form.

The administration did continue to press for and get direct assistance to specific industries. One of these was bituminous coal mining. It had long been sick, suffering from a multitude of small producers and overproduction. Both operators and miners had benefited from NRA, and now a similar program was authorized by the Guffey-Snyder Coal Act of August 1935. Drafted by the United Mine Workers and introduced by a senator and a representative from Pennsylvania, the legislation established a national coal commission representing both labor and management and empowered to develop a code concerned with prices, trade practices, marketing, wages, hours, and collective bargaining. The government's power to tax was used to obtain compliance. A 15 percent excise tax was imposed on the industry, and 90 percent of the money was returned to the companies that participated in the program.

Several other industries also received help. A program rather like the one for coal was developed for crude oil production, although the oil program relied less upon the federal government and more upon the states and paid less attention to labor. It emphasized production control as the means of raising oil prices. And an NRA-type program was established for the trucking industry. It was subjected to effective federal regulation with the passage of the Motor Carrier Act of August 1935 that attempted to stabilize the industry by bringing it under the Interstate Commerce Commission, controlling entry into it and regulating rates, financial conditions, safety, and labor practices. Related legislation passed by Congress and the states during the second half of the 1930s provided subsidies and controls for the shipping and airline industries and protection for small merchants from chain stores, mail-order houses, and other large retailers.

These laws did not involve efforts to work with and help the entire business world, and they reflected strong interest in small and medium-size firms and in the workers. Other measures of the period expressed concern about concentrated economic power. Included were laws involving progressive taxation with its emphasis on the use of the taxing power to affect the distribution of power and wealth. Such philosophy had been a part of the Progressive movement, had been put into practice by the Wilson administration, but had been repudiated by the Republicans during the 1920s. It had returned in the tax legislation of 1932, and that was now augmented in 1935 and 1936. This development was championed by Frankfurter, Corcoran, Cohen, Wheeler, and other critics of big business, and it hit upper-income groups and large corporations harder than they had been hit by postwar tax laws. Although social reform was a very large feature of the legislation, it also sought to reduce the deficit in the federal budget and encourage businessmen to invest rather than save. And the reform dimension was limited by strong opposition in and out of Congress, especially from business leaders and their spokesmen. Also, the equalizing tendencies of these laws were counteracted by other tax measures passed in the same period, especially the Social Security tax and the state sales tax laws. Thus, tax legislation as a whole did not have a significant impact on the distribution of income or the size of business organizations.

Another program in 1935 attacked the "money power." Promoted chiefly by Eccles, the Banking Act of August 1935 attacked the power of the private bankers, especially the giants in New York City. Opposed by Senator Carter Glass of Virginia, most leading bankers, and many economists, Eccles's ideas were not fully accepted, but the law did increase the power of the Federal Reserve Board over the regional banks, rediscount rates, and reserve requirements. A Keynesian like Eccles valued the law because it gave the central government more power to regulate the money supply and thus to affect the performance of the economy. The antitrusters were pleased with the law because it reduced the power of the giant banking houses.

Another new law attacked a more recently developed form of economic power—the giant holding companies in the electrical industry. By 1929, sixteen groups had gained control of 92 percent of the nation's electrical power output, and many of the companies had operations scattered over the country. Passed in August 1935, the Public Utilities Holding Company Act was influenced heavily by Roosevelt's own very strong hostility to these companies, drafted in part by Cohen and Corcoran, and introduced by Wheeler and Rayburn. In addition to enlarging the power of the Federal Power Commission, the law granted new powers to the SEC, including the power to dissolve many of the giants. Advocates of the law defended it as a means of enlarging economic freedom. Businesses were to be freed from domination by giants who controlled a very important commodity. Opponents, however, watered down the proposal before passage, and reorganization of the industry, which was firmly opposed by its leaders, did not begin until 1940. The advance of public power in the Tennessee Valley and elsewhere was a more effective means of reducing the power of the private companies in the electrical field and lowering rates for electricity.

A critical attitude toward business power and a desire to reduce it influenced the New Deal in 1935–1936. The new programs were not aimed at the overthrow of the business system. They sought to reform it—to destroy some concentrations of power and to alter some practices. One obvious consequence was the expansion of government power. The ability of the federal government to influence the behavior of business-men was increased.

At the same time, the administration developed a "welfare state." New programs dealt directly with some of the most pressing problems of lower-income groups and enlarged the social welfare role of the federal government.

One important step was the establishment in the spring of 1935 of the Works Progress Administration, directed by Hopkins. Allotted $1.4 billion of the nearly $5 billion provided by the Emergency Relief Appropriations Act, WPA was an enlargement of the New Deal's relief efforts and a victory for the idea of work relief. And the new agency created as many jobs as possible with the money.

The WPA's range was one of its most significant features. In addition to many blue-collar projects that built and improved public buildings, airfields, and the like, there was a theater project that produced plays, a writers project that turned out guides to the states and other publications, and an artists project that was especially notable for its murals. A closely related agency, the National Youth Administration, provided the part-time employment needed to keep thousands of young people in school and aided an even larger number who were not in school.

Hopkins regarded relief as a permanent need, produced by the expansion of productivity and of the work force. The program should expand and contract as the situation demanded, and it should supplement other government programs needed to solve the problems of the poor. He assumed that capitalism could wipe out poverty but not if the nation relied only on the policies of the businessmen.

The relief programs had only enough money to employ less than one-third of the jobless and were required to pay low wages. In making decisions about his relief programs early in 1935, Roosevelt rejected efforts by Hopkins, Ickes, and Eccles to raise the appropriation substan-tially and by Wagner, La Follette, Norris, the AFL, and others to pay high wages. Roosevelt was restrained by what he regarded as the requirements of sound finance. While Douglas was no longer around to press them, the

Secretary of the Treasury, Henry Morgenthau, was, and Roosevelt did not need a big push, for he did his own worrying about the consequences of unbalanced budgets. He assumed that most people believed in a balanced budget and argued repeatedly that big expenditures and big deficits weakened business confidence and retarded business recovery.

While Hopkins developed WPA, another social worker, Frances Perkins, worked for the establishment of a social security system. And she cooperated with Wagner, who introduced the administration's proposal into the Senate. The proposal was opposed by conservatives who charged that it would harm the American character and by Townsendites and others who insisted that much larger pensions were required. Nevertheless, the administration achieved a victory in August 1935 with the passage of the Social Security Act. Authorizing old-age pensions and unemployment insurance, in addition to federal grants for several deprived groups, the law was an attempt to compensate for the insecurities created by growing old and the unreliability of the economic system in a society in which most people worked for someone else and were heavily dependent upon the actions of other people. The pension program was financed by heavy taxes on workers as well as employers and excluded many groups of workers, including some of the poorest, but the entire program constituted a significant departure from previous practices.

Thus, more than ever before, the federal government had a social-democratic tinge. This was not an abrupt departure from the past. Important preparations for these moves had been under way for a generation, for they were influenced by more than the special conditions of the 1930s. The development of industry and the city had generated pressures for the establishment of a welfare state, and now the Great Depression accelerated the development of it. As a result, government now became much more active in the social welfare field.

The efforts to reform the business system and develop the welfare state were also illustrated by developments in farm policy in 1935–1936. The administration stepped up efforts to change the farm business and rural life as a whole but continued its efforts to make commercial farming profitable. In fact, early in 1935, leaders in the Department of Agriculture rejected the attempt by Jerome Frank and others to use AAA as an instrument of social reform.

To Chester Davis, the top administrator in AAA, the Legal Division's reinterpretation of the cotton contract seemed to be a threat to the entire farm program. The new ruling struck him as a dishonest distortion of the meaning of the contract and a threat to the farm program. He believed that his agency existed to bring higher prices to commercial farmers, not to reform the Southern social system. AAA's task was economic recovery, a task that seemed to him to be of fundamental importance and one that had to be completed before progress along other lines could take place. In addition, he doubted that the federal government could develop a new social order in the South. Thus, he decided that he must either dismiss the reformers or resign.

Wallace shared Davis's views of political realities. The Secretary had been working for more than a decade to develop a program capable of raising farm prices and had close ties with commercial farmers and their political representatives. He denied that the farm legislation gave the department the power to change the Southern social system, and he feared that if he followed the lawyers, there would be a break with the farm representatives in Congress and the agricultural program would be destroyed.

Thus, on February 5, 1935, Davis "purged" Frank and several others from AAA, and a week after the purge, Wallace ruled that the cotton contract did not bind landowners to keep the same tenants. The top officials were heavily influenced by concern about their relations with the leading farm groups and their allies. The commercial farmers were one of the business groups with which the administration remained on friendly terms.

Nevertheless, the administration did develop a larger and more active interest in the rural poor. The development took place outside AAA. In April 1935, Roosevelt established a Resettlement Administration, using relief funds. The new agency was headed by Tugwell, one of the boldest of the New Dealers and now a vocal critic of AAA. Resettlement tried to improve land-use practices and help those who suffered seriously from past mistakes in the use of the land, such as destitute groups living in once-thriving but now exhausted lumbering, mining, and oil regions, sharecroppers in the South, and farmers on poor land in the drought area of the Middle West and the Appalachians. Although Tugwell favored resettlement of the rural poor, his agency placed heavier emphasis on rehabilitation of them in the places they occupied. It did, however, purchase some submarginal land and resettle its occupants on better land or in new suburban communities developed by RA. It also constructed camps for migratory workers.

RA's programs assumed that rural poverty demanded an attack upon its causes, not just relief. The situations had taken years to develop, and only long-run programs could correct them. But solutions could not come entirely from indirect action, such as the expansion of urban employment. Rural poverty had to be dealt with directly through specially devised programs. And these programs needed to be devised because all Americans, not just the rural poor, suffered from poverty in agriculture, for it meant inadequate purchasing power, destruction of the land, disease, and costly social services.

Most important, the planned attack needed to be made because worthy human beings suffered directly from rural poverty. The programs rested on democratic rather than business assumptions, looking upon all men, not just those who had demonstrated abilities in business, as worthy of help from government. Involved was a concept of man that stressed the influence of environment upon behavior.

RA officials believed that rural America should be approached as something more than simply the home of rural businessmen and that government should do more than make their operations profitable. The program, in other words, challenged the dominant orientation of farm politics. The attack upon the problems of the rural poor was largely the work of intellectuals in government while the leading farm organization, the American Farm Bureau Federation, encouraged the rural poor to depend on the programs designed to raise farm prices. Not surprisingly, therefore, Tugwell and Resettlement came under heavy attack and were forced to tackle large problems with small sums of money.

While RA was taking shape, a major move was made to expand the supply of electricity in rural America. Only 10 percent of the nation's farms had electricity, for the private companies could not supply it to them at a profit; Washington, by establishing a Rural Electrification Administration in May 1935, said in effect that the private companies had failed to do what people had a right to expect from their society. Promoted chiefly by Morris Cooke, an engineer and long-time advocate of public power, the new program used funds from the RFC and made loans at low cost to nonprofit electrical cooperatives established by farmers. Within six years, the percentage of American farms with electricity jumped to 40, and many farmers could enjoy radios, household appliances, and other things previously restricted almost entirely to city people.

Also in 1935, the New Deal stepped up efforts to improve the nation's farmland. The great drought of the mid-thirties did much to stimulate interest in this, and one result was the establishment of the Soil Conservation Service as part of the Department of Agriculture. It was headed by Hugh Bennett, a veteran crusader for conservation of the soil, and it embarked upon a major campaign to change the ways in which farmers used their land.

At the same time, AAA's Program Planning Division developed four new activities. A regional adjustment project brought USDA and agricultural college officials together to study what adjustments in production were needed while a county planning project organized farmers into nearly 2,500 planning committees. And these efforts were supplemented by two educational programs, discussion groups for farmers and "schools of philosophy" for extension workers, that were designed to broaden the outlook of people involved in the farm programs.

The work of the Planning Division enabled the administration to respond quickly to the crisis created by the Supreme Court decision invalidating the basic farm law. Tolley became the driving personality behind the development of substitute legislation. He discovered that the justices had revived the old willingness to experiment among those administering AAA and benefiting from it. Thus, he was able to achieve things he had been trying to accomplish. Even the farm leaders, who had responded to the Court's action with determination to get new price-raising legislation, listened to the economist and endorsed his recommendations, which were based upon the division's work.

Congress quickly passed a new law that seemed capable of both conserving the soil and controlling production without running into trouble with the Court. The law established a scheme whereby payments obtained from general revenue would be made to farmers who shifted acreage from soil-depleting crops and employed soil-building practices. As the soil-depleting crops happened also to be the surplus crops, including wheat and cotton, while the soil-conserving ones, such as grasses and legumes, were not surplus commercial commodities, production seemed certain to be shifted away from surplus crops and brought into line with domestic needs and anticipated exports. Tolley, who now replaced Davis as administrator, was convinced that the new program would bring more benefits to the farmer and the nation than its predecessor had.

The New Deal for agriculture had become more complex. It continued its efforts to make farming a profitable business but enlarged its efforts to reform rural life. At the same time, the New Deal became more actively interested in the labor movement than it had been in 1933–1934.

In 1935, a major effort was made to enlarge that movement and make it more powerful. In July Congress passed Wagner's National Labor Relations Act. Roosevelt did not yet place a high value on labor unions, and he did not endorse the effort to provide stronger labor legislation than NIRA had supplied until Wagner had gained strong congressional backing for his proposal, the Senate had passed it, and the Supreme Court had invalidated the recovery act. The New York Senator and other promoters of new labor legislation, including the AFL, assumed that the development of powerful unions was more important than social welfare legislation and that such unions were the best safeguard of democracy and the best promoter of prosperity in an industrial society, for they were the best counterbalance to big business. Unions could guarantee an adequate supply of purchasing power and political influence for the workers. The promoters of the legislation also assumed that the government must come to the aid of unions to assure their development. Without such aid, unions could not overcome resistance by already powerful employers. In addition, the promoters assumed that the establishment of collective bargaining was the way out of the industrial warfare that had erupted in 1934 and a means of gaining and maintaining the loyalty of the workers to the American system.

The proposal encountered very vigorous opposition from business and the press. The opponents argued that the bill was unconstitutional, would interfere with recovery, and was unfair. Nevertheless, the measure passed by large margins.

The new legislation contained three major features. First of all, it recognized the right of industrial workers to organize and bargain collectively in independent unions chosen by a majority of the workers in each firm. Secondly, the Wagner Act placed restrictions on the activities of management that violated that right. Regarded as "unfair labor practices," they were practices that had been common in the past and designed to block the growth of unions. They included any type of interference with, restraint upon, or coercion of the organizing efforts of the workers, any attempt to dominate a labor organization, any discrimination against union members in hiring and firing, and any refusal to bargain collectively. Finally, the law established a new government agency—the National Labor Relations Board—to enforce the act. It was empowered to reduce the freedom and power of business leaders so as to encourage and facilitate collective bargaining. The agency could conduct elections of bargaining representatives and restrain unfair labor practices.

The federal government had been converted into a promoter of the labor movement. Most of the time prior to the New Deal the federal government had been hostile or indifferent. The NIRA had included provisions designed to protect the right of labor to organize, but they had not been enforced effectively. Congress, pressed in the final stages by the White House, had now passed a much stronger piece of legislation.

Rather than reject capitalism, the New Deal was seeking to promote the further development of an organizational or collectivistic type of capitalism. Leading New Dealers assumed that a system that already contained large-scale business organizations also needed large-scale labor organizations. And the New Dealers assumed that the government had to be enlarged in order to produce more and larger unions. Workers were to be fitted into the organizational system, rather than encouraged or forced to overturn it.

New Deal labor policy had become very bold. Fiscal policy remained more cautious. Boosted chiefly by the Emergency Relief Appropriations Act, federal expenditures did go up, moving from $6.5 billion in fiscal 1935 to $8.5 billion the following year. Receipts also increased as a result of economic advance and the increase in taxes, but they did not keep pace with expenditures. Thus, the deficit increased from $2.6 billion in 1935 to $3.5 billion the following year. This fiscal policy was about as bold as most people were willing to accept in 1935–1936.

Roosevelt did not advocate spending as a means of bringing recovery. In fact, in vetoing the veterans' bonus bill in 1935, he explicitly rejected the argument that the expenditure was desirable because it would stimulate the economy by increasing purchasing power. To get his support, expenditures had to be justified by other considerations, and he believed in relying on other methods of promoting recovery. Congressmen, interested chiefly in doing something for veterans in an election year, passed the measure over his veto in 1936.

By then, Roosevelt was still trying to persuade the public that his financial practices were "sound" and that he was reducing the deficit and moving toward a balanced budget as quickly as possible. This attitude exerted a restraining influence on his willingness to endorse expenditures. His concern about "business confidence" inhibited him in the area of fiscal policy while it was overwhelmed in other areas by other considerations, such as the need for reforms. Business was critical of the administration's fiscal policy by 1936 but would, it appears, have been less critical if the spending and borrowing had not been accompanied by tax policies that businessmen did not like.

In spite of inhibitions and resistance, the federal government was enlarged significantly in 1935–1936 and became more responsive to the needs of lower-income groups. The administration had become more critical of many business groups, but it had not become interested in abolishing capitalism. In fact, government programs included efforts to serve business interests. Also, reduction in the size of business organizations, while now a part of the New Deal, was only a small part. A substantial reduction in business power had become a major New Deal aim. This was to be accomplished, however, mainly by enlarging government and labor. Business organizations were to be made less powerful by enlarging labor organization and expanding the size and role of the federal government, using it to help groups that did not have as much power as business leaders had to help themselves. This redistribution of power would, the New Dealers assumed, result in a more equitable distribution of wealth and income and in prosperity.

SUGGESTIONS FOR ADDITIONAL READING

The thesis concerning the change in the New Deal in 1935 was introduced to historical writing by Basil Rauch in *The History of the New Deal, 1933–1938,* first published in 1944 and now available in a paperback edition, Capricorn Books, New York, 1963. To him, the change seemed so large that he argued that we should talk of two New Deals, not one. Since 1944, his thesis has exerted a large influence and stimulated controversy, as Otis L. Graham, Jr., and William H. Wilson have demonstrated in two articles, "Historians and the New Deals, 1944–1960," *Social Studies,* vol. 54, pp. 133–140, 1963, and "The Two New Deals: A Valid Concept?" *Historian,* vol. 28, pp. 268–288, 1966. On the controversy, one should see both Leuchtenburg and Schlesinger and also the books by Raymond Moley cited in Chapter 3 and another book by Tugwell, *The Democratic Roosevelt: A Biography of Franklin D. Roosevelt,* Doubleday, Garden City, N.Y., 1957. Rauch himself moved away from his thesis and emphasized "the unity of the New Deal more than its shift from early to later policies."

The books by Hawley and Parrish mentioned earlier remain very valuable on the business policies discussed in this chapter, and Stein's study of fiscal policy should also be consulted. Charles's study of Hopkins is important on WPA, and Bernstein's *Turbulent Years* and Huthmacher's biography of Wagner are very valuable on labor policy. On Social Security, see Theron F. Schlabach, *Edwin E. Witte: Cautious Reformer,* The University of Wisconsin Press, Madison, 1969; Daniel Nelson, *Unemployment Insurance: The American Experience, 1915–1935,* The University of Wisconsin Press, Madison, 1969; and Daniel S. Hirshfield, *The Lost Reform: The Campaign for Compulsory Health Insurance in the United States from 1932 to 1943,* Harvard, Cambridge, Mass., 1970. For discussions of developments in agricultural policies, see the books by Kirkendall and Grubbs and also Paul K. Conkin, *Tomorrow a New World: The New Deal Community Program,* Cornell University Press, Ithaca, N.Y., 1959; Bernard Sternsher, *Rexford Tugwell and the New Deal,* Rutgers University Press, New Brunswick, N. J., 1964; and Sidney Baldwin, *Poverty and Politics: The Rise and Decline of the Farm Security Administration,* The University of North Carolina Press, Chapel Hill, 1968.

Chapter 7

The Triumph
of the New Deal

In 1936, the New Deal achieved a spectacular victory. Most voters endorsed the man who had preserved and changed the capitalistic system, and their behavior suggests strong support for change but almost none for revolution. The voters wanted capitalism but not the capitalism of the 1920s. Anti-New Dealers proposed both the return to business dominance and the abolition of the business system, but the voters rejected these alternatives. Traditions explained some of their behavior but not all the important aspects of it, including the outcome. Roosevelt achieved a much bigger victory than any of his Democratic predecessors and a bigger victory than his own in 1932. Millions of voters changed their voting habits. Had the New Deal not conformed to their desires to a significant degree, they would not have behaved as they did. Other ways were available to them.

Roosevelt's strategy in 1936 was designed to win reelection by a substantial majority and thereby obtain overwhelming ratification for the New Deal. To accomplish this, he played down party affiliations. He rarely referred to his own party; he took the Democrats for granted, and he went out of his way to thank non-Democrats for their support. He supplied encouragement and support for the Farmer-Labor party in Minnesota, the Progressives in Wisconsin, the American Labor party in New York, and Republican Senator George Norris in Nebraska. Norris was one of the progressives outside the Democratic party who campaigned actively for Roosevelt.

FDR's strategy was influenced by the feeble character of the Democratic party from the 1890s to the 1930s. The President was aware that the old party scarcely existed outside the South, some parts of the rural West, and a few urban machines, such as Tammany in New York City and the Pendergast organization in Kansas City. The President knew

Figure 8   At the Peak of His Power—1936 (*Wide World Photos*)

that he could not tie himself too closely to the Democratic party and that
he could not count upon a sense of party loyalty to accomplish a defense
of the New Deal. His party, Schlesinger has observed, "could stay in
power only by attracting to itself traditionally non-Democratic groups."

There were other elements in Roosevelt's strategy. He ran against
Hoover, rather than the Republican nominee, Governor Alfred M.
Landon of Kansas. FDR repeatedly reminded the people of the conditions four years earlier and of the improvements that had been made since
then. Fortunately for him, the economy was improving. Recovery had
resumed again in 1935 and moved forward throughout 1936. By election
day, unemployment had been cut by 40 percent since 1932, industrial
output had nearly doubled, and the net income of farm operators was
nearly four times as high as it had been four years earlier.

Roosevelt also made a strong class appeal. He denounced "economic royalists" and "organized money" and represented himself as the
champion of the "forgotten man." "I should like to have it said of my first
Administration that in it the forces of selfishness and of lust for power
met their match," he proclaimed. "I should like to have it said of my
second Administration that in it these forces met their master." The New
Deal, he suggested, had only begun.

Roosevelt was building a new party. It was not the well-organized
type, united by an ideology, that some desired. James MacGregor Burns,
in his biography of Roosevelt, has been especially critical of him for
failing to build a liberal political coalition and party organization capable

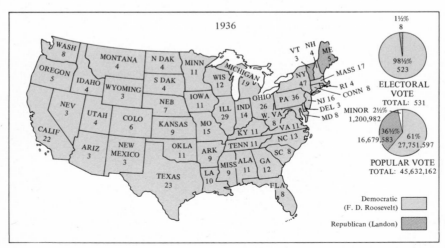

Figure 9 Election Results—1936 (*National Atlas, U.S. Geological Survey, Washington, 1970. Used by permission.*)

of sustaining and enlarging the reform movement and has argued that he
failed as a party leader because of "his unwillingness to commit himself to
the full implications of party leadership, . . . his eternal desire to keep
open alternative tactical lines of action, including a line of retreat." He
could not make the needed "continuing intellectual and political commitment to a set strategy. . . ." But Roosevelt had committed himself to the
construction of a much larger and much more vigorous party than the old
Democratic party had been. The party that was coming to be was
competing actively throughout the country, more closely tied to lower-
income groups and their organizations, and less dependent upon the
South. It was supported not only by traditional Democrats but also by
people who had been hostile or indifferent toward them.

The result was a landslide victory for Roosevelt and the new
Democratic party. While he received nearly 28 million votes, his leading
opponent, Landon, received less than 17 million. Landon carried only
Maine and Vermont, good for 8 electoral votes while Roosevelt picked up
523. State after state which had been strongly Republican in the past, such
as Pennsylvania, Michigan, and California, had become Democratic. In
contrast with Roosevelt's performance, no Democratic nominee for the
presidency from the 1850s to 1932 had received more than 50 percent of
the popular vote, and from 1892 to 1932, only Wilson had received close
to that amount. FDR received nearly 61 percent. And the Democratic
delegation in Congress increased from 69 to 75 senators and from 322 to
333 representatives. The party's congressional gains were made outside
the South.

Roosevelt's support contained a significant number of new voters.
The total vote was nearly 6 million above 1932, and Roosevelt's total was
nearly 5 million higher than it had been four years earlier. Many of the
new voters had become eligible since then, and they tended to prefer him
by a wide margin. Many others, however, had been eligible earlier but had
not been interested in voting. Now, they were attracted to the polls by
Roosevelt and his programs.

There was a substantial increase in turnout, and almost all of it took
place outside the South, outside the rural areas, and inside urban
working-class neighborhoods. Overall turnout increased by more than 4
percent, moving from less than 58 percent in 1932 to nearly 62 percent of
the nation's adults. Two important industrial states, Michigan and Pennsylvania, enjoyed especially large increases, in part because two-party
competition had been restored in those states after a generation of
Republican dominance and Democratic weakness. New voters constituted about 20 percent of the electorate, and most of them were members
of the urban working classes.

Most of those who switched from one party to another were also members of the urban working classes, and the latter formed the largest bloc in the "Roosevelt Coalition." Most workers, "old stock" as well as new, Protestants as well as Catholics and Jews, white as well as black, voted for Roosevelt. Class consciousness, at least among these people, was very strong in 1936. His proportion of the labor vote ranged from 61 percent of the white-collar workers to 81 percent of the unskilled and 84 percent of those on relief. The urban workers provided even more support for him than they had in 1932.

The voting behavior of these people enabled Roosevelt to carry the cities by even larger margins than he had four years before. His plurality in the twelve largest cities "leaped 80 percent, the biggest change in any single election," Samuel Lubell has pointed out. Twelve cities with more than 100,000 people, including Philadelphia, had not voted for him in 1932, but now all but two of them did, including the twelve largest. Those cities had supported the Republican party most of the time since the 1890s, but now Roosevelt won even in the big cities, Los Angeles, San Francisco, Seattle, Philadelphia, Pittsburgh, Baltimore, Chicago, and Detroit, that Smith had failed to carry.

Many of the urban voters for Roosevelt were immigrants from southern and eastern Europe and the children of those immigrants. They had long supported the repeal of prohibition that had come since 1932; they had long had an interest in social welfare programs as a consequence of their experiences in slums and factories, and they had become increasingly interested in government help as a result of the heavy impact of the Depression on them. Thus, they liked many features of the New Deal. They also applauded Roosevelt's appointment policy, which recognized that people who were not Anglo-Saxon Protestants could make important contributions to national life, and they appreciated the equalitarian ideology of many New Dealers, which rejected the racist assumptions involved in immigration policy and other features of American life.

While class was important in the "new immigrant" support for Roosevelt, more than class was involved. Most recent immigrants and their children were members of the working classes, but some were not, and they also preferred him.

Roosevelt's support from the new-stock Americans was much greater than it was from the nation as a whole and much greater than the support they had given earlier Democratic candidates. Most of these people were Catholics, and Roosevelt carried farther a tendency of Catholics to vote Democratic that had begun earlier. Many were Jews, and here the support for Roosevelt constituted a large change from their strong Republicanism in the 1920s.

Most black voters also supported Roosevelt. More than 20 percent of the nation's Negroes now lived outside the South, and the congressional elections of 1934 had supplied evidence that they were changing their voting habits. In that year, black voters sent a black Democrat to Congress for the first time. He was Arthur Mitchell of Chicago, a city in which only slightly more than 20 percent of the black voters had supported Roosevelt in 1932. Now, in 1936, blacks for the first time gave a majority of their votes to the Democratic presidential candidate. They voted 3 to 1 for Roosevelt.

Several influences produced the change. In part, it resulted from disgust with the Republicans, who had long taken the Negro vote for granted. "Abraham Lincoln is not a candidate in the present campaign," one Negro newspaper reminded its readers. The appeal to them by Landon and other Republicans could not compensate for the party's record in recent years.

The New Deal was even more influential. While signs of black discontent with Republican rule had been apparent in some places in 1932 and even earlier, the big, decisive change took place after the establishment of Roosevelt's policies. The Roosevelt administration did not develop programs designed to deal with the special problems of Negroes, such as lynching and disenfranchisement, and there was discrimination against blacks and segregation in New Deal programs. Nevertheless, blacks did benefit from parts of the New Deal, especially the relief programs, for most were members of the working classes and many were unemployed. Most of the benefits to blacks went to those who lived in cities and were able to vote.

Again, however, more than class was involved. The change was influenced also by the equalitarianism that some New Dealers expressed, the behavior of New Dealers such as Eleanor Roosevelt and Harold Ickes who were outspoken critics of racial discrimination, the appointment policy that placed more Negroes in important government jobs than Roosevelt's predecessors had, and the substantial role that Negroes played in the Democratic National Convention for the first time. Although Roosevelt himself approached race questions very cautiously, his departure from the practices of his Democratic predecessor in the White House, Woodrow Wilson, was striking.

In comparison with other groups, Roosevelt's party had become quite attractive to black Americans, at least the minority who could vote. The leading pressure group concerned with their problems, the National Association for the Advancement of Colored People, focused its attention on lynching and education and had only a small number of members. The Communist party continued to achieve almost no success in its efforts to gain black support, and the American Federation of Labor, except for A.

Philip Randolph's Brotherhood of Sleeping Car Porters, made almost no effort to recruit Negro workers.

Organized labor supplied more support for a Democratic presidential candidate than the movement had in the past. In 1932, John L. Lewis had supported Hoover, and Sidney Hillman and David Dubinsky had backed Thomas. Now, several leaders, including Lewis and Hillman, formed Labor's Non-Partisan League for Roosevelt. Labor liked the social welfare programs and the assistance to the movement itself and wanted additional legislation that would benefit the workers and the unions. The labor leaders worked hard and successfully to persuade their members to vote for Roosevelt. Eighty percent of them did so.

The labor movement filled the void created by the alienation of the businessmen. A few prominent businessmen, including Joseph P. Kennedy, Edward Filene, A. P. Giannini, and Thomas Watson, did support Roosevelt, convinced that the New Deal was actually enlarging business opportunities. Corporations had, after all, moved from losses of $2 billion in 1933 to profits of $5 billion in 1936. Nevertheless, most business leaders, including most large newspaper publishers, opposed Roosevelt's reelection, and their financial contributions to the Democratic campaign fell far below the 1932 level. Some of the unions, however, especially Lewis's United Mine Workers, compensated for this decline by contributing heavily to Roosevelt's campaign.

At the same time that city people voted overwhelmingly for Roosevelt, most farmers also cast their ballots for him. They were in the Roosevelt Coalition in spite of the strength of the cultural factors that had promoted urban-rural conflict in the 1920s and in spite of some unhappiness with acreage controls. Farmers also supported Roosevelt in spite of the efforts of an affiliate of the Liberty League, the Farmers' Independence Council. A propaganda organ for industry, the meatpackers, and some large cattle interests, it preached an individualistic philosophy and tried to turn the farmers against the New Deal. And farmers supported Roosevelt in spite of the strength of Republican traditions in the rural Middle West. In Iowa, for example, Roosevelt received better than 60 percent of the farm vote whereas Democratic presidential candidates in the 1920s had averaged less than 30 percent. Obviously, the benefits of New Deal farm programs were very persuasive.

The Democrats also made a strong and successful appeal for the female vote. Women were now more active in politics and in the Democratic party than ever before. Molly Dewson, a social worker interested in equal opportunity for women, headed the Women's Division of the Democratic National Committee and played a leading role in this development, while Frances Perkins, the first woman to serve in the

Cabinet, and Eleanor Roosevelt, the President's wife, were also important. Mrs. Roosevelt, a liberal influence on her husband, represented him very actively throughout the country.

Most intellectuals, a small but articulate group, supported Roosevelt. Only a few, such as Reinhold Niebuhr and John Dewey, supported Thomas. Intellectuals had long resented the power of business in America and believed in an active government. They also liked Roosevelt's use of intellectuals as advisers and administrators.

In addition, two traditional props of the Democratic party, the urban machines and the South, supported Roosevelt. The Hague machine in Jersey City, the Kelly machine in Chicago, the Pendergast machine in Kansas City, and others like them backed him in spite of their limited interest in reform. What did interest them was the enlargement of patronage that accompanied the expansion of government. Organizations with good relations with the administration, such as the Pendergast machine, gained strength by staffing New Deal agencies and distributing New Deal benefits. In Pittsburgh, the New Deal actually helped the Democrats, with Senator Joseph Guffey and David Lawrence as leading figures, to build an organization that was much like the Republican machine that had lost power in 1933. Republican machines and Democratic organizations like Tammany Hall that had bad relations with the national administration declined in the New Deal period, but the old-time boss remained a part of American politics. He was not destroyed by FDR.

Long-time Democrats in the South also formed an important part of the Roosevelt Coalition. Most Southerners were enthusiastic supporters of the New Deal. Their representatives had played important roles in its development. The Speakers of the House—first Joseph W. Byrns of Tennessee and then William B. Bankhead of Alabama—were Southerners, as were the Senate majority leader—Joseph T. Robinson of Arkansas—and most committee chairmen. One of the latter, Sam Rayburn of Texas, had sponsored some of the most important New Deal legislation. Senator James F. Byrnes of South Carolina was another influential Southerner who cooperated closely with the President. Not surprisingly then, he received 76 percent of the Southern vote. Also, one of his outspoken Southern critics, Senator Thomas P. Gore of Oklahoma, was defeated for reelection by a New Dealer, Josh Lee.

There was some dissatisfaction in the South, and Southern critics of the New Deal also had representatives in Washington. Some Southerners disliked the new importance of the Northern cities in their party. Many Southerners also feared the new relations between Democrats and blacks, and some believed that Roosevelt's policies threatened important interests in the South and betrayed the traditions of the party. Senators Carter

Glass and Harry Byrd of Virginia, Walter F. George of Georgia, and Ellison D. "Cotton Ed" Smith of South Carolina had been critical of the New Deal, but all these men recognized Roosevelt's popularity and avoided a break. Governor Eugene Talmadge of Georgia had been much less cautious in his anti-New Deal efforts; he ran for the Senate in 1936 against a Roosevelt supporter, Senator Richard Russell, and lost.

Some Southerners voted for anti-New Dealers when they had a chance, as they did in North Carolina in 1936. There, the voters in the Democratic senatorial primary rejected a New Dealer and endorsed a cautious anti-New Dealer, Senator Josiah W. Bailey. Thus, the North Carolinians returned to Washington a senator who recognized that his political future did not demand that he follow the lead of the President. The same voters, however, supported Roosevelt. He was the only Democrat running for the presidency.

Some anti-New Deal Democrats outside the South were less inhibited by party tradition and deserted their party in 1936. The list included two former presidential nominees, Smith and John W. Davis; a former senator, James Reed; and a former chairman of the party's national committee, Raskob. They were unhappy with changes in the policies of their party and were convinced that it had deserted them.

The Democratic losses, however, were insignificant when compared with the troubles of the old ruling party. The Republicans had experienced bitter frustrations since 1929, and their party was wracked by internal conflict over the response that should be made to the New Deal and the steps that should be taken to regain the dominant position the party had held for many years.

The Grand Old Party selected a moderately progressive member of its ranks to lead the ticket. Landon's ties with progressive Republicanism ran back to the days of Theodore Roosevelt, and his election victories in 1932 and 1934 set him apart from most Republicans. His record in Kansas politics included support for civil liberties and social and economic reform, and he accepted much of the New Deal and promised more government help to farmers and old folks and a constitutional amendment permitting the states to pass social welfare legislation. He was certainly not as conservative as the support for him from the Liberty League made him appear. Yet, he called for cuts in government spending and a balanced budget, criticized the growth of the central government and the presidency, and warned of dangers ahead, and Republican campaigners emphasized his disagreements with the New Deal. He did supply the voters with a choice. Less than 37 percent of them, however, selected the alternative that he offered.

To many voters, the GOP seemed to be the party of big business.

Business leaders did provide very generous support for the Republican party, which reported expenditures of $14 million compared with $9.2 million for the Democrats. Republican funds financed a slick advertising campaign that strengthened the impression that the party spoke for business leadership.

The Republican party was not the only political organization that experienced frustration in 1936. The broad coalition that endorsed Roosevelt and defeated Landon also rejected the right and the left. The Liberty League had become increasingly active during 1935 and 1936 as the members had grown even more furious as a result of the legislation of the period. Organization leaders had thought of forming a third party and attempted to disrupt the Democratic party by supporting Al Smith. In the end, however, the Liberty Leaguers supported Landon, and they played a large, loud, and expensive role on his behalf. The effort embarrassed Landon, for it encouraged the people to associate him with the league. The Democrats contributed by concentrating much of their fire on that organization.

The Liberty Leaguers were demoralized by the size of Roosevelt's victory. It suggested that most people liked the New Deal and wanted nothing to do with the philosophy of this right-wing group. As a consequence, it ceased to function actively in 1937.

A similar fate befell the Socialist party. Thomas received fewer than 200,000 votes. Party membership dropped nearly 50 percent soon after the election, falling below 7,000 in 1937.

This development was a consequence of the New Deal. Roosevelt, Thomas was convinced, had cut the ground out from under him and his party, and the historian of the party has concluded that the "story of the decline of the Socialist Party since 1933 is, for the most part, the story of the political success of the New Deal." Prominent members, such as Hillman and Dubinsky, deserted the party and led others out of it and into the Roosevelt ranks. Some Socialists had concluded that the New Deal was a fulfillment of their dreams; others realized it was not socialism but accepted it as "half a loaf," convinced that half was better than none at all; and others concluded from the experiences of the 1930s that socialism had no chance in America and became enthusiastic New Dealers, regarding the New Deal as in harmony with American conditions. Hillman argued that the Socialist party had failed to build the labor movement and was incapable of doing so whereas the New Deal had helped the movement make important gains. He also argued that "the defeat of Roosevelt and the introduction of a real Fascist administration" would "make the work of building a labor movement impossible."

The New Deal's impact on potential Socialists was especially

Figure 10   Gerald L. K. Smith (left), Father Coughlin (center), and Dr. Townsend (right)
(*United Press International Photo*)

important. Millions of people who might have become Socialists if conservatism had been the only alternative that American politics supplied felt no need to become Socialists. Especially important were the people upon whom the party was counting for success, the working classes. They did not behave as Socialists had predicted. Consequently, as David Shannon has pointed out, "the party of Debs, which had predicted the collapse of American capitalism, itself collapsed during the worst crisis American capitalism ever had."

Other representatives of the left also failed. In the fall of 1935, the most popular of the radicals, Huey Long, had been assassinated, forcing Coughlin, Townsend, Gerald L. K. Smith, and others to seek a substitute to run against Roosevelt. They found Congressman William Lemke of North Dakota and hoped to unite behind him Long's followers in the South, Townsend's in the Far West, and Coughlin's in the Middle West and East. Coughlin believed that the combination would produce 9 million votes, and many assumed that it could decide a close election. But the leaders quarreled with one another; most radicals and progressives denounced them, and Coughlin received much criticism from the Catholic hierarchy and clergy, many of whom endorsed Roosevelt. Lemke also suffered from the party's failure to get on the ballot in fourteen states, including some where his allies had large followings. The candidate of the Union party, Lemke ran on a rather confusing platform that faced right as well as left, and the campaign denounced the New Deal as both "bent on communistic revolution" and dominated by "international bankers." The most successful third-party candidate, Lemke received less than 1 million votes, about 2 percent of the total. The outcome prompted Coughlin, who had promised to take "a Communist from the chair once occupied by Washington," to announce his retirement from politics and to disband his National Union for Social Justice.

Once again, the left had failed to gain the support of lower-income Americans, including those who did not support either the Republican or the Democratic party. Although turnout increased in 1936, it remained far below its potential. Many adults—nearly 40 percent of them—did not participate actively in the politics of 1936. Turnout was especially low among the poorest people in both urban and rural areas. Educational deficiencies, restrictions on the franchise, social isolation, and other factors limited their participation, but many people apparently found nothing in the programs and proposals of the period that seemed significant to them. Roosevelt had reduced the number of the alienated by only a small percentage, but none of his rivals appealed effectively to them. His competitors were, in fact, less effective than he in attracting people who had not voted in the past.

The American response to the great crisis of the 1930s had been influenced by desires for change and also by traditions. Almost all Americans were too heavily influenced by traditional attitudes, including political apathy and alienation, to endorse advocates of revolutionary change, but most of the voters supported a promoter of nonrevolutionary change. To do so, millions of Americans either switched parties or changed from nonvoters to voters. Clearly, the New Deal seemed significant and desirable to them. They liked the changes that the New Dealers had promoted.

As a consequence, the relations between the two major parties changed. Roosevelt, with his program and his personality, had successfully exploited the opportunities for party realignment that existed in the 1930s. Rather than the year in which the Republicans regained their status as the majority party, as they had after the Wilsonian interlude, 1936 was the high point in a "critical period" or "realigning electoral era" that had begun several years earlier. The Democrats had maintained and strengthened their hold on the position they had established in 1932. They had become the nation's majority party.

This new position of the Democratic party was, however, a result of the influence of tradition as well as a desire for change. The party not only added voters but held on to most of its traditional support. Some Roosevelt supporters were influenced decisively by traditional attitudes toward the Democratic party. They voted for him, not because he was a promoter of change, but because he was a Democrat and so were they. Those who voted for Roosevelt in spite of their dislike for the New Deal apparently did not feel that the changes of the 1930s were sufficiently large to justify a change in their party affiliation.

Many other Americans—better than one-third of the voters—were so heavily influenced by traditions that they voted Republican. Most of these were old-stock, Protestant Americans in the rural areas, towns, and suburbs. Few were poor. Some had been influenced by the Depression to vote for Roosevelt in 1932 but now returned to their traditional party. Some had been Democrats. Some were influenced most of all by their traditional attitude toward the Republican party, while for others, hostility toward the ways in which the country was being changed was decisive. To many of his supporters, Landon seemed to symbolize an older, simpler, and better America.

American voters of the 1930s had not broken all ties with the past, and they had rejected revolution. But they were experiencing changes that seemed significant to them, and they gave the period's most effective promoters of change the power needed to go forward.

SUGGESTIONS FOR ADDITIONAL READING

Leuchtenburg's essay in Schlesinger and Israel, eds., *History of American Presidential Elections*, is the best survey of the subject. See also his larger work on the New Deal and the third volume of Schlesinger's *Age of Roosevelt*. Landon's career has been examined with sympathy and intelligence by Donald R. McCoy in *Landon of Kansas*, University of Nebraska Press, Lincoln, 1966. The essays in the book by Clubb and Allen (see Chapter 3) help one see the historical significance of the 1936 election. See also the outstanding essay by E. E. Schattschneider, "United States: The Functional Approach to Party Government," in Sigmund Neumann, ed., *Modern Political Parties*, The University of Chicago Press, Chicago, 1956. George Tindall, *The Emergence of the New South, 1913–1945*, Louisiana State University Press, Baton Rouge, 1967, discusses Southern attitudes toward the New Deal. See also Elmer E. Puryear, *Democratic Party Dissension in North Carolina 1928–1936*, The University of North Carolina Press, Chapel Hill, 1962. Lyle Dorsett, *The Pendergast Machine*, Oxford University Press, New York, 1968; Bruce M. Stave, *The New Deal and the Last Hurrah: Pittsburgh Machine Politics*, The University of Pittsburgh Press, Pittsburgh, 1970; and Richard Polenberg, "Franklin D. Roosevelt and the Purge of John O'Connor: The Impact of Urban Change on Political Parties," *New York History*, vol. 49, pp.

306–326, 1968, are very important on the New Deal and the political machines. On the Catholics, see George Q. Flynn, *American Catholics and the Roosevelt Presidency, 1932–1936,* University Press of Kentucky, Lexington, 1968; on blacks, see Leslie H. Fishel, "The Negro in the New Deal Era," *Wisconsin Magazine of History,* vol. 48, pp. 111–126, 1964–1965; Rita Werner Gordon, "The Change in the Political Alignment of Chicago's Negroes during the New Deal," *Journal of American History,* vol. 56, pp. 584–603, 1969; and Raymond Wolters, *Negroes and the Great Depression: The Problem of Economic Recovery,* Greenwood, Westport, Conn., 1970. The essays by Lane and Burnham recommended in Chapter 3 remain very helpful on voter turnout.

Most of the relevant work on the failure of the left and the right has already been cited. See especially the books by Wolfskill, Shannon, Seidler, and Johnpoll. See also James C. Carey, "The Farmer's Independence Council of America, 1935–1938," *Agricultural History,* vol. 35, pp. 70–77, 1961; Edward C. Blackorby, *Prairie Rebel: The Public Life of William Lemke,* University of Nebraska Press, Lincoln, 1963; Charles J. Tull, *Father Coughlin and the New Deal,* Syracuse University Press, Syracuse, N.Y., 1965; and David H. Bennett, *Demagogues in the Depression: American Radicals and the Union Party, 1932–1936,* Rutgers University Press, New Brunswick, N.J., 1969.

Chapter 8

The Court Fight and the Emergence of the Roosevelt Court

Two highly significant changes took place soon after the 1936 election. One involved the behavior of the United States Supreme Court. After achieving his spectacular victory, Roosevelt set out to reform the one institution that had been frustrating him and the one remaining threat to the New Deal. His effort produced his first major defeat in Congress, but the Court changed its ways. In 1935–1936, it had limited the New Deal's efforts to enlarge the role of government, but thereafter it stopped offering resistance to the growth of government in economic affairs and began itself to promote change in other areas.

Roosevelt's court reform proposal was influenced by the traditional progressive distrust of the Court as an undemocratic institution, a theory that had been developed long before and had been expressed frequently in 1935 and 1936. The proposal was influenced even more by his concern about the immediate situation. New challenges to the New Deal were moving up in the judicial system, and Roosevelt feared that the Court might invalidate additional New Deal measures. To FDR, the future of democratic institutions was at stake. If his reforms were defeated, society might degenerate, revolutionary movements might grow, and fascism might triumph. He valued reform for its ability to perform a conservative function in a crisis situation, and now the Court seemed likely to destroy reforms like the Wagner Act and Social Security and prevent passage of still other essential reforms, such as national wage and hour legislation. In addition, he resented the way in which the Court had treated him and the likelihood that it would cause him to fail as president.

Two decisions in the spring of 1936 had clearly suggested that more trouble for the New Deal lay ahead. One invalidated the Guffey-Snyder Coal Act, and the other declared that New York's minimum wage law for women was unconstitutional. In the Carter case involving the coal act, Sutherland, speaking for the majority, relied upon the distinction between direct and indirect effects on interstate commerce and insisted the employer-employee relations in the mining industry were subjects that could be regulated only by the states. All the justices, except Brandeis, Stone, and Cardozo, agreed. In the New York case, the Chief Justice joined the liberals, but Roberts stayed with the conservatives, enabling them to reaffirm the Adkins decision of 1923.

The Court had attacked both national and state efforts to solve problems of the workers. Stone believed that it had been "needlessly narrow and obscurantist in its outlook" and had "tied Uncle Sam up in a hard knot." In his view, the majority had read its own economic beliefs into the Constitution and did not recognize that "ours is a nation which should have the powers ordinarily possessed by governments, and that the framers of our Constitution intended that it should have."

The majority seemed deeply offended by the New Deal and seemed to prefer a policy of laissez faire. "I am happy to report," Hughes told a conservative audience, "that the Supreme Court is still functioning."

Roosevelt moved carefully and secretly toward a decision. He considered and for a time favored a constitutional amendment imposing restrictions on the Court or enlarging the power of Congress. Some suggested that an open appeal for such a change would have broad popular support. In the end, however, he concluded that it would be extremely difficult to persuade the necessary number of states to ratify such an amendment. He decided instead to rely upon well-established powers: the power of Congress to set the size of the Court and the power of the President to appoint its members. He decided also to stress the need to make the judicial system more efficient, rather than to argue that the nation needed a liberal majority on the Court. Many observers were seriously concerned about the judiciary's slowness, and Roosevelt and his top adviser on the issue, Attorney General Homer Cummings, shared this concern. The careful study given to alternatives persuaded Roosevelt that one method was constitutional, could be adopted quickly, and would produce the desired results.

Roosevelt's proposal of February 5, 1937, called for a law authorizing the President to appoint a new justice to supplement any justice who was more than seventy years old and chose not to retire. The law would limit the number of additions to six. The proposal recognized that some of the laws had been invalidated by narrow majorities, a fact that persuaded Roosevelt the problem lay in the composition of the Court, not in the institution itself. Furthermore, some critics of the Court frequently stressed the ages of the justices and suggested seventy as the proper age for retirement.

Unfortunately for Roosevelt, he did not handle the issue very well. The problem posed by the Court and possible solutions to it had been discussed in the administration for two years, and action was delayed by a desire to allow public sentiment for change to reach full strength, but he did not actively prepare the public. He seldom discussed the Court publicly in 1935–1936 and did not make an issue of it in the campaign. Also, he did not discuss his plan with congressional leaders before introducing it.

Nevertheless, at the time the plan was announced prospects for its acceptance seemed rather good. The public desire for a plan to change the Court seemed very strong, and there seemed to be substantial support for a plan of the type selected. Many people and many congressmen applauded the proposal after Roosevelt made it.

Yet Roosevelt suffered a serious defeat on the issue. Americans had long been ambivalent in their attitudes toward the Court, regarding it as both undemocratic and the essential safeguard of freedom, the Constitution, and the rights of minorities, and now the positive attitude rose to the surface, even among liberals who were unhappy with the Court's economic decisions. It was effectively exploited by Roosevelt's opponents, and he, for the first time, became vulnerable to attack as critics charged that his proposal proved that he had dictatorial ambitions. Much of the opposition came from members of his own party, including not only fairly persistent critics like Glass and Byrd of Virginia but men such as Connally of Texas, Bailey of North Carolina, and George of Georgia, who had been reluctant to express their criticisms of the President, and also previously consistent supporters, including O'Mahoney of Wyoming and Wheeler of Montana. Still other strong New Dealers, such as Wagner, stayed out of the fight, and Vice President Garner deserted his chief on the issue, going home to Texas in the middle of the fight. With Democrats battling against the President, the Republicans were able to hold back. The foes received help from the justices, including a persuasive challenge to the inefficiency argument by Hughes, and Roosevelt's top lieutenant in the Senate, Robinson of Arkansas, died while the battle was under way. It consumed much of the Senate's time from February to July and ended when Roosevelt surrendered.

A substantial change in the Court's behavior contributed to Roosevelt's defeat. In a series of decisions from March to May, the Court moved away from the principles that had dominated it in 1935–1936 and had dominated its history since the 1890s. One decision overturned the minimum wage decisions of 1923 and 1936, criticized the freedom of contract doctrine in upholding a state of Washington minimum wage law, and thereby affirmed the power of the states to pass social welfare legislation. Another decision upheld the National Labor Relations Act, recognizing the right of organization and collective bargaining as a "fundamental right" and its protection as an appropriate concern of legislative power and discarding the distinction between direct and indirect impact on interstate commerce. The majority insisted that the corporation involved in the case, the Jones & Laughlin Steel Corporation, presented "in a most striking way the close and intimate relation which a manufacturing enterprise may have to interstate commerce." Still another decision upheld the old-age feature of the Social Security Act, discarding the doctrine that had restricted the use of the tax power, and another upheld unemployment insurance.

The change in the Court's behavior took place before any changes in personnel were made. It resulted from shifts by two justices, Hughes and Roberts. Roberts had voted with the majority against New York's minimum wage law in 1936, and then voted in favor of Washington's law in 1937, enabling the liberals, plus Hughes, to win in 1937. And the decision on the Wagner Act, which in effect overruled the decision on the coal act, was supported not only by the three dissenters in the 1936 case, but also by Roberts and Hughes, who had voted with the majority the year before. Roberts had been the Court's spokesman in the Butler case, which had included an attack upon the use of the tax power, and Hughes had voted with him, but now they voted to uphold the old-age pension system.

The decisive influence was a desire to protect the Court and other established institutions. Roosevelt's plan, the behavior of the voters in 1936, and the intensification of labor-management conflict in late 1936 and early 1937 suggested to Hughes and Roberts that further refusal to accept reform legislation could create a very dangerous situation. Roosevelt's plan seemed to them to be a serious threat to the Court, and the people seemed very interested in social and economic change and likely to turn in radical directions if the reforms were destroyed by the Court. Thus, the justices changed their behavior in order to avoid much more undesirable changes, including possible destruction of the institution in which they served. Like Roosevelt, the two justices now endorsed the theory that reform could perform a conservative function.

Most of the major decisions in the spring of 1937 were reached by narrow 5-to-4 votes, but the trend that they announced was strengthened by personnel changes in the next four years. In the fall of 1937, Roosevelt was able to make his first appointment to the Court, and he chose Senator Hugo Black of Alabama to replace Willis Van Devanter. The latter had been appointed by President Taft in 1910 and had been one of the most conservative members of the Court during the 1930s. Black, on the other hand, was a strong New Dealer. As a senator, he had battled for regulation of hours and wages, the abolition of child labor, and the reduction of government subsidies for certain business groups, had attacked the political practices of business groups, and had criticized the anti-New Deal decisions of the Court.

In 1938, Roosevelt replaced another conservative with a New Dealer. George Sutherland, perhaps the most intelligent and perceptive of the conservative justices, resigned. He had voted with the majority against the New Deal in 1935–1936 and with the minority against it in 1937. To replace him, Roosevelt selected Stanley Reed. He had been counsel for the Farm Board and for the Reconstruction Finance Corporation before becoming Solicitor General in 1935 and had defended New Deal legislation before the Court. Reed believed in government action in economic affairs and in judicial restraint. The elected branches of government, not the judiciary, should, he insisted, have the power and responsibility for governing.

A short time later, Roosevelt appointed one of his top advisers, Felix Frankfurter. He replaced one of the liberals, Cardozo. Frankfurter had been heavily influenced by Holmes and Brandeis and believed very strongly in judicial restraint. He had confidence in elected officials and had been critical of the Court in 1935–1936, arguing that the justices should change their behavior.

In 1939, the President substituted another liberal for another member of the Court's liberal bloc when Brandeis decided to retire. Roosevelt chose William O. Douglas. He had moved from the Yale Law School in 1934 to work for the Securities Exchange Commission, had become a commissioner in 1936 and the chairman the following year, and had become an important member of the administration. Very critical of the conservatives on the Court, he was very close intellectually to the man he replaced.

Early in 1940, Frank Murphy replaced Pierce Butler, who had died a short time before. Butler had been an unrelenting, rigid foe of the New Deal, while Murphy was a passionate New Dealer. As mayor of Detroit in the early 1930s, he had stressed relief for the unemployed; as governor general and high commissioner of the Philippines from 1933 to 1936, he had shown the same passion for reform, and as governor of Michigan in 1937, he had refused to use force against the sit-down strikes. Following his defeat in 1938, he had served briefly as Roosevelt's Attorney General.

Roosevelt made two more appointments in the summer of 1941. One was Senator James F. Byrnes. He had been a rather strong supporter of Roosevelt in spite of his reservations about the New Deal. He was more conservative than Roosevelt but not as conservative as the man he replaced, James C. McReynolds. The latter had voted against more New Deal measures than any other member of the Court and strongly opposed the post-1936 trend, writing 119 dissents in his last four years.

Also in the summer of 1941, the retirement of Charles Evans Hughes enabled Roosevelt to make two moves. To fill the vacancy on the Court, he selected Robert Jackson. He had become a government lawyer in the Treasury Department in 1934 and had worked on tax matters, including the legislation of 1935. Then, he had moved to the Justice Department, where he devoted some of his time to the enforcement of the Public Utilities Holding Company Act. Elevated to Assistant Attorney General, he became a strong advocate of more effective enforcement of the antitrust laws. He was also a critic of the Court majority of 1935–1936, regarding it as out of touch with conditions and as preventing the administration from dealing effectively with them. He believed very strongly that justices should use their power in a restrained way.

Hughes's retirement also enabled Roosevelt to appoint a Chief Justice. He elevated Harlan Fiske Stone to the post. Stone had been on the Court since 1925 and had been close intellectually to Holmes and Brandeis. He was now the only remaining member of the liberal bloc of the mid-thirties.

Thus, by the fall of 1941, every member of the Court but Roberts owed his position to Roosevelt. The situation was very different from what it had been from 1933 to 1937, when every member had owed his position to FDR's predecessors.

Thus, the Court was transformed from 1937 to 1941. The new men had been critics of the old Court and had been influenced by Holmes and Brandeis and other critics of government by judiciary. What had been dissenting opinion supporting government action in economic affairs, challenging such action in intellectual matters, and insisting that law must change as social and economic conditions changed now rose to the top in the late 1930s and early 1940s.

The change in the Court's behavior amounted first of all to a retreat from the economic arena. The new majority called for judicial self-restraint in economic matters and ceased to provide strong protection for businessmen. Like Holmes before them, the justices now insisted that the Court "was not the only agency of government that must be assumed to have the capacity to govern" and that "the criterion of constitutionality is not whether [judges] believe the law to be for the public good." The majority now emphasized the "presumption of constitutionality" in the economic field. When faced with economic legislation, they assumed that it was constitutional, and the assumption was not easily shaken. Economic policy, in other words, was left largely in the hands of elected officials serving in the legislative and executive branches.

The change in the Court appeared in numerous decisions in the period. The justices, in upholding agricultural legislation, overturned the Butler ruling that agricultural production was "a purely local activity." They enlarged the federal government's power over navigable waters, protected striking workers, refused to use the Sherman Antitrust Act against labor, and upheld minimum wage legislation for men. Repeatedly, the Court overturned recent decisions that had invalidated measures similar to the ones now accepted, causing conservatives to complain about the uncertainty that had been introduced as well as about the enlargement of government power.

At the same time that they retreated from the economic field, the justices enlarged their concern for civil rights and civil liberties. In 1937, they revived the clear and present danger test as the standard for judging questions of free speech and overturned the convictions of Communists. "The power of the state to abridge freedom of speech and assembly is the exception rather than the rule and the penalizing even of utterances of a defined character must find its justification in a reasonable apprehension of danger to organized government," Roberts insisted. "The greater the importance of safeguarding the community from incitements to the overthrow of our institutions by force and violence," Hughes declared, "the more imperative is the need to preserve inviolate the constitutional right of free speech, free press and free assembly in order to maintain the opportunity for free political discussion, to the end that government may be responsive to the will of the people and that changes, if desired, may be obtained by peaceful means." Three years later, the clear and present danger rule protected the Jehovah's Witnesses, and the Court for the first time ruled explicitly that religious freedom is a liberty protected from state interference by the Fourteenth Amendment.

In 1938, the Court for the first time enforced the equal protection clause of the Fourteenth Amendment on behalf of Negro claims in the field of education. The case had begun in 1935, when four graduates of Lincoln University in Jefferson City, Missouri, the state university for blacks, had applied for admission to professional schools in the all-white state university in Columbia. They were denied admission on the ground that it was "contrary to the constitution, laws and public policy of the State to admit a negro as a student in the University of Missouri," and they were advised that the state would pay a portion of their expenses in schools outside of Missouri in those fields, such as law, in which education was available in Columbia but not in Jefferson City.

One of the four, Lloyd L. Gaines, challenged the university in the courts. He was a Missouri citizen and an honors graduate, and he argued that lack of opportunity to receive his education in his own state would hamper his efforts to establish a legal practice there. In making his challenge, he received help from the National Association for the Advancement of Colored People.

The Supreme Court ruled late in 1938 that Missouri had violated the separate but equal rule of the Plessy case (1896) and thus the equal protection clause. "By the operation of the laws of Missouri a privilege has been created for white law students which is denied to negroes by reason of their race," Hughes concluded in his opinion for the Court. " . . . That is a denial of the equality of legal right to the enjoyment of the privilege which the State has set up, and the provision for the payment of tuition fees in another State does not remove the discrimination." Gaines "was entitled to the equal protection of the laws, and the State was bound to furnish him within its borders facilities for legal education substantially equal to those which the State there afforded for persons of the white race . . . " Only McReynolds and Butler dissented from a decision that forced Missouri and other states to enlarge educational opportunities for Negroes.

Another development of the time recognized the civil liberties dimension of labor union activities. In a 1939 case involving Boss Hague of Jersey City and the Congress of Industrial Organizations, the Court invalidated a city ordinance prohibiting outdoor assemblies in streets and parks without official permit. The Court declared that such use "has, from ancient times, been a part of the privileges, immunities, rights, and liberties of citizens" and, though it could be "regulated in the interest of all," it could not be "abridged or denied." Two decisions the following year interpreted picketing as a form of speech, not merely an economic act, and extended to some aspects of this means of expression the protection of the First and Fourteenth Amendments. In 1941, the majority indicated clearly that the picketing must be peaceful. The Court, speaking through Frankfurter, held that a state court could enjoin picketing when past violence in the dispute convinced the court that future picketing could not be peaceful, and Reed in dissent maintained that "the right to picket peacefully in industrial disputes is a recognized means for the marshalling of public opinion on the side of the worker."

A new "preferred freedoms" doctrine emerged in this period. Having rejected the doctrine that the Court should protect property as *the* preferred freedom, some of the justices now began to assume that they had special responsibilities to protect civil rights and civil liberties. Stone suggested the doctrine in 1938 in the Carolene Products Company case. In cases involving rights guaranteed by the first ten amendments, basic political processes, and legislative attacks on minorities, he suggested, there would "be narrower scope for the operation of the presumption of constitutionality," "more exacting judicial scrutiny," and "more searching judicial inquiry."

Stone spelled out the doctrine more fully in dissent in 1940. The case (*Minersville School District v. Gobitis*) concerned a Pennsylvania statute requiring students to salute the flag, a requirement that was challenged by the Jehovah's Witnesses and upheld by the Court, 8 to 1. In speaking for the majority, Frankfurter relied upon the rule of judicial self-restraint, explaining in a letter to Stone that his intention was to "use this opinion as a vehicle for preaching the true democratic faith of not relying on the Court for the impossible task of assuring a vigorous, mature, self-protecting and tolerant democracy . . . " But Stone insisted that in a case of this sort, involving religion and a minority that could not effectively protect itself against prejudice in the political arena, the Court had an especially large responsibility. Stone lost, but the Court was now frequently behaving as he suggested that it should.

A very significant change had taken place. The Supreme Court had ceased to be an opponent of reform and had become an instrument of reform. The justices had become tolerant of the efforts by the President, the Congress, and the states to change the economic system and had themselves begun to change life in other areas.

The changes in constitutional law were, to a significant degree, part of the New Deal. They did have roots in the past, especially in the work of Holmes and Brandeis, but the Court was influenced by criticism of it that resulted from its invalidation of New Deal laws, by Roosevelt's impressive victory in 1936, by his proposal for change in the Court, and by his appointments to it. And one result was judicial acceptance of the New Deal. The development was also influenced by the new momentum in the labor movement, which the New Deal stimulated and which in turn affected it.

SUGGESTIONS FOR ADDITIONAL READING

The work by Friedman and Israel, cited in Chapter 5, discusses each of the justices mentioned. The works by McCloskey and Mason noted there are also very useful. Leuchtenburg discusses the subject briefly in his book on the period, while Burns and Tugwell in their biographies of Roosevelt provide very critical accounts of his handling of the issue. Morton Frisch, in the article to which reference is made in Chapter 3, presents a much more favorable interpretation.

There are also some very useful specialized studies. Lionel V. Patenaude, "Garner, Summers, and Connally: The Defeat of the Roosevelt Court Bill in 1937," *Southwestern Historical Quarterly*, vol. 74, pp. 36–51, 1970, and Gene M. Gressley, "Joseph C. O'Mahoney, FDR and the Supreme Court," *Pacific Historical Review*, vol. 40, pp. 183–202, 1971, deal with the opposition to the plan. Robert Cortner, *The Wagner Act Cases*, The University of Tennessee Press, Knoxville, 1964; John W. Chambers, "The Big Switch: Justice Roberts and the Minimum Wage Cases," *Labor History*, vol. 10, pp. 44–73, 1969; Charles A. Leonard, *A Search for a Judicial Philosophy: Mr. Justice Roberts and the Constitutional Revolution of 1937*, Kennikat Press, Port Washington, N.Y., 1971; and Sidney Fine, "Frank Murphy, The Thornhill Decision, and Picketing as Free Speech," *Labor History*, vol. 6, pp. 99–120, 1965, are important on the changes in the Court.

Some of the most important work on the Court fight has been done by Leuchtenburg. See "The Origins of Franklin D. Roosevelt's 'Court-Packing' Plan," *Supreme Court Review*, 1966; "Roosevelt's Supreme Court 'Packing' Plan," in Harold M. Hollingsworth and William F. Holmes, eds., *Essays on the New Deal*, University of Texas Press, Austin, 1969, and "The Constitutional Revolution of 1937," in Victor Hoar, comp., *The Great Depression: Essays and Memoirs from Canada and the United States*, Copp Clark, Toronto, 1969.

Chapter 9

The Advance of the Labor Movement

The second highly significant change that came soon after the election of 1936 was a very substantial increase in the size and strength of the American labor movement. It became a large and strong part of American life. The mood of the workers, the orientation of the national government, and the recovery of the economy produced large opportunities for labor leaders, and they discarded some of the ideas that had hampered labor's progress and seized the opportunities that existed. Most businessmen continued to resist, but their resistance was much less effective than it had been earlier. Thus, labor moved forward rapidly, and the advance was deeply troubling to business leaders. To them, as well as to many other people, the change seemed to be a major development.

Passage of the Wagner Act, although very important, was not enough to build a strong labor movement. Many employers continued to employ antiunion weapons, and were advised by lawyers, including those affiliated with the Liberty League, that the law was unconstitutional. The Supreme Court decision on the Guffey-Snyder Act in 1936 seemed to confirm this interpretation. Thus, many corporations defied the law and the National Labor Relations Board.

The defiant companies continued to employ their economic power to combat unions. They fired union members and strikers, evicted them from company-owned housing, denied them credit at company-owned stores, and employed spies and armed guards, whom they supplied with weapons and ammunition. Investigators discovered that General Motors, a company determined to maintain the power of management, spent nearly $1 million on Pinkerton agents and other spies from 1934 to 1936 and that Republic Steel, headed by one of the most militant antiunion executives, Tom Girdler, was the nation's largest purchaser of tear and sickening gas in 1937. One of Ford's lieutenants, Harry Bennett, used a band of toughs, called the Service Department, against organizers like Walter Reuther of the United Auto Workers, beating him severely when the UAW tried to organize the auto company in 1937.

Antiunion employers also used more peaceful methods of persuasion. These included sophisticated personnel programs designed to convince workers that they could depend upon businessmen and did not need to turn to nonbusiness organizations for help. Employers also expanded public relations programs, using such schemes as the Mohawk Valley Formula that was developed by Remington Rand in 1936 and propagated by the National Association of Manufacturers. The formula was designed to win public support for management's side in a dispute and mobilize the community against a strike. The formula involved efforts to brand union leaders as subversives and to portray the workers as eager to cooperate with their employers. It also involved a threat to remove the affected firm from the community if local interests stood by and allowed the "outside agitators" to win control of the workers. Several giants, including Bethlehem Steel and General Motors, employed this weapon, and it was used against such important parts of the labor movement as the Steel Workers Organizing Committee, the Textile Workers Organizing Committee, and the UAW.

Almost all employers tried to remain free of dealings with independent unions, especially large ones determined to bargain about a long list of questions. Businessmen with a positive attitude toward unions were very rare. Most looked upon them as a threat to management's right to control the firm. Management alone, most businessmen insisted, had the right to make the decisions governing the work force.

In many communities, especially in the South, industrialists successfully appealed for public support against unions. Community leaders feared that established industries would move out and that campaigns to recruit new ones would fail if unions moved in. Thus, communities passed laws and waged propaganda campaigns against the unions; local police forces worked against union organizers and strikers, and private citizens used vigilante and mob action against union organizers, seeking to drive them out of town. Violence, bloodshed, and loss of life continued to be features of American economic life.

The Supreme Court, however, upheld aid to the labor movement by the federal government. In its decision in *NLRB v. Jones & Laughlin Steel Corporation* on April 12, 1937, the Court validated the Wagner Act and in the process recognized the organizational character of the economy and the need to extend the organizational tendency. "Employees have as clear a right to organize and select their representatives as the respondent [the steel company, the fourth largest in the industry] has to organize its business and select its own officers and agents," the Court declared. Labor organizations were "organized out of the necessities of the situation." A single employee was "helpless in dealing with an employer." He was "dependent ordinarily on his daily wage for the maintenance of himself and family" and if his employer refused to pay him the wages that he thought fair, "he was nevertheless unable to leave the employ and resist arbitrary and unfair treatment . . . " Organization "was essential to give laborers opportunity to deal on an equality with their employer." The decision put pressure on companies to recognize unions and bargain with them.

In addition to the decisions on the Wagner Act, the Supreme Court helped the labor movement in other ways. It sharply reduced the vulnerability of unions to attack under the antitrust laws, and it reconstructed the law of picketing, upholding legislation supporting peaceful picketing and overturning an antipicketing law as an abridgment of free speech.

Labor also received significant help from the NLRB. Prior to the Supreme Court's action, the board was largely ineffective, but the 1937 decision and a subsequent one in 1938 enabled the agency to do the job that Congress had intended and to become a promoter of the movement. Unions now turned to it frequently, usually with charges of unfair labor practices. It declared that most of the antiunion practices of the past were now illegal and must be stopped. While its rulings were frequently challenged by employers, the board was usually upheld by the courts. Wagner and other congressional friends of the board and the basic legislation also successfully defended unions against their many enemies.

Senatorial investigators in the La Follette Civil Liberties Committee helped labor. Formed in 1936, it investigated the struggles of the period, demonstrated that corporations and other private groups and state and local governments often violated the civil liberties of workers in preventing them from organizing, and maintained that the power of the federal government could and should be used to safeguard those liberties. Revealing the use of spies, private police, strikebreakers, and the suppression of free speech and assembly, the investigations damaged the public relations of management, generated sympathy for workers, and put pressure on employers and local communities to change their ways.

In addition, what governments did not do was important. The states and the national government did not use force as regularly as they had in the past to break strikes. The most famous example was the refusal by Governor Frank Murphy of Michigan and the President to use troops to break the sit-down strikes. In similar fashion, Governor Bibb Graves of Alabama rejected demands that he use state troops against strikers in the textile industry in 1938.

Thus, governments contributed in several ways to the growth of unions. An economic factor also exerted an influence. This was recovery. It enabled employed workers to think about more than survival and to consider ways of raising their standard of living, and it made employers eager to come to terms and avoid a strike. They did not want to miss opportunities for profit, which, since 1929, had been hard to find. Labor's progress correlated rather closely with the business cycle, moving forward in the rather good situation of late 1936 to early 1937, falling off with the recession that came later that year, advancing once again when recovery resumed in the summer of 1938, and receiving a new push from the defense spending of 1940–1941.

Labor's progress, however, was not merely a consequence of government aid and improving economic conditions. Labor's leaders also made major contributions. They took full advantage of the opportunities that existed.

Leaders made beneficial structural changes in the movement, discarding the old emphasis on the organization of workers along craft lines. The change took place after a bitter fight from 1933 to 1935. The adversaries were the dominant and inflexible advocates of craft unions in the AFL, led by William Green, John Frey, Dan Tobin, Big Bill Hutcheson, and Matthew Woll, and the champions of industrial unionism, including John L. Lewis, Sidney Hillman, and David Dubinsky. Lewis pressed the issue most boldly, even striking Hutcheson after an angry verbal battle at the AFL convention in 1935. The logic of industrial development dictated the move to industrial unions, for as industry had moved forward, it had increased the number of unskilled and semiskilled workers, but the AFL had made almost no effort to organize them and resisted the idea that they should be united in a union with the skilled workers who worked with them.

The result was the formation in 1935 of a new labor organization. It was called the Committee for Industrial Organization when hope for

Figure 11   John L. Lewis (*Copyright by Harris & Ewing*)

affiliation with the AFL and avoidance of "dual unionism" was still high. Lewis served as chairman of the committee. It became the Congress of Industrial Organizations in 1938 following the failure of efforts to unite the two major parts of the labor movement. Lewis then became president with Hillman and Philip Murray as vice presidents.

The structural change was extremely significant. It opened a new range of opportunities for the labor movement. It enabled labor to organize workers who had been largely ignored by the AFL. The CIO organized workers along industrial lines, paying no heed to individual skills, such as the skills of a machinist or a carpenter, and combining into one union all workers in a particular industry, such as automobiles or steel. Here was a way to build large unions with concentrated strength and to serve the interests of every class of workers.

In its efforts to organize all workers in each industry, the CIO also departed from the racial practices of the AFL. The new labor organization welcomed and organized black workers. The CIO was not free of racial discrimination and segregation, but the new organization did draw many blacks into the labor movement.

Lewis and his allies pressed their organizing efforts very boldly. After forming the CIO, they did not sit back and wait for the Supreme Court to uphold the Wagner Act. They moved into the major antiunion industries with huge organizing campaigns financed on a scale that was far above AFL levels. In 1936–1937, much of the money came from Lewis's United Mine Workers. The leaders staged massive strikes, including the sit-down strikes in General Motors late in 1936 and early in 1937. These extremely significant strikes came when the Wagner Act was widely regarded as unconstitutional and demonstrated that progress depended upon more than help from government. The quality of labor's leadership was also important.

The workers as well as their leaders contributed significantly to labor's rise. Many, especially in the South, remained too individualistic, too respectful of and grateful to their employers, or too fearful, but millions were now determined to join unions. They responded readily to appeals from organizers and eagerly engaged in strikes, including the many sit-down strikes from 1936 to 1938. In them, workers did not walk out but instead occupied factories and refused to move out. The workers resisted efforts to check their progress, using force when necessary, as in Flint when police attempted to remove the sit-down strikers. Given the techniques used by many employers and many communities, the advance of unions depended upon courage as well as determination.

Even AFL leaders revealed a new dynamic spirit. The largest organization at the beginning of the decade, the AFL remained the largest after the great activities of the 1930s. In 1933, its membership had been lower than at any point since 1916. By 1936, however, it had recouped its depression losses, and then, stimulated by the rise of a rival, the old organization made strenuous, expensive, and successful efforts to enlarge itself, developing in the process a much greater interest in organizing the unskilled into industrial unions. By 1941, the AFL had nearly twice as many members as the CIO, and the former ranged over most of the economy while the latter was confined to manufacturing and mining and had better than 70 percent of its membership concentrated in six unions.

Thus, labor moved forward. As time passed, employers found themselves forced increasingly to discard old antiunion practices, recognize unions, and accept collective bargaining. General Motors, the largest manufacturing corporation in the world and a firm that was linked closely with another giant, Du Pont, and with the Liberty League, responded to the

Figure 12 Class Conflict (*United Press International Photo*)

sit-down strikes by coming to terms with the UAW on February 11, 1937. The organization of this industrial giant that had firmly opposed unions led to the organization of other major firms. The United States Steel Company reached an agreement with the Steel Workers Organizing Committee on March 2, 1937, and Chrysler and the UAW agreed to terms a month later. Even Ford, quite suddenly in 1941, surrendered to the great pressures favoring unionism. For Ford, the pressures were a series of NLRB rulings against the company for unfair labor practices, a major organizing drive by the UAW, a big strike, an election favoring the UAW by a wide margin, hopes for more sales, including sales to the federal government, and fear of new NLRB investigations of charges against the company. At the same time, pressures from the SWOC, the NLRB, and the United States Supreme Court resulted in the organization of four of the six members of "Little Steel," including Girdler's Republic.

Labor was becoming a much more powerful part of American life. One base was the enlarged membership. After growing slowly from the

2.8 million level to which it had declined in 1933, the movement doubled in size from 1936 to 1941, jumping to more than 8.4 million members, or 23 percent of nonagricultural employment. While far below this level in the South, organized labor was substantially above it in the Pacific, East North Central, and Middle Atlantic regions.

More than growth in membership was involved in the expansion of labor's power. Also very important was the movement's penetration of strategic sectors of the economy. Unionism in 1935 was confined largely to the needle trades, coal mining, public utilities, the railroads, and the building trades. Heavy industry was largely unorganized. By 1941, in addition to gains in the areas it had occupied earlier, especially transportation, mining, and construction, unionism had invaded the centers of heavy industry. Less than 10 percent of the manufacturing employees had been organized in 1930, but better than one-third of them were ten years later. The centers that were organized included formerly antiunion cities like Pittsburgh, Detroit, and Akron and formerly antiunion or nonunion industrial giants such as General Motors, United States Steel, Chrysler, Ford, Firestone, Goodrich, United States Rubber, Goodyear, General Electric, Republic Steel, Bethlehem Steel, Inland Steel, and Westinghouse. The labor movement now had strength in some of the most important parts of the economy.

Labor used its enlarged economic power to accomplish several objectives. One was higher wages. But the movement also obtained the establishment of the seniority principle in decisions about layoffs, promotions, and the like and the creation of grievance procedures that reduced management's ability to discipline and fire workers. Some important decisions could no longer be made exclusively by management.

Most businessmen regarded the change as undesirable and perplexing. It reduced their power to make some very important decisions concerning the operations of their firms, and it also challenged the businessman's belief that he had taken good care of his employees. When his workers joined a union, a businessman usually regarded the move as an act of disloyalty and ingratitude. He looked upon NLRB elections as tests of loyalty and of confidence in management, and he found a majority vote in favor of joining a union a painful and distressing as well as surprising experience, difficult to explain. To explain it to himself and others, he often argued that the workers had been led astray by outsiders.

Labor's power was not limited to the economic arena. As the movement grew, it also became more important in American politics. Gompers had preached that workers, at least adult males, must rely upon the union, the union must rely upon itself, and neither should rely upon the state. Some labor leaders had rejected that philosophy of "voluntarism" before the 1930s; more discarded it in the early years of the Depression, and now almost all the leaders did so. Leaders in the AFL as well as the CIO became much more willing to join forces with social reformers in support of social welfare legislation, such as unemployment insurance and old-age pensions, convinced that collective bargaining could not solve all the worker's problems, and they also became more willing to accept government protection and participation in the organizing and collective bargaining processes. One traditionalist complained that "under Mr. Gompers' regime, the trade union movement stood upon its own feet; now it must depend, to a large extent, upon the support of State and Federal administration." Both the seriousness of the situation and the new friendliness in Washington encouraged this change. Workers were desperate; employers were strong, and the government was willing to help.

Critics inside the movement had long insisted that labor should endorse government help for the worker and the movement and that it should play a larger role in politics, and now the new CIO became especially active in politics, announcing that it represented "the hard core around which all progressive political action must be based." The change involved the creation of permanent political machinery rather than the reliance on temporary mechanisms, created only for an election year. Also involved was a vastly increased commitment of time, money, and personnel to politics and much closer ties with one political party, the Democrats. One stimulus was the enlargement of government's economic role as it forced labor to pay more attention to politics. The change also resulted from labor's growing self-confidence. The new leaders in the CIO had confidence that the growing movement could have a large political influence. They rejected the theory that politics was inevitably dominated by business groups. Most leaders of the AFL also became more active in politics and more closely associated with the Democratic party than they had been in the past.

In spite of the many changes, a procapitalist philosophy remained the dominant philosophy of the American labor movement. Most of the leaders believed in the main features of the system, and they continued to value labor power chiefly as a means of obtaining for wage earners a larger share of the benefits of a highly industrialized capitalistic system, not of overthrowing it.

There were radicals in the labor movement in the late 1930s. Trotskyites had some strength, based on control of the Teamsters local in Minneapolis, and other Communists were important in other places. Some had important staff positions in the national office of the CIO, and some performed effectively as organizers. Communists made serious but unsuccessful efforts to gain control of some unions, including the UAW, and did gain control of some others, such as the CIO's United Electrical Workers, the largest union under Communist control. Communist-controlled unions had less than 6 percent of the union members in 1941, and those unions were mostly weak and broke, and Communist only at the top. Almost all their members as well as almost all other workers were not interested in revolution. And while Lewis was quite willing to use Communists, most labor leaders, including Dubinsky and Murray as well as AFL leaders like Tobin, were strongly anti-Communist.

The Communist party remained active in the United States after 1936. It had changed its behavior just before that election year, dropping its self-defeating denunciation of Socialists and New Dealers as fascists and foes of the workers and switching to efforts to cultivate all possible groups. It tried to create a "Popular Front" against fascism. In this new phase, the party sought to appear 100 percent American. The party was, its leader Earl Browder maintained, "the only party entitled by its program and its work to designate itself as 'sons and daughters of the American Revolution.' " The party benefited in these years from its ability to identify with the desire for reform and from Communist opposition to Hitler and fascism while many others held back, and it made some progress in peace, youth, and church groups and some government agencies, as well as the labor movement. The party in the United States, however, had to contend with the revelation of the authoritarian structure of Stalinism supplied by the bloody purges in Russia as well as with the popularity of the New Deal. Although some intellectuals were attracted to the party, most were not, and it had no influence on government policy.

Nonradical leaders dominated the labor movement. Almost all of them functioned within the established party system and opposed the formation of a labor party committed to radical change. Hillman, Dubinsky, and some other labor leaders had moved away from the Socialist party after the New Deal began to evolve, and others continued to do so during the years of rapid growth of the labor movement. Walter Reuther, for example, a young and rising member of the UAW, resigned from the Socialist party in 1938 as labor's opportunities within the system were expanding. By then, that party had no strength in the labor movement.

Most labor leaders rejected the theory that class conflict was an inevitable feature of a capitalistic system and argued instead that unions and management could cooperate and that the organization of the workers could stabilize labor relations. "A CIO contract is adequate protection against sit-downs, lie-downs, or any other kind of strike," Lewis assured management, and Hillman advised textile manufacturers that the organization of the workers would eliminate "unnecessary stoppages and interruptions in production." A few managers endorsed the argument, concluding that unions were necessary and good, and attempted to build constructive and harmonious relations with organized labor. "The union has scrupulously followed the terms of its agreement and . . . the Corporation subsidiaries, during a very difficult period, have been entirely free of labor disturbance of any kind," Myron Taylor of United States Steel announced in 1938.

New Deal labor policy had succeeded. Promotional in nature, its goal was a strong labor movement. By the beginning of the 1940s, the movement was more powerful than ever before. Since the passage of the Wagner Act, it had grown more rapidly than it had in any earlier period.

Labor leaders, helped by the New Deal and other forces, had altered power relations in the American system of economics and politics. Business leaders had lost some of their power. They remained very strong, and capitalism survived. Nevertheless, the change was not insignificant.

The growth of the labor movement in the 1930s formed a highly significant part of a long-term transformation of American capitalism. Organization of the labor sector took a great leap forward in the decade, giving the wage earners more power to deal with previously established business organizations. The rise of the latter had meant new controls over the workers' lives, often by bureaucracies centered in a big city outside the workers' communities. Now, workers turned to labor organizations with their bureaucracies, frequently centered in Washington. The workers made this move not to destroy capitalism but to obtain a larger share of its benefits for themselves. They hoped to find ways of fulfilling old desires to acquire the goods that the system produced, desires that had been frustrated by the Depression and seemed now to depend for their fulfillment on new institutional developments.

SUGGESTIONS FOR ADDITIONAL READING

Histories of American labor, such as Henry Pelling, *American Labor*, The University of Chicago Press, Chicago, 1960; Joseph G. Rayback, *A History of American Labor*, Free Press, New York, 1966; and Philip Taft, *Organized Labor in American History*, Harper & Row, New York, 1964, provide useful introductions to this important subject, but Bernstein's *Turbulent Years* carries the reader far beyond them in a long, rich, impressively researched, thoughtful, and well-written account. In spite of his accomplishment, other broad studies remain useful, including Milton Derber and Edwin Young, *Labor and the New Deal*, The University of Wisconsin Press, Madison, 1957, and David Brody, "The Emergence of Mass Production Unionism," in John Braeman et al, eds., *Change and Continuity in Twentieth-Century America*, Ohio State University Press, Columbus, 1964, both of which caution against overemphasis on change in interpretations of American labor in the 1930s.

Other, more specialized accounts are also very valuable. James O. Morris, *Conflict within the AFL: A Study of Craft versus Industrial Unionism, 1901–1938*, Cornell University Press, Ithaca, N.Y., 1958, traces the lengthy debate that led to the formation of the CIO. Walter Galenson details the rise of CIO unions and the AFL's response in *The CIO Challenge to the AFL: A History of the American Labor Movement, 1935–1941*, Harvard, Cambridge, Mass., 1960. Also on the AFL's split and recovery see Philip Taft, *The AFL from the Death of Gompers to the Merger*, Harper, New York, 1959. Brody makes a major contribution in a study of one group of workers, *The Butcher Workmen*, Harvard, Cambridge, Mass., 1964. Sidney Fine's book, *Sit-down: The General Motors Strike of 1936–1937*, The University of Michigan Press, Ann Arbor, 1969, demonstrates the large importance of this strike and of the men involved in it, and Jerold S. Auerbach calls attention to the contributions of the La Follette committtee in *Labor and Liberty: The La Follette Committee and the New Deal*, Bobbs-Merrill, Indianapolis, 1966. On the slow development of labor in the South, see, in addition to Tindall's *Emergence of the New South*, F. Ray Marshall, *Labor in the South*, Harvard, Cambridge, Mass., 1967; on the organization of black workers see James S. Olson, "Organized Black Leadership and Industrial Unionism; The Racial Response, 1936–1945," *Labor History*, vol. 10, pp. 475–486, 1969; and on developments in one firm consult the work of Robert Ozanne, *A Century of Labor-Management Relations at McCormick and International Harvester*, The University of Wisconsin Press, Madison, 1967. Howe and Coser's study of the Communist party, noted in Chapter 3, remains useful for this period.

Bernstein and most labor historians write with great sympathy for the labor movement, and their insights should be compared with those of the business historians. One of the best works of this kind concerned with the 1930s is Allan Nevins and Frank Ernest Hill, *Ford: Decline and Rebirth, 1933–1962*, Scribner, New York, 1963. For a guide to others, see Richard S. Kirkendall, "The Great Depression: Another Watershed in American History?" in Braeman et al., eds., *Twentieth-Century America*, pp. 179, 184. On business personnel and public relations programs, see, in addition to the book by Cochran cited in Chapter 1, Otis Pease, *The Responsibilities of American Advertising: Private Control and Public Influence, 1920–1940*, Yale, New Haven, Conn., 1958; Loren Baritz, *The Servants of Power: A History of the Use of Social Science in American Industry*, Wesleyan, Middletown, Conn., 1960; and Morrell Heald, *The Social Responsibilities of Business: Company and Community, 1900–1960*, The Press of Case Western Reserve University, Cleveland, 1970.

Chapter 10

Recession and Recovery

As changes were made in the constitutional law and the labor movement, the economic situation also changed. The economy, which had been moving forward since 1933, slipped into a serious recession in 1937. This economic downturn generated pressures for policy changes and resulted in an enlargement of antitrust activities and even more significant developments in fiscal policy. The latter turned the economy around once again, but the progress of recovery fell far short of full employment by 1940.

The recession began late in the summer of 1937 and continued into the following summer. Industrial production had moved above the 1929 level by the end of 1936; unemployment had dropped below 15 percent of the labor force; but from September 1937 to June 1938, employment in manufacturing dropped more than 20 percent; 4 million workers lost their jobs, and unemployment moved back to 20 percent.

A change in fiscal policy contributed, perhaps decisively, to the coming of the recession. Henry Morgenthau, the Secretary of the

Treasury, had become the leading advocate within the administration of a substantial cut in federal spending. In late 1936 and early 1937, he supplied both economic and political reasons for a reduction in expenditures that would balance the budget, and he found Roosevelt very receptive. As one student of economic thought has suggested: "The 'great spender' was in his heart a true descendant of thrifty Dutch Calvinist forebears." He had never been happy with the level of federal spending and with the deficits in the federal budgets. Furthermore, as he was in the middle of the Court fight, he hoped to take some step that would appeal to conservatives.

Spending for fiscal 1937 was nearly $1 billion below the $8.5 billion of the year before, and Roosevelt now cut back still more. He made cuts in relief spending as well as other areas and promised that the combination of the cuts plus the increase in revenue due to recovery and the new Social Security tax would result in a balanced budget for fiscal 1938. Actually, the budget was moving toward balance even more rapidly than the President realized, for on budgetary matters he and his advisers thought in terms of fiscal rather than calendar years and did not have a clear understanding of the significance of the financial aspects of the Social Security program. Almost all of the veterans' bonus was paid out in calendar year 1936; Social Security revenue became substantial in 1937, and Social Security payments remained small. As a consequence, the deficit moved from $3.5 billion in calendar 1936 to $0.2 billion in 1937. Thus, the federal government sharply reduced its contribution to investment and purchasing power and did so at a time when businessmen were not yet investing at a high level. Morgenthau and other fiscal conservatives assumed the move toward a balanced budget would encourage private investment, but it did not. Perhaps developments in constitutional law and labor-management relations in 1937 alarmed businessmen.

The new economic situation generated demands for changes in the power of both government and business. Advisers bombarded Roosevelt with suggestions about the moves he should make. Some, including Morgenthau, Joseph Kennedy, and Daniel Roper, the Secretary of Commerce, blamed the recession on deficit spending, the encouragement of labor, hostility toward business, and the destruction of business confidence. They urged the President to conciliate business by balancing the budget, revising the tax laws, and declaring a recess on reform. Then business would bring the country out of the recession.

Budget balancing continued to be the policy in late 1937 and early 1938, as Roosevelt and Morgenthau announced in several speeches. At the beginning of 1938, the President called for a further cut in expenditures in fiscal 1939 that would compensate for the fall in revenue resulting from the recession and result in only a small deficit—even a surplus if the financing of the Social Security program were considered. But businessmen continued to hold back. Apparently, government spending policy was not the decisive influence on business confidence.

Planning proposals emerged once again. Baruch, Richberg, and others advocated an NRA-type program involving the relaxation of antitrust activities, a reduction in competition in the business world, and an increase in cooperation and planning with government helping business cooperate and plan. Still others, such as Mordecai Ezekiel in the Department of Agriculture, called for cooperation among all economic groups, a large role for government, and planned expansion of production and of purchasing power.

By now, Roosevelt had too many doubts about businessmen to endorse any of these suggestions. He did hold conferences with some business leaders but found them fearful of even the Baruch-Richberg proposal. It seemed likely to give government too much power.

The President was more receptive to suggestions for a renewed attack upon business power. The recession stimulated concern about it. Corcoran, Cohen, Ickes, Jackson, and others maintained that the downturn was the result of high "administered" prices by corporations and a sit-down strike by capital. This suggestion made more sense to Roosevelt than the one that his antibusiness policies had caused the recession.

One consequence of this line of advice was the establishment of the Temporary National Economic Committee. Recommended by Roosevelt in April 1938, the TNEC was composed of representatives of Congress and the administration, and they made a lengthy and thorough investigation of the distribution of power in the economy.

At the same time, the Antitrust Division of the Justice Department was given new life. It was headed by Thurman Arnold, a colorful and iconoclastic professor from the Yale Law School. Obtaining greater appropriations for his division, he enlarged and upgraded his staff and embarked upon the biggest antitrust campaign in the nation's history.

The recession also helped the Keynesian theories rise to new prominence in the administration. Eccles was still there, as were other "spenders," including Lauchlin Currie and Mordecai Ezekiel, and Keynes himself sent advice to the President. The English economist had published his great work, *The General Theory of Employment, Interest and Money*, in 1936, and he already had American disciples in the economics profession and was gaining more at a rapid pace. Keynes's influence in Washington, however, was not yet very large. "The New Deal and Keynes were developing along parallel lines," Herbert Stein has written, "but no substantial influence from Keynes on the New Deal has been found."

Hopkins was the most effective promoter of this brand of economics within the administration at this point. He was one of the members of the administration whose power and status depended on the scale of the spending programs they managed and who controlled machinery that could be used to bring about a large increase in spending. Two senators, La Follette and Wagner, and one of Hopkins's lieutenants, Aubrey Williams, among others, advised Hopkins late in March that he must make another attempt to sell the theory of deficit financing to FDR, and the relief administrator then spoke to his chief in terms that he could understand. With relief rolls expanding rapidly and with commentators blaming Roosevelt for the recession as Hoover had been blamed for the Depression, Hopkins spoke of soup lines, apple peddling, and the like. He insisted that only the government could provide the purchasing power that the economy now needed, and he convinced the President that he should drop Morgenthau's budget-balancing program and expand federal spending substantially. It was the only available way of producing recovery quickly, and it was just a new way for the federal government to play its old role as a promoter of economic growth, helping private enterprise to function.

Roosevelt endorsed this economic philosophy in messages to Congress and the people in April. He called for the spending and lending of several billion dollars in fiscal 1939 by WPA, CCC, PWA, NYA, FSA, and several other agencies. Furthermore, he provided a clear expression of the theory that the government could and should promote economic growth and stability. "The prosperity of the United States is of necessity a primary concern of Government" he announced. " . . . It is because the course of our economics has run adversely for half a year that we owe it to ourselves to turn it in the other direction." Government spending, he now assumed, would do that, and he expressed no concern about the deficit that would result.

The behavior of Congress and then the economy was in line with Roosevelt's hopes. Few opponents now argued that spending was unacceptable as a recovery measure. Instead, their main argument was that spending should be supplemented by programs, especially tax cuts, designed to promote business confidence and investment. In May, Congress passed over Roosevelt's opposition a tax measure reducing the capital gains and undistributed profits taxes and providing for the expiration of the latter in 1939, and then in June, Congress passed a Recovery-Relief Act that was in line with his recommendations on spending. Federal spending moved from $6.8 billion for fiscal 1938 to $8.9 billion the following year, and the deficit from $1.2 billion to $3.9 billion, less the Social Security surplus. The economy began to recover once again in the second half of 1938, and unemployment began to decline.

While the spending program affected the performance of the economy, the antitrust activities had almost no impact on the structure of American business. TNEC investigations, which lasted nearly three years, produced only a timid report calling for minor changes in the antitrust laws and patent procedures, and Arnold was not really concerned with the size of business organizations.

Arnold was concerned about economic behavior, especially pricing policies. He tried to use the government power that antitrust laws supplied as a weapon to restore and maintain price competition in American business. He was more concerned about the consumer than about the small businessman and the decentralization of the system. The antitrust program, in his view, was important for the smooth and prosperous functioning of the economy. It was a way of guaranteeing an adequate supply of purchasing power. If used, the existing antitrust laws could, he assumed, give the federal government important managerial powers. They could force changes in business behavior even though the government did not attack all giants or win all antitrust cases.

Arnold did use his power more vigorously than any earlier chief of the antitrust program. He selected his cases with great care, seeking maximum impact, and relied heavily on consent decrees, fully satisfied to reach an agreement with a firm prior to the point of judicial decision. He moved against entire industries, such as home building, attacking labor as well as business. And he moved against the giants of the auto, dairy, movie, tire, oil, aluminum, and tobacco industries and also against the American Medical Association.

Arnold's effectiveness was limited by the opposition of very strong groups. His support came chiefly from dissident businessmen who hoped to strengthen their competitive positions, while most businessmen opposed him, insisting that the program weakened business confidence and punished businessmen for doing things they had been encouraged to do only a few years earlier by NRA. They also maintained that the program was based on a ·false theory, the theory of administered prices. Big businessmen did not administer prices; they were determined by the forces of supply and demand. The American Federation of Labor was also hostile, and many planners regarded the program as futile and harmful. They believed that the government should coordinate and provide direction for the economic system.

Arnold's effectiveness was limited also by the way in which

government spending was promoting recovery. It suggested that the government need not deal directly with the structure and behavior of the business system. If government managed its fiscal affairs properly, then business would be encouraged to behave in a desirable fashion.

The performance of the economy from 1936 to 1939 gave the Keynesians new importance in the economics profession and in the administration. Keynes obtained a major American disciple with the conversion of Alvin Hansen of Harvard University, the president of the American Economics Association, in 1938. Currie became an economic adviser to the President, and he and Hansen testified before the TNEC in 1939 that private investment could no longer be relied upon to achieve full employment, especially as income was concentrated in the hands of wealthy individuals and large corporations who tended to save a large portion of their money, and thus government should supplement private investment by spending and should redistribute income so as to get it into the hands of spenders. A number of Keynesian economists, including Hansen, moved into government positions in 1939 and 1940. One center for them was the Department of Commerce, which was now headed by Hopkins. If FDR had been no more than partially converted, and most Americans had not moved even as far as he, Keynesian economics was making progress in the United States.

The economy was also making progress, but the New Deal failed to produce complete recovery. By 1940, unemployment was nearly 50 percent less than it had been when Roosevelt came to power, but 8 million people—nearly 15 percent of the work force—were still out of work.

The New Deal's failure to accomplish more is explained in part by its fiscal policy. The administration had failed to spend enough and to run sufficiently large deficits. According to the traditional way of figuring the budget, federal spending moved only from $3.3 billion in fiscal 1929 and $4.6 billion in fiscal 1933 (Hoover's last year) to $9.1 billion in 1940. At the same time, receipts were raised from $4 billion to $5.1 billion. The method now used reveals a somewhat different but essentially similar picture, with expenditures moving from $2.6 billion in 1929 to $3.2 billion in 1932 and then to $10.1 billion in 1940 while receipts moved from $3.8 billion to $8.6 billion. Thus, although federal spending was increased and the budgets did move from surplus to deficit, the increase and the deficits were small, reaching a peak of $3.5 billion in 1936.

The federal government pursued no more than a moderately expansionary fiscal policy. It, however, was not solely responsible for the New Deal's failure to produce more change in economic conditions. The behavior of state and local governments was also significant. Their fiscal policies actually counteracted New Deal fiscal policy. State and local governments increased spending but increased taxes even more and moved from deficit to surplus, thus having a negative impact during New Deal years.

The nation as a whole moved away from deficit financing during the decade. All governments combined had a deficit in 1929. Together, they either had a surplus or had an approximately balanced budget each year but one (1936) from 1933 to 1939. Frequently during the decade, the governments removed larger sums in taxes from the community than they returned to it in expenditures. "Fiscal policy," E. Cary Brown has concluded, " . . . seems to have been an unsuccessful recovery device in the 'thirties—not because it did not work, but because it was not tried."

Business investment policies also contributed significantly to the failure to achieve full employment. Although investments increased after 1932, they did not come close to the 1929 level of $16 billion before the 1940s. New Deal experimentation contributed to this. The expansion of government and of labor troubled almost all businessmen and encouraged them to hold back. But businessmen were influenced also, and perhaps even more, by awareness of the tremendous increase in American productive capacity during the 1920s, which suggested that additional investments could not be profitable, and by memories of the bitter experiences of the early 1930s. Some businessmen did finance impressive developments in such fields as chemicals and aviation and in the South, where the growth psychology survived and opportunities for investment seemed quite large. Many businessmen, however, assumed that industrial expansion had reached or gone beyond its limit, and, as a group, businessmen failed to create a new industry to play the extremely stimulating role that the automobile and other new industries had played after World War I.

Thus, recovery was far from complete by 1940. The recession was over, and it had been a significant episode. In response to it, the administration had rejected both the do-nothing philosophy and centralized planning of the NRA type and had reduced business power and expanded the role of government. The changes in the distribution of power resulted chiefly from the enlargement of the federal government and its expenditures rather than from reductions in the size of business organizations. The episode provided evidence of the effectiveness of government spending and strengthened the convictions of New Dealers about the importance of government action. The action that was taken, however, was not bold enough to produce complete recovery at a time when state and local governments were working against federal fiscal policy and business leaders were holding back and not playing the role of large and bold investors still required for the successful performance of the American economic system.

SUGGESTIONS FOR ADDITIONAL READING

Many of the works already cited, including Leuchtenburg's survey and Tugwell's biography, remain useful on the recession and its significance. Burns is especially critical of Roosevelt's reluctance to endorse Keynesian economics, and Hawley and Stein are essential items on antitrust and fiscal policies. On the latter, see also Robert Lekachman, *The Age of Keynes*, Vintage Books, New York, 1966; John M. Blum, *From the Morgenthau Diaries: Years of Crisis, 1928–1938*, Houghton Mifflin, Boston, 1959; and E. Cary Brown, "Fiscal Policy in the 'Thirties: A Reappraisal," *American Economic Review,* vol. 46, pp. 857–879, 1956. John Chamberlain, *The Enterprising Americans: A Business History of the United States*, Harper & Row, New York, 1963, and Douglas North, *Growth and Welfare in the American Past: A New Economic History,* Prentice-Hall, Englewood Cliffs, N.J., 1966, should also be seen on the failure to achieve complete recovery.

Chapter 11

The Waning
of the New Deal

Change moved forward after 1936, but resistance mounted in Congress and the Democratic party and reduced the ability of the political system to pass reform legislation. Foes of the New Deal had been present during Roosevelt's first term, but then they had been quite ineffective. Now, without help from the Liberty League, a much more effective conservatism emerged. Roosevelt's hopes for substantial enlargement of the New Deal were largely frustrated, and he was forced to fight—even to run for a third term—in order to preserve what had already taken shape.

Roosevelt had interpreted his victory in 1936 as a mandate to carry his program farther and to make more vigorous efforts to improve the lot of lower-income Americans. His opportunities by January 1937 had seemed very good, for the Democratic majorities in Congress were very large. "Give your mind seriously to the question of the Second Coming, the signs and portents are upon us," H. L. Mencken had warned.

By the summer of 1937, however, signs pointed to the emergence of a new reality in American politics, a conservative coalition in Congress. It was replacing the Court as the major obstacle to change. The conservatives in Congress had not had much strength during Roosevelt's first term, but some of them learned in 1936 that they did not need to support the President in order to succeed in American politics. Then his attack upon the Court, while helping him with the Court, hurt him on Capitol Hill. The sit-down strikes, which alarmed many middle-class Americans, also contributed to the growth of opposition. And the recession strengthened the conservative cause.

The conservative coalition had several characteristics. It was bipartisan, loosely organized, and informal. It was composed mainly of politicians who did not face strong challenges at home and felt secure. They represented "safe" states or districts. They also represented rural areas. Many of the conservatives were Southerners, men such as Garner of Texas, Bailey of North Carolina, Smith of South Carolina, George of Georgia, Byrd and Glass of Virginia, but not all of them were. Tydings of Maryland, Copeland of New York, Gerry of Rhode Island, Austin of Vermont, and Vandenberg of Michigan were also prominent members of the coalition. And not all Southerners were conservatives. The liberal bloc in Congress contained such men as Rayburn, Maverick, and Johnson of Texas, Hill of Alabama, Pepper of Florida, and Barkley of Kentucky.

Several features of the existing situation troubled the conservatives. They resented the sharp increase in the power and influence within the Democratic party and the national administration of the North and of urban groups, such as intellectuals and organized labor. They also disliked many features of the expanding government, including the centralization of power, heavy government spending, the deficits in the budgets, the relief and welfare programs, the taxes, the controls over business, and the encouragement of labor unions.

Conservatives also feared the changes that seemed to be ahead. The one that seemed most likely was change in race relations, for blacks had gained new importance in American politics. In fact, a civil rights proposal had been brought to the Congress as early as 1934. The Depression had revived lynching, and that had revived the antilynching movement. The NAACP made this its top priority item and brought forward a bill to make lynching a federal crime. Wagner became the chief congressional sponsor of the measure; the House passed it in 1937, and it was on the Senate's agenda at the beginning of 1938. By then, a majority of the senators were ready to vote for it, but they did not get a chance to do so because a Southern filibuster prevented it from coming to a vote.

Most Southerners were determined to maintain the system of race relations that had been established long before, and they were alarmed by what seemed to be a rising threat. They were alarmed even though

Roosevelt himself refused to endorse the bill. He feared that his endorsement would harm his relations with Southern Democrats and hurt his chances of getting other legislation that seemed more important.

Both Roosevelt and the bill's proponents may have been right. Lynching was no longer the large feature of American life that it had been in the late nineteenth century, and economic problems were very large in the 1930s. But lynching remained an unusually ugly feature and an unusually brutal form of social control. There could be little hope of strong black pressure for change in the South as long as lynching remained one of the realities there. Agitation of the issue may have contributed to decline in the size of that reality. The number of lynchings dropped from eight in 1937 to six in 1938 and three in 1939.

The effectiveness that conservatives demonstrated on the antilynching issue also appeared in others during 1937–1938. They were strong enough in a special session of Congress late in 1937 to defeat all of Roosevelt's proposals, and they reduced taxes on upper-income groups in 1938. They also contributed to the defeat of his proposal for the reorganization of the executive branch. The proposal had been developed by a group of social scientists headed by Louis Brownlow, who devised plans to make the executive branch more effective by enabling the President to shift the locations of executive agencies. Influenced by his appraisal of political realities, Roosevelt did not accept all the ideas of the social scientists, but conservatives still professed to see in his proposal additional evidence of his desire to make himself and the presidency all-powerful. They received help from government agencies that feared the impact of reorganization upon them and from groups who hoped to safeguard particular agencies with which they had close ties, and the combination produced another defeat for Roosevelt in 1938.

There were limits, however, on the power of the conservative coalition. Its effectiveness was limited by the conflicting interests of the men of conservative inclinations. As a result, membership in the coalition expanded and contracted from issue to issue. Effectiveness was also limited by partisan traditions that prevented the members from establishing a formal organization. Thus, liberals achieved some congressional victories after 1936, such as the Wagner Housing Act of August 1937, which authorized the development of a small public housing program.

Another New Deal victory attacked rural poverty. Tugwell's experiences in the Resettlement Administration and other frustrations had helped to persuade him to resign after the 1936 election, but programs for the rural poor did not stop with his departure from Washington. In 1937, a President's Special Committee on Farm Tenancy made a comprehensive analysis of the problems of low-income farm groups and a set of proposals

Figure 13   A Sharecropper's Family (*Wide World Photos*)

relating to them, and the Farm Security Act was passed in the summer. It contained provisions on rural rehabilitation and the retirement of sub-marginal lands and an emphasis on loans to tenants to enable them to buy farms, and the Farm Security Administration was established as a substitute for RA.

There were several New Deal victories in 1938. Conservatives did not block the establishment of TNEC, the enlargement of the Antitrust Division and its activities, and the expansion of federal spending. Roosevelt also obtained a Fair Labor Standards Act that put a floor under wages and a ceiling over hours, regulated working conditions, and attacked child labor. Although many industries were granted exemptions and the minimum wage was very low (25 cents per hour), the law forced many industries, mainly in the South, to raise wages for many workers.

Hoping to strengthen the forces of resistance, some conservatives in both parties considered party realignment. They wanted to unite con-servatives into one party. Realignment, however, failed to take place. Most Southern Democrats opposed the idea, for they did not feel sufficiently threatened by the administration, did not want to break with party traditions, and wanted to hold on to the positions they had in the Democratic party.

Some of Roosevelt's liberal advisers also advocated realignment. The President had long thought that it would be desirable to reorient the Democratic party along ideological lines, and now, after defining himself as the leader of a liberal party, he entered several primaries in hopes of "purging" conservative Democrats from Congress. While he may have helped two established liberals, Senator Barkley of Kentucky and Senator Thomas of Oklahoma, and did contribute to the defeat of Congressman O'Connor of New York City, the conservative chairman of the powerful House Rules Committee, FDR failed to bring about the defeat of several established conservatives: Senators George of Georgia, Smith of South Carolina, and Tydings of Maryland. He suggested that they hampered the development of the South, which he labeled "the nation's No. 1 economic problem"; he expressed concern about the widespread poverty there and about disenfranchisement, and he endorsed efforts to repeal the poll tax. His targets, however, and their supporters portrayed the attempted purge as fresh evidence of his dictatorial ambitions and meddlesome tendencies and an insult to the South. They forced him to continue to live with the broad, decentralized, and complex party that had taken shape by 1936.

Roosevelt failed even though he still had many admirers in the South and the region was not thoroughly conservative. Two-thirds of the Southerners approved of his performance as president, and there were more than a few very articulate liberals in the region. Some of them joined forces with radicals to form the Southern Conference for Human Welfare, a group eager to push the New Deal much farther in the South.

The tide was not running in that direction, however. In the congressional elections in the fall, the Republicans made an impressive comeback. Helped by the recession and by growing middle-class alarm about the advance of the labor movement, the Republicans made gains in the East and the Middle West, increasing their contingents in the House by 75 and in the Senate by 7 so that the Democrats now had 261 representatives and 69 senators and the Republicans had 164 members in the lower house and 23 in the other. Most of the incumbents who were defeated were liberals, such as Congressman Maury Maverick, a leading figure in a liberal bloc in the House.

Democrats won most of the congressional races, and liberals, including Wagner, scored some victories, but the outcome suggested to Roosevelt that he must now move cautiously and encouraged him to relax his pressure for reform. "We have now passed the period of internal conflict in the launching of our program of social reform," he announced to Congress in January 1939. "Our full energies may now be released to invigorate the processes of recovery in order to preserve our reforms, and to give every man and woman who wants to work a real job at a living wage." The message did not mean that he had deserted the New Deal. He was determined to "preserve" it.

The conservative coalition had been strengthened by the elections. The Democratic component had gained confidence, and the Republican contingent had been expanded with the addition of men like Senator Robert A. Taft of Ohio, the son of a former president. The conservatives believed that expenditures must be cut and that the system the New Dealers had established must be reformed. Tax programs, labor policy, and other features, the conservatives believed, discouraged investment and must be altered in order to speed economic advance. Business investment, not government spending, seemed the only way of producing complete and lasting recovery. Thus, prodded by the conservatives, Congress in 1939 slashed relief appropriations, cut taxes, defeated new public works and public housing proposals, imposed restrictions on the political activities of federal employees, and launched a special investigation of the NLRB.

One consequence of the increase in conservative strength was the destruction of WPA's Federal Theater Project. Staffed by ambitious people who hoped to change the American theater and enlarge its importance in American life, the project encountered foes, especially in the House Committee on Un-American Activities. HUAC was a product of the rising resistance to change. Established in 1938, it was chaired by Martin Dies of Texas, a Democratic congressman. His committee focused its attention on charges of Communist infiltration in many aspects of American life and tended to see the New Deal and the CIO as products of the Communist conspiracy. Influenced by HUAC's investigations, Congress now denied the theater project the funds needed for survival. Roosevelt let it die without a fight. In this small but not insignificant area, opponents of change demonstrated great strength.

Roosevelt and the congressional liberals had not given up. They did obtain some improvements in social security, made some liberal appointments, including Hopkins as Secretary of Commerce, Murphy as Attorney General, and Frankfurter and Douglas as Supreme Court justices, and protected the Wagner Act and the NLRB against their critics. FDR also obtained passage of a bill authorizing him to reorganize the executive branch. Prior to submission of it, however, he had scaled down his original proposal in response to his defeat in 1938, and thus the final result was not only less than Brownlow and his associates had recommended but also less than Roosevelt wanted.

Activities in farm politics from late 1938 to late 1940 illustrated the continuing pressures for change and the growing resistance to it. FSA remained active, seeking chiefly to increase the number of small but efficient family farms, and it became a significant participant in farm politics, especially in the South, challenging the status quo and putting pressure on others to match the efforts of the agency. Yet, its concrete accomplishments were small relative to the size of rural poverty. Congress provided only small support for efforts to increase the number of family farmers. In its early years, FSA was able to provide loans for fewer than 5 percent of the applicants and only 2 percent of the nation's tenants. The number of tenants in the South declined from 1.8 million in 1935 to 1.4 million in 1940, but the number of farm operators also dropped by 400,000 while the number of day laborers increased by nearly 300,000 and many Southerners moved out of agriculture. Although there were more than 1 million Negro tenants and day laborers in the South, FSA made less than 2,000 tenant purchase loans to blacks. Nationally, tenant farmers were increasing at the rate of 40,000 per year, while the law allowed FSA to make fewer than 10,000 loans per year.

The administrator of FSA, Dr. Will Alexander, a prominent Southern liberal, had a strong interest in poor blacks as well as poor whites. His agency distributed a significant share of its benefits to blacks, but it did discriminate against them, dealt cautiously with racial problems, and seldom challenged the system of segregation, fearing that boldness would reduce still more its ability to grapple with the problems of poverty. Yet, FSA was bold enough to arouse opposition. In June 1940, Alexander resigned in part because his appearances before congressional appropriations committees were being made increasingly difficult by the opposition of conservative congressmen who feared FSA's threat to class and race relations. Such congressmen favored only those farm programs that benefited commercial farmers.

While FSA was taking shape, Tolley and other ambitious New Dealers obtained a new opportunity to promote their hopes for agricultural planning. In the fall of 1938, Wallace elevated the USDA's Bureau of Agricultural Economics to the role of central planner for the department and appointed Tolley chief of the bureau. During 1939 and 1940, Tolley and his lieutenants, with assistance from M. L. Wilson, first as Under Secretary and then as director of the Extension Service, devoted most of their time and energy to the construction of a planning program involving cooperation among the national agricultural agencies, the agricultural colleges and their extension services, and the farmers.

Tolley and his aides hoped to change both farm policy and the way in which it was made. The BAE pushed many proposals for change in AAA. Believing it had not done nearly enough to improve the lot of lower-income groups, the social scientists pushed for changes in this area. Recognizing that AAA officials were interested first of all in making payments to farmers and raising farm prices and farm income, the BAE battled for proposals designed to get more conservation from the program.

The efforts to change the policy-making process included efforts to enlarge the role of the farmers and was illustrated most significantly by the county planning committees. They were organized by the extension services and composed of farmers and state and national officials serving in the counties. Most members were farmers, and a farmer served as chairman.

One feature of the committees troubled Tolley and others. They did not represent all groups in their communities. The county agent usually selected the farmers who served on the committees, and as those agents tended to work most closely with the more substantial members of their communities, the committees seldom included representatives of the rural poor. Tolley and his close associates favored the establishment of elected committees and tried to influence the extension and farm leaders to take the steps needed to make the committees more representative.

Although the planning committees failed to conform perfectly with the planners' ideals and many officials in the agricultural agencies and colleges resisted the pressures from Tolley and his aides, they were optimistic. Farmer participation was growing; planning committees were taking shape and participating actively in the planning process, and various educational programs were at work, seeking to promote participation in and support for planning. The work of the planning committees, the schools of philosophy, and the discussion groups might change the ideas of enough farmers, county agents, and administrators and generate enough support for planning to enable it to triumph over hostility and develop a better farm program.

Yet, the ambitious efforts to improve the lot of the rural poor and develop a system of agricultural planning had alienated the most influential farm organization, the American Farm Bureau Federation. Formed after World War I, the organization had quickly become the largest farm organization with a membership of more than 300,000 farm families throughout the 1920s, most of them in the Middle West. It made no effort to organize all of the people who lived on the land; it was interested only in the rural businessman, the farmer who produced and sold a substantial crop. And the "farm problem," as the organization defined it, was the most obvious problem faced by this type of farmer: low farm prices. The organization's aim was to make the farm business profitable and keep it so.

The organization had provided strong support for the major New

Deal farm programs. For Edward A. O'Neal of Alabama, the national president, one of the most attractive features of the New Deal was the many opportunities it provided to strengthen his organization. He applauded the administration's practice of working with farm leaders in drafting farm laws and claimed credit for obtaining the legislative benefits for the commercial farmers. He liked the use made of the Farm Bureau's allies—the extension services—in the administration of the program. Often, extension officials helped the Farm Bureau recruit new members and appointed Farm Bureau members to the committees that looked after the farm programs on the local level.

In the second half of the 1930s, however, the AFBF grew increasingly unhappy with the New Deal. To the organization's leaders, the Roosevelt administration seemed to have become dominated by urban liberalism and biased against the farmer, and Wallace and his department seemed to be drawing away from the Farm Bureau and rejecting the view that their job was to serve the interests of commercial farmers. The officials seemed too interested in the rural poor and the urban consumers. Furthermore, the department's tendency to develop committees of farmers to plan and administer farm programs seemed capable of creating groups that would replace the farm organizations in the policy-making process, depriving the Farm Bureau of its status as the leading spokesman for the farmer and providing department officials with the power needed to dominate farm politics and alter the orientation of farm policy.

Thus, in the late 1930s, Farm Bureau leaders began to make suggestions for changes in the planning and administration of the farm programs, and late in 1940, the organization proposed the establishment of a five-man nonpartisan board, representative of agriculture, to plan and administer farm programs on the national level and reliance on the extension services in handling those functions on the state and local levels. The farm organization felt both threatened and capable of expanding its power. As a consequence of the power of the Farm Bureau among farm organizations and its influence upon the extension services, the proposal, if put into effect, would inevitably produce a large increase in the power of that farm organization. It did not want to remove the government from agriculture. The organization wanted only to guarantee that it would shape the role the government played.

The Farm Bureau that had become highly critical of the New Deal was a larger group than the one that had supported it earlier. Under the impact of the Depression, membership had dropped from more than 320,000 in 1930 to less than 165,000 in 1933. Then, massive membership drives, involving efforts to exploit the organization's ties with Extension and AAA, had been very successful, especially in the South. By 1940, it had nearly 450,000 members and had established itself as the strongest farm organization.

The Farm Bureau had become a very substantial obstacle in the path of New Dealers who hoped to serve more than the business interests of commercial farmers, and it could count on very strong support in Congress. The organization had close ties with the conservative coalition. Thus, New Dealers who advocated additional innovations faced opponents who offered powerful resistance to further change.

By 1940, conservatives were strong enough in the Democratic party to threaten New Dealers with loss of control of the White House and destruction of many of their programs, and the threat forced Roosevelt to break with the anti-third term tradition. Fearful that Garner or some other conservative Southern Democrat would be nominated, New Dealers pressed FDR to run again, believing that only he could protect the New Deal. This concern, as well as the international situation and his failure to find a suitable substitute with a substantial following, persuaded Roosevelt that he must make the break with tradition. He obtained his own renomination and forced the convention to nominate an ardent New Dealer, Henry Wallace, as his running mate. Fortunately for the liberals, they received important support from another faction of the party—the big city organizations, especially the Kelly machine in the convention city, Chicago. They regarded Roosevelt as the only person capable of leading the party to another victory, urged him to run, and helped him obtain the nomination.

In spite of the troubles inside his party and the growing opposition to the New Deal elsewhere, Roosevelt maintained his control of the White House. But he did not do it on the basis of the New Deal alone. Foreign policy issues were very important by 1940, and the opposition failed to challenge him clearly on domestic issues. The Republican candidate, Wendell Willkie, was a corporation lawyer, a president of a giant public utility holding company, and a former Democrat who had broken with his party chiefly on the issue of public versus private power in the Tennessee Valley. While devoting much of his time to attacks upon Roosevelt's foreign and military policies, Willkie also criticized the New Deal, arguing that its antibusiness bias had resulted in failure to promote recovery and economic growth, but he ran on a platform that called for the continuation of much of the New Deal. Also, he endorsed much of it in his campaign, thereby helping to make Roosevelt's programs more secure.

Perhaps the international crisis, which was very serious by the fall of 1940, enabled the Democrats to maintain their majority position. Roosevelt's portion of the popular vote (less than 55 percent) was smaller than it had been in 1932 and 1936 and might have fallen farther if the

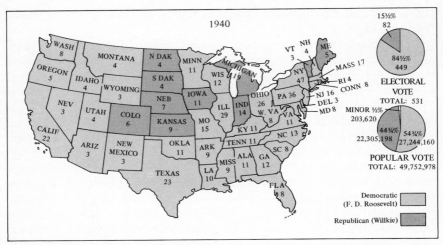

Figure 14 Election Results—1940 (*National Atlas, U.S. Geological Survey, Washington, 1970. Used by Permission.*)

international situation had not provided help. It supplied the Democrats with new arguments, gave Roosevelt new opportunities for action, and stimulated economic growth.

Roosevelt's victory, however, depended very heavily on the support for the Democratic party in the big cities that had been produced to a significant degree by the New Deal. He had lost much of his support outside the big cities. Most farmers in the Middle West, for example, returned to the Republican party. His victory margins were so large in New York City, Chicago, Milwaukee, and Cleveland, on the other hand, that they enabled him to carry their states in spite of his losses in other parts of those states. Contributing to those victory margins was even greater support from the black voters than he had received in 1936. Of all the groups of Americans in 1940, they were most eager for additional changes. And the workers, who liked the changes of the 1930s and wanted more, gave Roosevelt almost as much support as they had in 1936, even though Lewis deserted him and endorsed Willkie. The other leaders in the CIO and most of its members did not do so, causing Lewis to resign as president and enabling Murray to replace him.

Roosevelt's dependence on the urban workers was even greater than it had been earlier. In 1932 and 1936, he had received more support from farmers, businessmen, and professionals than he did in 1940. By then, their unhappiness with many of the recent changes and their eagerness to repeal them had been growing for several years.

Foes of the New Deal were growing stronger. Although it has been suggested that the New Deal "ran out of fuel not because of the conservative opposition, but because it ran out of ideas," the most ambitious New Dealers such as Wagner, Arnold, men in the FSA and the BAE, the advocates of government spending, and many men around the President still had many ideas for change, but the forces of resistance had become very strong.

There were limits on the effectiveness of the conservatives. It was limited by the strength of the President and other New Dealers, including the CIO, and by the urban machines, a combination that helped the New Dealers maintain control of the White House. Conservative effectiveness was limited also by the hold that traditional attitudes had upon the conservatives. They were partisans as well as ideologues, and their attachments to their parties hampered efforts to develop a formal conservative coalition in Congress and to realign the political parties.

Nevertheless, the conservatives were much stronger by 1940 than they had been in Roosevelt's first term. They had enlarged their ability to check and restrain the New Dealers. And now, the situation in which the struggle took place was changing rapidly. Economic crisis was giving way to international crisis, and the latter would soon be the major influence shaping American life.

SUGGESTIONS FOR ADDITIONAL READING

Leuchtenburg's survey and Huthmacher's biography remain useful on the waning years of the New Deal, while Burns in his biography provides an especially critical account of Roosevelt's performance in the period.

The development of resistance to the New Deal in the late 1930s has inspired some very good work. The most important book is James T. Patterson's *Congressional Conservatism and the New Deal: The Growth of the Conservative Coalition in Congress, 1933–1939*, University Press of Kentucky, Lexington, 1967. But one should also see Dewey W. Grantham, Jr., *The Democratic South*, University of Georgia Press, Athens, 1963; Frank Freidel, *F.D.R. and the South*, Louisiana State University Press, Baton Rouge, 1965, and John Robert Moore, *Senator Josiah Bailey of North Carolina: A Political Biography*, The Duke University Press, Durham, N.C., 1968.

Robert L. Zangrado, "The NAACP and a Federal Antilynching Bill, 1934–1940," *Journal of Negro History*, vol. 50, pp. 106–117, 1965, is the major study of that subject. Barry Dean Karl, *Executive Reorganization and Reform in the New Deal: The Genesis of Administrative Management, 1900–1939*, Harvard, Cambridge, Mass., 1963, and Richard Polenberg, *Reorganizing Roosevelt's Government: The Controversy over Executive Reorganization, 1936–1939*, Harvard, Cambridge, Mass., 1966, are the major books on an important part of the period.

Jane DeHart Mathews has written a superb monograph on *The Federal Theater, 1935–1939: Plays, Relief, and Politics,* Princeton University Press, Princeton, N.J., 1967.

Southern liberals have been studied by Thomas A. Krueger, *And Promises to Keep: The Southern Conference for Human Welfare,* Vanderbilt, Nashville, Tenn., 1967; Richard B. Henderson, *Maury Maverick: A Political Biography,* University of Texas Press, Austin, 1970; and Stuart L. Weiss, "Maury Maverick and the Liberal Bloc," *Journal of American History,* vol. 57, pp. 880–895, 1971.

Charles M. Price and Joseph Boskin have reappraised "The Roosevelt Purge . . . ," *Journal of Politics,* vol. 28, pp. 660–670, 1966, while "The Republican Congressional Comeback of 1938" has been studied by Milton Plesur in *Review of Politics,* vol. 24, pp. 525–562, 1962.

On farm politics, see, in addition to the books by Baldwin, Kirkendall, and Tindall, Christiana McFadyen Campbell, *The Farm Bureau and the New Deal: A Study in the Making of National Farm Policy 1933–1940,* The University of Illinois Press, Urbana, 1962; Louis Cantor, *A Prologue to the Protest Movement: The Missouri Sharecropper Roadside Demonstration of 1939,* The Duke University Press, Durham, N.C., 1969; and Donald Holley, "The Negro in the New Deal Resettlement Program," *Agricultural History,* vol. 45, pp. 179–193, 1971.

Bernard Donahoe has taken a close look at the struggle within the Democratic party in *Private Plans and Public Dangers: The Story of FDR's Third Nomination,* University of Notre Dame Press, Notre Dame, Ind., 1965. Robert E. Burke surveys the 1940 election in Schlesinger and Israel's multivolume book on the elections. On Roosevelt's foe in 1940, see Donald Bruce Johnson, *The Republican Party and Wendell Willkie,* The University of Illinois Press, Urbana, 1960.

Chapter 12

Beyond Washington

Beyond Washington, resistance to change was even stronger throughout the 1930s than it was in the nation's capital. There were reformers in state politics, but most of the leading politicians who operated below the national level were not vigorous promoters of change. There were many intellectuals who advocated the transformation of American life, but most Americans did not endorse their proposals or even bother to investigate them. Most Americans were interested in other matters.

There were only a few active and successful reformers at work in the governors' mansions in the 1930s. Only two, Floyd Olson of Minnesota and Philip La Follette of Wisconsin, were much more ambitious than Franklin Roosevelt. Several others, including Herbert Lehman of New York, Paul V. McNutt of Indiana, George Earle of Pennsylvania, Ed Rivers of Georgia, and Frank Murphy of Michigan, developed New Deal-type programs—"little New Deals"—in their states. Most of these New Dealers served in predominantly urban states that had relatively high per capita wealth and relatively high political interest. These conditions, including increased political participation by lower-income groups, favored reform, but reform also depended upon the strong leadership that these politicians supplied.

In addition to the reformers, several of the governors of the 1930s were at least mildly sympathetic with Washington's efforts to change the nation. Several Republican governors, including Landon of Kansas and George D. Aiken of Vermont, tended to move with rather than against the New Deal, and several Democratic governors, such as John C. R. Ehringhaus of North Carolina, Wilbur Cross of Connecticut, and Henry Horner of Illinois, also did so, although in rather restrained and ineffective ways.

These militant and moderate reformers did not dominate the state politics of the 1930s. Some of the reformers, in fact, had but a small impact on their own states. Rivers succeeded only briefly and was hampered throughout his term by a shortage of money; Murphy obtained but one term, and it lasted only two years, and La Follette was replaced by a conservative, Julius Heil, who repealed some of the Progressive's accomplishments. Anti-New Dealers, including Eugene Talmadge of Georgia, Harold Hoffman of New Jersey, Homer A. Holt of West Virginia, Charles E. Martin of Oregon, Clarence D. Martin of Washington, Martin Davey of Ohio, and W. Lee (Pappy) O'Daniel of Texas, served as governors of other states. And most of the governors were, James T. Patterson has pointed out, neither New Dealers such as Earle nor reactionaries such as Talmadge. Instead, they were "nobodies— moderate, undramatic, yawn-inspiring men with legislative programs as pedestrian as they were unsuccessful."

The result of this political configuration was some change but not a spectacular amount. The states did increase their spending on welfare and relief, chiefly in response to the establishment of federal programs in these areas that contained provisions for state action. In 1932, only 5 percent of the funds spent by the states was devoted to welfare, but the percentage jumped to 13 by 1942. Some of the states also passed laws designed to encourage the growth of the labor movement, abolish child labor, protect working women, raise wages, and benefit workers in other ways. Yet, state relief programs were less adequate than federal programs, and states rejected most of the prolabor proposals, repealed some of their prolabor laws, and enacted laws restricting the rights of labor to organize and bargain collectively. Also, the states moved away from deficit financing by raising taxes even more than they increased spending, and they relied chiefly on the regressive sales tax, rather than the progressive income tax, to obtain the additional revenue.

Conflict as well as cooperation characterized the relations between the states and the New Deal agencies. State leaders welcomed federal funds that could be used for relief, public works, and the like, but they clashed frequently with federal officials over such issues as the amount of money that the states should spend on relief. "The New Deal," Patterson has concluded, "produced neither federal dictation, a completely cooperative federalism, nor a new state progressivism. . . . For all the supposed power of the New Deal, it was unable to impose all its guidelines on the autonomous 48 states."

While the New Dealers in Washington and the reform governors in the states worked to promote change in them, other forces offered resistance. Money was a factor. The states did not have the funds needed to pay for all the proposals made by the reformers. Also, pressure groups representing business and agricultural interests fought against programs for the unemployed and for the urban workers. And many of the politicians, Democrats as well as Republicans, were hostile to the proposals for change, in part because the politicians had ties with farm and business groups, and many other state politicians were indifferent to the proposals and interested only in patronage. Democrats dominated state politics during the decade, but the state Democratic parties were split into factions and had difficulty uniting on programs.

Traditional attitudes and ideas maintained great strength in state politics throughout the decade. They included the belief in a balanced budget and the distrust of government, especially the federal government. Confidence in business also remained a large element in this part of American life, and the old beliefs in self-help and material success were far from dead there.

These attitudes and ideas had many critics in the 1930s. In fact, social criticism was a major characteristic of American intellectual and artistic life during the decade. Writers of fiction and nonfiction, poetry and plays, and also artists and photographers produced an abundant supply of social criticism, and it was often radical rather than mild. Many social scientists, for example, called for a planned society, and many writers of American fiction advocated very large changes in the capitalistic system or the destruction of it. One historian of the intellectual life of the period, Charles C. Alexander, has suggested that "perhaps a majority of American writers during the thirties were influenced by theories of economic determinism, class struggle, capitalist decadence, and proletarian revolution."

The writers and artists on the left, however, reached only a small audience. Only a few of their works, such as John Steinbeck's *Grapes of Wrath*, found a place on the best seller lists, and Steinbeck's book, which was published in 1939, did not appear until the opportunities for changes in the American system were in decline. The most ambitious planners, including Rex Tugwell, who advised the men of power and even possessed some for a time, experienced many frustrations and found the New Deal far from satisfactory.

The biggest seller of the decade was not a book of protest. It was Margaret Mitchell's *Gone with the Wind*, a romantic tale of the South during the Civil War and Reconstruction. Published in 1936, it sold 4 million copies and became a very successful movie. This widely read and discussed book supplied escape from the present, not inspiration or a blueprint for transformation of it.

The Depression increased the amount of leisure time available to the average American, and Americans could have spent the time reading social criticism and proposals for large-scale changes. Few did so, however. Certainly the American workers, the people upon whom the left depended for revolution, did not give themselves a chance to be influenced by the radical writers. They were read instead by other intellectuals.

The children of the working classes spent more time in school than they had in the past. High school enrollment shot up sharply during the decade. New laws attacking child labor and requiring school attendance contributed to this, and the financial aid to students available from the National Youth Administration during the second half of the 1930s also helped. The biggest influence, however, was the shortage of jobs. Young people did not have as many alternatives to school as they had earlier, and thus the working-class children and others had greater opportunities to come into contact with the intellectual influences of the period.

Varieties of radicalism and reformism did have impacts on the schools. Some of the most prominent intellectuals, such as John Dewey of Columbia University's Teachers College, had a very large interest in these institutions. Dewey, George S. Counts, and others tried to transform them into instruments for the construction of a new, more democratic, and more highly collectivized society. And some students and teachers participated in radical movements.

Radicals and reformers in the schools, however, had to contend against very strong forces. Conservative groups dominated the local school boards and the governing boards in higher education, and they regulated the expression of political ideas by teachers and insisted that only the "right things" should be taught. Many states required teachers to take loyalty oaths, and many teachers with radical ideas lost their jobs.

Radicalism was a part of student life during the 1930s, but not a very large part. Some of the radicals of the period were young people; some were on the college campuses, but the numbers involved in protest organizations, like the American Student Union, were small. Campus radicals, if not lonely figures, were not very numerous. One social historian has suggested that the Harvard student who swallowed a large goldfish in 1935 "aroused greater undergraduate excitement in the nation than any of the radical social causes could manage to muster." And more than a few observers complained about the conservatism of the young. "To the generation of strivers before them," Caroline Bird has written, "the 'Lost Generation' of the Depression young seemed amiable, pliant, and uncritical."

Young Americans devoted most of their time to matters other than political action and the transformation of American society. Religion was not one of their big interests. Some observers expected that the Depression would stimulate a great revival, but the churches actually lost members. Religion did, of course, remain a large interest for millions of Americans, and a number of minor cults, like the Jehovah's Witnesses, grew in size. Most young people, however, had other concerns.

Interest in college football also declined from the high peak of the 1920s. At least, attendance dropped, and many schools had trouble paying for the large stadiums that they had constructed earlier. Students had less money to spend on such activities, and college life was somewhat more austere than it had been in the preceding decade. One of the most famous gridiron heroes was Byron "Whizzer" White of the University of Colorado. White won a Phi Beta Kappa key and election as a Rhodes scholar in the same year that he was selected for All-American honors.

As the goldfish episode suggests, the college student of the Depression era was not interested only in work. Dancing maintained the popularity that it had gained during the 1920s, and drinking, which was freer after 1932 than it had been for more than a decade, enjoyed an increase in popularity, although most of the increase took place in other parts of American society, for the college student had not been intimidated by prohibition. Repeal did result in the rapid building of cocktail lounges, bars, and night clubs, and they supplied music and dancing as well as alcohol. Radio and the phonograph also increased the supply of music, and before the end of the decade, college students and other Americans were listening and dancing to a new form of jazz—"swing"—and to the big bands of Benny Goodman, Count Basie, Duke Ellington, the Dorsey brothers, and many others. The popular music of the day did not challenge the dominant values of American society.

The evidence does not suggest that interest in sex declined among young Americans. There was, apparently, less bold talk about it than there had been in the roaring twenties, and the Depression did increase the fear of pregnancy, force young people to postpone marriage, and encourage a further drop in the birthrate. Some of the evidence from the world of feminine fashion suggests a more cautious approach to sex. "Women," Gilman Ostrander has written, "lowered their skirts . . . to their calves and, amid the sobering experience of the Great Depression, more or less left them there until World War II." "Girls adapted by turning down the heat," another social historian has observed. "The jazz-baby went out with the boom." Yet, other evidence from the world of fashion pointed to a renewal of interest in the mature female form. "The flat-busted little girl of the nineteen-twenties had attained maturity and was proud of it," Frederick Lewis Allen maintained; "indeed so striking was the change between the ideal figure of 1929 and that of 1933 that one might almost have thought that a new anatomical species had come into being." Also, the desire to have no more than one or two children did not force Americans to abstain from sexual activities. Instead, they turned increasingly to birth-control methods and practiced "planned parenthood." And, while the birthrate continued to decline for a few more years, the marriage rate began to rise once again before the middle of the decade.

Thus, the reformer and the revolutionary faced stiff competition. Much of it came from the mass media. Two old forms, the newspaper and the magazine, were antirevolutionary forces. Even more than in the past, they were a part of big business, for the Depression killed many publications and stimulated the process of consolidation in these industries. Almost all the newspapers and magazines that Americans read were dominated by business attitudes and were conservative, timid, or evasive in their handling of public issues.

The newer forms of the mass media, radio and the movies, also were not champions of a new social and economic system. They did experience changes of their own, such as the development of technicolor. Radio increased the amount of classical music and opera available to its audience. The National Broadcasting Company, for example, established and presented regularly a distinguished symphony orchestra conducted by Arturo Toscanini. Radio also increased its supply of news and commentary, but they were dominated by conservative points of view. This medium of mass communication devoted most of its time to entertainment and diversion. The comedy programs were very popular, and so were the serials, including the soap operas that suggested to the millions of housewives and unemployed workers who had time to listen that their problems could be solved by personal adjustments, rather than social reform. Radio also increased the time devoted to advertising, and many of the radio advertisements, and also those in newspapers and magazines, promised that the products advertised, such as Listerine, Pepsodent, and Lifebuoy, would solve the problems of the individual that stood in the way of success.

The movie business—and it was essentially a business enterprise—emphasized entertainment, fantasy, and escape. Sex was a central feature, but by the middle of the decade, the sexual content of American films was rigidly censored. Only a few movies expressed a critical attitude toward American society. Movies produced dreams, not revolutions. As Allen observed, the films dodged "the dissensions and controversies of the day" and supplied almost no record "of the ordeal through which the United States went in the nineteen-thirties" and "hardly a glimpse of the real America." Instead, they "took one to a never-never land of adventure and romance uncomplicated by thought."

Both radio and the movies enjoyed great and growing support during the decade. Radios dropped in price, and thus, whereas only 12 million families had owned sets in 1929, 28 million did so by 1940. They were then available in the homes of more than 85 percent of the population. And millions of Americans, perhaps as many as 85 million per week, watched the products of Hollywood. A pollster in 1940 challenged this high estimate and maintained that the number was "only" 54 million. (The total population was slightly above 130 million.) This large American habit suggested to Allen that "in the back of their minds there was room for an Horatio Alger paradise where young men of valour rose to the top and young women of glamour married the millionaire's son, and lived happily ever after."

The Depression increased the amount of leisure time, and radio and movies moved in to fill a large part of it. Other activities also became more popular. Gambling, especially in forms like Bingo and slot machines that required only small stakes, became a larger part of American life; bridge playing increased sharply, and family games, like Monopoly, were enjoyed in many homes. There was a great increase in participation in sports, seen, for example, in the democratization of golf as municipal courses became much more numerous. The flourishing of softball was another sign of the times. The public works programs supplied the American people with many more parks, swimming pools, and other facilities that they could use in their hours away from work.

Spectator sports also remained popular, in spite of the money problems of the American people. If the college game suffered for a time, professional football moved forward rapidly after economic recovery began. And the decade had its sports heroes, such as Lou Gehrig, "Pepper" Martin, "Dizzy" Dean, Joe DiMaggio, and Joe Louis, to match the greats of the 1920s in the minds of the sports enthusiasts.

Those who could afford to do so used some of their leisure time in travel. By the middle of the decade, streamlined trains became available, as did faster ocean liners, such as the *Normandie* and the *Queen Mary*, and faster airplanes, including the Douglas DC3 and the China Clipper.

Automobiles increased in number, owing mainly to the tendency to keep them for longer periods, and house trailers appeared on the American road.

Thus, the Americans remained a very busy people even though their economic system could not keep them as busy as it had in the past. The intellectual who wanted to change the system or substitute a new one for it had to contend against diversions as well as foes. And the established system's ability to supply diversions even in a period of economic adversity added to its attractiveness.

The Depression challenged traditional beliefs and values but did not destroy them. It did not destroy the old American belief in social mobility. Many people during the dark days looked forward to the time when it would begin again for them. And many forces in their culture assured them that they would be able to move up the social ladder if they had the necessary qualities and that they should want to do so.

While some writers supplied social criticism, others produced success literature that resembled the work that had been available in days of more rapid economic growth. One of the most popular books of the decade was Dale Carnegie's *How to Win Friends and Influence People.* Published in 1936, it became a best seller. Three million copies were sold. Like Horatio Alger and others of the past, Carnegie presented the individual as responsible for his own fate. The popularity of the book indicated, Alexander suggests, "that for millions of Americans the myth of rags-to-riches endured." Many maintained an "attachment to an older America, to a time when economic and social opportunity and mobility were taken for granted."

For an increasing number of Americans, "getting ahead" meant moving away from the central city and building a home in the suburbs. The process had begun before the 1930s, and it continued during the decade, although not at a rapid pace. The continued growth of suburbia indicated that for at least a few the old American dream of success was more than a dream, and the movement up the social ladder involved in a move to suburbia helped to keep the dream alive for others.

The Depression challenged that dream; the challenge influenced the New Deal, but the New Deal also helped the dream survive. Much of the New Deal was designed to revive faith in the dream of success and to make it a reality. Many people, including many Americans of "new immigrant" backgrounds, liked Roosevelt's programs because they seemed to open doors for them. The New Deal did so by promoting the growth of labor unions and by other acts of government. It restructured the system in a way that would permit its beneficiaries to get ahead.

Thus, the advocates of large-scale social and economic changes in the 1930s had to contend against massive forces of resistance in American culture. There were reformers and radicals at work in state politics and in American intellectual life, but they encountered strong hostility and widespread indifference to their proposals. Most Americans had other interests and lived in a society that supplied many activities and left little time for political action. Few people spent their hours dreaming about a new social order and making plans for the construction of it. Most dreamed instead of moving up in the existing system and enjoying a larger share of its benefits. They were interested only in changes that seemed likely to increase their chances of accomplishing these objectives.

SUGGESTIONS FOR ADDITIONAL READING

Increasingly in recent years, historians of the New Deal era have been shifting attention away from national politics and policies and emphasizing activities outside of Washington and social and intellectual developments. This is not to say that these matters were ignored earlier. Early students of the era, such as Frederick Lewis Allen and Dixon Wecter, examined its social history and, in *Since Yesterday: The Nineteen-Thirties in America*, Harper, New York, 1940, and *The Age of the Great Depression 1929–1941*, Macmillan, New York, 1948, published books that are still useful. Other historians at work in the early years of New Deal historiography, such as George H. Mayer and Robert E. Burke, looked at state politics. See Mayer, *The Political Career of Floyd B. Olson*, The University of Minnesota Press, Minneapolis, 1951, and Burke, *Olson's New Deal for California*, University of California Press, Berkeley, 1953.

Recently, however, much more work of these types has been published. Some scholars have studied specific participants in state and local politics. Examples are Allan Nevins, *Herbert Lehman and His Era*, Scribner, New York, 1963; Bernard Bellush, *He Walked Alone: A Biography of John Gilbert Winant*, Mouton, The Hague, 1968; Donald R. McCoy, *Landon of Kansas*, University of Nebraska Press, Lincoln, 1966; J. Woodford Howard, Jr., *Mr. Justice Murphy: A Political Biography*, Princeton University Press, Princeton, N.J., 1968; Keith L. Bryant, Jr., *Alfalfa Bill Murray*, University of Oklahoma Press, Norman, 1968; and Michael P. Malone, *C. Ben Ross and the New Deal in Idaho*, University of Washington Press, Seattle, 1970. Other works, such as Elmer L. Puryear's *Democratic Party Dissension in North Carolina 1928–1936*, The University of North Carolina Press, Chapel Hill, 1962, and Francis W. Schruben, *Kansas in Turmoil, 1930–1936*, University of Missouri Press, Columbia, 1969, supply other ways of looking at developments outside of Washington. And James T. Patterson has written an early and very useful and significant interpretive essay in this area: *The New Deal and the States: Federalism in Transition*, Princeton University Press, Princeton, N.J., 1969.

New Deal historiography has also been enlarged recently by social and intellectual historians who have challenged the almost complete domination of the field by political historians. Large and valuable examples are Caroline Bird, *The Invisible Scar*, New York, 1966; Gilman M. Ostrander, *American Civilization in the First Machine Age: 1890–1940*, Harper & Row, New York, 1970; and Warren I. Susman, "The Thirties," in Stanley Coben and Lorman Ratner, eds., *The Development of an American Culture*, Prentice-Hall, Englewood Cliffs, N.J., 1970. Charles C. Alexander's *Nationalism in American Thought, 1930–1945*, Rand McNally, Chicago, 1969, gives a synthesis of the intellectual history of the period that is comparable in significance to Patterson's work on state politics.

Chapter 13

Change and the New Deal

As part of their effort to describe, measure, and explain change in human affairs, historians have developed three basic interpretations of the New Deal. One emphasizes change and sees the New Deal as a revolution; a second emphasizes continuity and denies that the New Deal changed American life in fundamental ways; and the third stresses both change and continuity and presents the New Deal as a promoter of significant although not revolutionary changes. The third interpretation seems most successful. The New Deal did not revolutionize American life; yet the changes that it produced were not insignificant. The New Dealers themselves limited the amount of change in American life during the 1930s but would have accomplished more if they had not been resisted and frustrated by other people and other forces.

Much has been made of the New Deal's failure to move the economy from depression to prosperity. Substantial progress was made. By 1940, unemployment had been cut in half. Yet, 8 million people were still out of work!

The New Deal's failure to accomplish more is explained in part by one of its own shortcomings. It pursued a timid fiscal policy. This defect has been very sharply criticized by historians who have viewed the New Deal from the left and regretted that it did not produce much larger changes.

The problem of recovery was, however, much more difficult than is suggested by those who criticize the timidity of the Roosevelt administration in the area of fiscal policy. One needs to consider more than national spending policies in attempting to explain the failure to achieve full employment. The state and local governments, with fiscal policies that counteracted New Deal fiscal policy, and also businessmen, with seriously inadequate investment policies, shared responsibility with the national government.

In seeking to promote recovery, Roosevelt had a very difficult task. He was restrained by his own attitudes about government spending and the attitudes of most people and most politicians. They did not believe in spending and deficits on a grand scale, nor did they have many economists during the decade to tell them that they should believe in such methods. And the small-scale spending and deficits that were acceptable were offset by the practices of the state and local governments. To overcome them, the federal government would have had to be very bold. Furthermore, the men of power in the economic world would have had to embrace the same economic philosophy. To produce recovery, massive deficit financing would have had to be acceptable to business leaders so that they would have been stimulated rather than frightened by it.

In fact, the attitudes of business leaders hampered recovery efforts. If the administration was timid, so was the businessman. Although investments increased after 1932, they did not come close to the 1929 level.

In retrospect, it seems clear that Americans faced a dilemma in the 1930s. The old economic system had serious defects, as the Depression proved, and the system needed to be reformed. The reforms, however, alarmed businessmen, reinforced the cautious tendencies that the Depression had produced in them, and thus impeded recovery. "If a government is resolved to operate through the mechanisms of private capitalism," Robert Lekachman has written, paraphrasing Keynes, "that government should refrain from upsetting the delicate state of confidence of businessmen. . . . " Both reform and recovery seemed essential to the administration. In fact, its members were inclined to believe that the system must be reformed in order to recover. Given the importance and the mentality of the businessmen, however, reform and recovery were not harmonious objectives.

Thus, there is more than one part to the explanation of the failure during the 1930s to recover completely from the Great Depression.

Turning to other questions, the New Deal had an impact on class relations, although hardly a revolutionary impact. By providing relief agencies and encouraging the growth of labor unions, it did reduce the degree of dependence of the lower classes upon upper-income groups. It also redistributed income but by only a small amount. The top 5 percent of the population had 31 percent of the disposable income in 1933 and 26 percent at the end of the decade. The share held by the top 1 percent also dropped but only from 13 to 12 percent. The American class structure, while affected by the New Deal, was not destroyed by the crisis of the 1930s and the political developments of the decade.

The New Deal reduced the amount of poverty, but poverty continued to be a large part of American life. Those who emphasize the shortcomings and failures of Roosevelt's programs stress one of these facts, the second one, the survival of poverty, but they ignore the fact that it did decline during the period. They also seem to assume that a classless society was a realistic expectation. In 1929, about 60 percent of the population lived below the poverty line (an income of $3,000 in 1954 dollars), and nearly 63 percent did so in the mid-thirties. By 1941, however, the percentage had dropped below 50.

By the beginning of the 1940s, poverty rates were especially high among several groups, including, of course, the unemployed. A high percentage of old people were poor, as were most service and domestic workers. Poverty also remained a major characteristic of the lives of tenant farmers and migratory workers, and the percentage of blacks below the poverty line was much greater than the percentage of white Americans.

Poverty remained a very large part of rural life in spite of the efforts of AAA, FERA, RA, and FSA. New Deal agricultural expenditures, as Leonard Arrington has demonstrated, were "directed not so much toward the poor farm states but at those states which, though with comparatively high farm incomes, experienced the greatest drops in income as a result of the depression." Those expenditures were "primarily relief-oriented," not "reform-oriented or equality-oriented." They aimed primarily at "the restoration of income for individual farmers rather than the achievement of a greater equality." The New Deal, in other words, tended to raise out of poverty farmers who had been impoverished by the Depression, not those who lived below the poverty line before the Depression hit.

The distribution of benefits revealed that farm politics during the 1930s was dominated by men interested first of all in higher farm prices. Some of the New Dealers hoped to serve more than the business interests of the commercial farmers, and, although their efforts were partially successful, these New Dealers encountered major obstacles that limited their accomplishments.

In the cities, antipoverty efforts were more successful. There, lower-income groups received help from unions as well as government. The groups had more political strength than the rural poor, many of whom did not and could not vote.

Throughout the nation, however, many poor people did receive benefits from the New Deal. Many of the poor were neglected, and most of them did not receive enough help to escape poverty, but the benefits did reduce suffering. Without help from such agencies as WPA, FSA, and CCC, suffering would have been much greater.

Change, though not revolutionary change, also took place in race relations. The New Deal tolerated both discrimination and segregation in its own programs and did not enact any civil rights programs. The Jim Crow system remained in place in 1940. Yet, the New Deal did provide benefits for black Americans, especially in the relief programs, and did increase substantially the number of blacks in important government jobs. Also, the CIO organized some of the black industrial workers. Furthermore, preparation for an attack upon Jim Crow were made during the decade. Blacks became more important in politics as the national parties, especially the Democratic party, concluded that they needed the support of black voters; the Supreme Court became more receptive to arguments by the leading civil rights pressure group, and Northern congressmen developed an interest in civil rights legislation.

The New Deal also changed the structure of American capitalism. This was its most fundamental accomplishment.

Roosevelt did not abolish capitalism. In fact the New Deal protected and maintained it in a crisis situation that seemed to threaten the existence of the system, a fact that has not been given enough attention by those who argue that the New Deal was a revolution and that has been deplored by some historians who regret that it was not. Some Americans of the 1930s hoped that capitalism would be replaced and assumed that the economic conditions would produce such a revolutionary develop-ment, but the American government came to the rescue of American business. And most politically active Americans approved. They were less radical than the left hoped and the right feared, but they might have behaved differently if they had not assumed that reform could make capitalism work satisfactorily and if a reform movement had not emerged. The New Deal developed in a situation that generated hopes and fears about the future of capitalism, and it demonstrated that reform and relief could undercut radicalism in America. The New Deal performed a conservative function. Rather than a revolutionary response to a revolutionary situation, as some have suggested, the New Deal was a politically successful nonrevolutionary and antirevolutionary response to a situation that had revolutionary potentialities.

Furthermore, the New Deal did not reduce the size of business units significantly. The inability of the Roosevelt administration to decide how it should reform America helped big business survive. A conflict over economic policy that had been going on since the rise of industrial America continued throughout the decade both inside and outside the administration. At the center of the conflict was the question of what to do about "monopoly." The New Deal, and the American people in general, gave conflicting answers that ranged from destruction of big business to cooperation with it. As the battle raged, large business organizations continued to function. In spite of the severe depression, big business was not destroyed or reduced in size.

The New Deal also strengthened parts of the business system, including agriculture. Farming was extremely depressed in 1933, and the New Dealers worked to raise farm prices and restore profits to the farm business. They tried to do even more. They tried to fit the farmer into the collectivistic type of capitalism that had been developing for half a century and involved major roles for large organizations, both public and private, in the operations of the economy. Both the development of the production control program and the growth of the American Farm Bureau Federation represented ways in which the New Deal promoted the development of collective capitalism. Rather than destroy business organizations and business power, the New Deal tried to fit the farmer into the system. He was encouraged to organize as other businessmen organized and to regulate production as powerful corporations did. Above all, the New Deal made government much more important in his life. Public organizations such as AAA and the Soil Conservation Service became very active in rural America. The farmer was encouraged to move with rather than against the development of a collectivistic type of capitalism, and he did so. He came out of the 1930s less independent and more dependent on others than he had been before the New Deal.

The Roosevelt administration was committed to capitalism. It did not try to break with that aspect of the American past. But the administration did not merely accept the system as it had evolved by 1933. The administration was determined to make changes in it, as well as to preserve it, and the changes in American agriculture were some of the New Deal's most important accomplishments.

Even more important was the substantial enlargement of organized labor. The New Deal functioned as an effective promoter of labor's growth, and the movement nearly tripled in size from 1933 to 1940. Some of the unions achieved recognition only and were not yet engaged in collective bargaining, and most wage earners, including the agricultural laborers, remained unorganized. Nevertheless a very significant change had taken place. Historians who challenge this stress the large number of workers who were not organized and argue that the labor leaders were not truly representative of union members, but the fact remains that labor-management relations after the 1930s were very different from what they had been earlier. Management had lost a substantial amount of power.

Also of major importance, the New Deal involved a substantial enlargement of the federal government and its power in economic affairs. This development has been emphasized by historians who interpret the New Deal as a revolution. According to them, the federal government suddenly became a very active force and an independent power, not merely the servant of powerful economic interests. Some of these historians also see the new government as a benefactor of the lower-income groups. Some critics of this view argue that the element of continuity is more important than the change in the size and activities of the federal government. The leading business groups dominated it as they had in the past. Still other critics see the growth of government as a long-term development that began long before the New Deal and emphasize the contributions of the Progressive movement to this development and to the New Deal. Proponents of this thesis also often see the people as a whole, not the leading business groups, as major beneficiaries of the enlargement of government.

Several facts seem undeniable. One is that the federal government did grow. Federal expenditures nearly tripled from 1929 to 1940. During the same period, the number of employees on the regular payroll of the federal government increased by nearly 50 percent, and if the WPA is also included, the increase becomes at least 400 percent. At the same time, however, the country did not move from laissez faire to big government. Laissez faire had never characterized the relations between government and the economy, and government had been growing for a long time. Furthermore, the New Deal did have links with the Progressive movement, and ideas that had been in the air for a long time were translated into action under the pressure of the Depression. In other words, change did take place, but important preparations had been made for it. Also, business groups did receive direct and indirect benefits from the New Deal. And finally, they were not the only beneficiaries, and nonbusiness groups received more benefits than they had in the past, certainly more than they had received in the 1920s.

In the end, too much power remained in business hands to call the New Deal a revolution; too much had been shifted to government and labor to regard the New Deal as an insignificant promoter of change. Business organizations and their leaders had been demoted. They had new restrictions on their activities, and they were less important in the total scheme of things in the United States. Business organizations could not do things that they had been able to do previously; their power was limited more effectively than in the past by the power of government and the power of labor.

The loss of power was a consequence of the loss of prestige. The Depression had reduced the prestige of the business system and its leaders. Most politically active Americans had concluded that they could no longer rely as heavily on business leaders and business institutions as they had in the past. Most voters had concluded that they needed to rely more heavily on political and labor organizations.

The New Deal was a significant stage in a large-scale transformation of American capitalism that had been under way for half a century before the 1930s. During those pre-New Deal years, American business had lost its individualistic character and, although some unsuccessful attempts were made to restore that, somewhat more successful efforts sought to bring government and various economic groups into harmony with the collectivistic trends. Then in the years of the Great Depression and the New Deal, big government emerged and promoted the rise of big labor. The changes in size and power of the federal government and organized labor were significant changes, but significant preparations for them had been made prior to the 1930s, indicating that they constituted only a stage in developments long under way and responses to more than the special conditions of the 1930s. Furthermore, New Dealers as well as anti-New Dealers, uncertain about the course they should follow and clinging to traditions in a crisis situation, successfully resisted many of the pressures for change in the decade and preserved major institutions, including big business. It lost some of its power but little of its size. The New Deal had developed big government and big labor and had not destroyed big business.

Historians of the left assume that much more could and should have happened. They assume that the situation in the 1930s was very flexible and fluid and that therefore revolutionary changes could have taken place, and they emphasize weaknesses in the New Deal itself, especially intellectual deficiencies, in their efforts to explain why a desirable revolution did not occur. The deficiencies that they find include lack of firm commitments, inconsistencies and contradictions, and severely re-stricted ambitions for change. These deficiencies, according to this interpretation, explain why the changes that were needed and within reach were not made.

There are serious difficulties in this interpretation. First of all, it exaggerates the intellectual weaknesses of Roosevelt and his aides and does not recognize their strengths. They had the strengths as well as the weaknesses of the tradition of modern American reform that had been taking shape since the late nineteenth century. That tradition was broad and complex. It supplied room for maneuver, and Roosevelt did maneuver and make compromises. He even endorsed contradictory policies and was often less than bold. He did, however, have ideas and principles that were reasonably coherent and had a significant influence on his behavior. They emphasized the use of government power to solve social and economic problems. He was not doctrinaire and dogmatic and was not inhibited by the belief that capitalism meant a very small role for government. He was willing to experiment and was capable of learning from experience.

Furthermore, the interpretation fails to comprehend some of the major realities of the 1930s. It seems to assume that political leaders can be successful as well as wise at every point and fails to recognize that the realities of the time limited as well as stimulated change. Roosevelt is compared with John Maynard Keynes, Norman Thomas, or John Dewey or with an abstraction called the "creative leader" rather than with the real alternatives to him in the 1930s. Compared with the men who had a chance to get the Democratic nomination and thus to become president—men such as Al Smith and John Nance Garner—he was quite bold. And the interpretation compares the New Deal with a vision of the good society rather than with the accomplishments of actual American administrations. Compared with others, the Roosevelt administration promoted a large amount of change.

The interpretation fails to deal adequately with the distribution of political power and the state of public opinion. One of the realities of the period was the conservatism of important elites. New Dealers were much bolder, much more democratic and humanitarian, and much more interested in social and economic reform than they, but the conservatives had power in the economic system, the Supreme Court, the Congress, the party system, state and local governments, and in the administration itself. Another reality was the antiradical orientation of the great majority of ordinary Americans. They rejected the radical proposals of the day.

The interpretation also fails to appreciate the importance of the time factor. The growth of conservative opposition—plus the diverting pressures from the international crisis—meant that the New Dealers had only a short period of time in which to change the country. Before the end of the 1930s, after only a half decade of power, they faced large and frustrating obstacles. They had not run out of ideas for change, but the forces of resistance had become very strong.

The left, in short, fails to recognize that Roosevelt had only a limited amount of power that he could use to produce social and economic change. The historian should, I assume, have realistic expectations, but historians who have viewed the New Deal from the left have not. They have assumed that the opportunities for change were much greater than they actually were.

In support of their assumption that a revolution could have taken place, these historians employ two quite unsatisfactory arguments. One is that a more ambitious program would have rallied the underprivileged and thereby gained the power needed to move forward. It seems unlikely, however, that a political leader could have freed himself from the confusion and inconsistency that were present in the administration's policies on big business, committed himself to one policy, pursued it consistently, and carried a majority of the people with him. The confusion and inconsistency were rooted in the culture. It also seems unlikely that Roosevelt could have gained adequate support for a very bold policy of deficit financing. And it seems even more unlikely that he could have gained adequate support for a truly radical program. The anticapitalist left of the 1930s attempted that and failed dismally. The realities of the situation in the 1930s, while supporting significant change, blocked revolution.

Those who deplore the fact that Americans failed to enjoy a revolution in the 1930s also suggest that Roosevelt and the New Dealers deceived the masses and led them astray. They did not know what was good for them, were seduced by rhetoric and style, and persuaded that they were benefiting significantly from the New Deal when they actually were not. Voter behavior at the time, however, suggests somewhat more rationality than this. Faced with a wide range of alternatives, the voters made decisions and choices and did not behave just as they always had. Many entered the electorate, and many moved from one party to another. They appear to have concluded that significant changes were being made. And lower-income groups were not the only people who reached this conclusion. Businessmen also did so. Apparently, experiences as well as rhetoric were influencing behavior.

Perhaps Roosevelt should have pressed for revolution. He would surely have failed, however, for the voters would have rejected him. Equally important, he was incapable of doing so. If the American people wanted revolution, they would have had to elect one of the revolutionaries. They did not do so; they selected instead a man who had more limited ambitions. He shared the nonrevolutionary aspirations of almost all politically active Americans.

Roosevelt was highly sensitive to the realities of the 1930s and tried to accomplish what he could within the situation that existed. As a consequence, the American people entered the 1940s with an economic system that was structured differently from the one that had existed ten years before. The new system was dominated by the interplay among large public and private organizations. A complete appraisal of the New Deal would include a consideration of the performance of the economic system after the 1930s and a comparison of that performance with that of the pre-New Deal system. That task would be difficult, however, for one would need to sort out post-New Deal influences. The system continued to evolve in response to new experiences, new situations, and new leadership after the 1930s.

SUGGESTIONS FOR ADDITIONAL READING

Students will wish to make their own appraisal of the positions in the debate over the historical significance of the New Deal. For a sample of the literature, see Richard S. Kirkendall, ed., *The New Deal: The Historical Debate*, Wiley, New York, 1973.

Several historians have argued that the New Deal was a revolution. They include Charles Beard in William Beard, ed., *The Economic Basis of Politics and Related Writings*, Vintage Books, New York, 1957; Louis M. Hacker, *American Capitalism: Its Promise and Accomplishment*, Van Nostrand, Princeton, N.J., 1957; Mario Einaudi, *The Roosevelt Revolution*, Harcourt, Brace, New York, 1959; and Carl N. Degler, *Out of Our Past: The Forces that Shaped Modern America*, Harper, New York, 1959. Two books already cited, Robinson's study of Roosevelt's leadership and Leuchtenburg's survey of the period, also develop versions of this interpretation. In addition, see Hofstadter's *Age of Reform*. He emphasizes change although he does not call the New Deal a revolution.

The second interpretation referred to in the first paragraph of this chapter also has a long history. It was developed by Hacker in *American Problems of Today: A History of the United States since the World War*, Crofts, New York, 1938; William Appleman Williams, *The Contours of American History*, World Publishing, Cleveland and New York, 1961; Howard Zinn, ed., *New Deal Thought*, Bobbs-Merrill, Indianapolis, 1966; Zinn, "The Grateful Society," *Columbia University Forum*, vol. 10, pp. 28–32, 1967; Paul K. Conkin, *The New Deal*, Thomas Y. Crowell, New York, 1967; and Barton J. Bernstein, "The New Deal: The Conservative Achievements of Liberal Reform," in Bernstein, ed., *Towards a New Past: Dissenting Essays in American History*, Pantheon, New York, 1968. Three works already cited, Mitchell's book on the 1930s, Hofstadter's essay on Roosevelt, and Burns's biography of him, also fit into this category.

The third interpretation has also been developed by several historians, including Arthur M. Schlesinger, *The New Deal in Action 1933–1938*, Macmillan, New York, 1939; Henry Steel Commager, *The American Mind: An Interpretation of American Thought and Character since the 1880's*, Yale, New Haven, Conn.,

1950; Eric Goldman, *Rendezvous with Destiny: A History of Modern American Reform*, Knopf, New York, 1953; Arthur S. Link, *American Epoch: A History of the United States since the 1890's*, Knopf, New York, 1955; and Andrew Scott, "The Progressive Era in Perspective," *Journal of Politics*, vol. 21, pp. 685–701, 1959.

For discussions of New Deal historiography, see Richard S. Kirkendall, "The Great Depression: Another Watershed in American History?" in Braeman et al., eds., *Twentieth-Century American*; Kirkendall, "The New Deal as Watershed: The Recent Literature," *Journal of American History*, vol. 54, pp. 839–852, 1968; William E. Leuchtenburg in John A. Garraty, ed., *Interpreting American History: Conversations with Historians*, 2 vols., Macmillan, New York, 1970; Alfred B. Rollins, Jr., "Was There Really a Man Named Roosevelt?" in George Athan Billias and Gerald N. Grob, eds., *American History: Retrospect and Prospect*, Free Press, New York, 1971; Jerold S. Auerbach, "New Deal, Old Deal, or Raw Deal: Some Thoughts on New Left Historiography," *Journal of Southern History*, vol. 35, pp. 18–30, 1969; and Otis L. Graham, Jr., "New Deal Historiography: Restrospect and Prospect," in Graham, ed. *The New Deal: The Critical Issues*, Little, Brown, Boston, 1971, pp. 171–179.

Most of the work that one should consult in order to appraise the controversy and reach a conclusion about the New Deal has been cited in earlier chapters. Attention should also be called to Leonard J. Arrington, "Western Agriculture and the New Deal," *Agricultural History*, vol. 44, pp. 337–354, 1970.

Part Two

The Second World War

Chapter 14

The International Crisis and American Isolationism

By the beginning of the 1940s, a new crisis dominated American life. It was an international crisis; it resulted from the militaristic imperialism of Germany, Italy, and Japan, and it led to a vast enlargement of the American role in the world. That change, in turn, produced major changes in life inside the United States.

The new crisis had been taking shape since early in the 1930s, but the United States had moved slowly and reluctantly toward large-scale efforts to deal with it. In fact, through most of the decade, the nation was dominated by the Great Depression, and it , and also the emergence of the international crisis itself, encouraged Americans to reduce rather than enlarge their role in world affairs. In the early and middle 1930s, American isolationism regained much of the strength that it had lost since the late nineteenth century, and the United States made almost no effort to influence developments abroad.

The two crises were closely related. In fact, the international crisis was largely an outgrowth of the Depression. Economic troubles provided the militarists and the expansionists in Japan and Hitler in Germany with the help that they needed to gain power, for the troubles weakened the established regimes. Economic factors also provided motives for expansion. Japan, for example, looked to the Asian mainland for markets, raw materials, and room for her surplus population, and the expanding nations welcomed the jobs provided by armament factories, the armed forces, and the imperial bureaucracies. Desires for revenge and an interest in containing communism also influenced expansionists.

The international crisis emerged first in Asia and soon spread into Europe and Africa. Japan seized Manchuria in 1931 and established the new government of Manchukuo and soon began to look for new opportunities for expansion at China's expense. Germany, soon after Hitler came to power in 1933, embarked upon a program of rapid rearmament and reoccupied the Rhineland, both in violation of the Treaty of Versailles; Italy conquered Ethiopia, and the two expanding nations formed an alliance. Then, they intervened in the Spanish civil war on the side of Francisco Franco, the Fascist leader of a rebellion against the republican regime.

The expanding nations encountered almost no resistance from the other major nations of the world. Busy with the domestic problems created by the Depression, Great Britain and France had little time or energy to devote to international affairs. They were also restrained by fear of war and by hope that Germany, Italy, and Japan would save the West and its empires from the Communists. Russia did intervene in the Spanish civil war on the side of the established government.

Americans in the early and middle 1930s were not inclined to work actively against the expanding nations. In fact, old ideas about a small role for the United States in international affairs took on new life. The overlapping crises stimulated a revival of American isolationism.

The Depression contributed significantly to the revival. The economic crisis created giant problems at home and focused attention upon them. For a time, they seemed more important to most Americans than any other problems.

At the same time, the march of events abroad revived attitudes toward foreigners that had long been a part of the isolationist pattern of thought. For years, Americans had distrusted foreigners, regarding them as incapable of behaving properly, inclined toward war and other evils, and a potential source of corruption and destruction for the American experiment, not people worthy of close association with Americans. Thus, many Americans had long believed that they should stay out of world affairs. Events in the 1930s seemed to confirm the wisdom of this tradition. And the behavior of England and France, as well as Germany, Italy, and Japan, seemed tainted. Great Britain and France seemed to be "have" nations whose selfish and imperialistic behavior had forced the "have-nots" to resort to aggression. Thus, the United States should not be concerned about the outcome of the rivalries or try to influence it.

Depression at home and violence abroad also influenced other factors that contributed to the popularity of isolationism in the 1930s. One was disillusionment with World War I. While Wilson had interpreted it as a democratic force, his war now seemed to be a result of selfish rivalries and a source of antidemocratic trends, such as the rise of fascism. The war was also viewed as a source of the Depression. Since wars produce such undesirable consequences, many Americans reasoned, the United States should not participate in them. It could not convert them into events with desirable consequences.

The decline in the prestige of business leaders also contributed to the isolationist revival. During the 1930s, ambitious foreign policies were often seen as products of business influence upon the policy makers, and American participation in World War I was explained as a consequence of the behind-the-scenes activities of international bankers, such as the House of Morgan, and munitions makers, the "merchants of death." Eager for the profits of war, they willingly accepted the sacrifices that it meant for other men. Popular magazines and books and a Senate investigating committee, headed by a progressive Republican, Gerald P. Nye of North Dakota, and composed mainly of isolationists, including Home T. Bone of Washington, Bennett C. Clark of Missouri, and Arthur H. Vandenberg of Michigan, publicized this historical interpretation.

The United States should, the isolationists insisted, avoid grand adventures in other parts of the world. They warned against large-scale economic activity abroad and against a large professional army, arguing that they would lead inevitably to political involvement and war, and they insisted that the United States did not need to spend large sums on a military establishment. It needed no more than a *defense* force that would supplement the defenses—the broad oceans—supplied by nature.

Above all, the isolationists insisted, the United States must avoid involvement in "foreign wars." They could lead the United States into dangerous alliances and permanent entanglements and would have very undesirable consequences at home. Some isolationists envisioned the destruction of democracy in America and of opportunities for social and economic reconstruction, while others foresaw the destruction of free enterprise and the substitution of an all-powerful government.

Thus, most Americans did not believe that the developments abroad threatened them and demanded their active opposition. Most believed instead that the United States should concentrate upon domestic problems and the improvement of American institutions.

The Presidents of the period did not seriously challenge the isolationist revival and did not try to offer strong resistance to the expanding nations. They did not even though neither Hoover nor Roosevelt was himself a thorough-going isolationist. Each shared some isolationist assumptions, but each rejected others.

Hoover's disagreement with isolationism came chiefly in the realm of economic policy, but even here his challenge was not bold and consistent. Prior to his years as president, he had acquired much experience in world affairs as an engineer, a businessman, a relief administrator, and a cabinet officer actively concerned with the American business system abroad as well as at home, and he had developed strong convictions about the importance of foreign trade and investment. As president, however, he rejected advice to veto the Hawley-Smoot Tariff of 1930. It raised American tariff barriers and encouraged other nations to turn to nationalistic schemes. The British, for example, ended free trade and established an imperial preference system that sharply reduced the market for American goods inside the British Empire.

After that, Hoover brought his actions into line with his theories. Concluding that the weaknesses of the European economy were the chief cause of the Depression, he recommended a one-year moratorium on the payment of war debts and reparations, and the American Congress and other nations went along with his recommendation. The only alternative was cancellation, and Hoover and almost all Americans opposed that. But before the moratorium came to an end, the European nations virtually repudiated their debts. By then, Hoover championed a World Economic Conference to discuss stabilization of currencies, the reduction of trade barriers, and related matters.

Hoover's economic theories meant that he rejected the isolationist assumption that large-scale economic involvement abroad would lead inevitably to undesirable political involvement. He did fear political involvement, however, especially when it took on military form. Like the isolationists, he had a strong distrust of military power. He preferred reliance on the moral force of public opinion, regarding it as capable of exerting a much larger and much more desirable influence. America, he assumed, should supply moral leadership, not rely on military power. Thus, he worked for the reduction of military expenditures, regarding them as an especially undesirable type of government spending, and actively promoted international disarmament.

In line with his theories, Hoover developed a good-neighbor policy for Latin America. He made a large effort to improve relations with Latin American countries by discarding the policies of military intervention and nonrecognition of revolutionary regimes. He refused to intervene in the revolutions of the early 1930s, recognized the regimes that gained control, and removed American Marines from Nicaragua.

Like Hoover, Roosevelt had disagreements with the isolationists, but he was not inclined to play a large role in world affairs during his first term in the White House. Influenced by earlier critics of isolationism, such as Alfred Thayer Mahan, Theodore Roosevelt, and Woodrow Wilson, he tended to think of international affairs in terms of power, the danger that domination of Europe and Asia by a hostile and aggressive nation would pose for the United States, and the importance of international trade; and he assumed that his nation should promote peace, democracy, and a better way of life elsewhere. As Assistant Secretary of Navy, he had been a strong advocate of expansion of the Navy and an early advocate of American intervention in World War I; in 1919 and 1920, he had worked actively for American membership in the League, and now he was troubled by the behavior of Germany, Italy, and Japan.

Criticisms of isolationism, however, were not the only influence on Roosevelt's thinking about foreign affairs in his early years as president. Influenced also by the tradition of domestic reform, he was very interested in attacking domestic problems. Furthermore, as a politician, and one who had witnessed Wilson's defeat on the League of Nations and experienced a related defeat in a bid for the vice-presidency in 1920, he feared getting out ahead of public and congressional opinion on foreign policy. In addition, he shared isolationism's hostility toward war and its conviction about the importance for other nations of the American example.

In one of his earliest acts in foreign affairs, Roosevelt hampered efforts by the internationalists at the World Economic Conference in London in 1933. Concerned with such matters as the low level of international trade and monetary instability, they had high hopes for this conference. Stabilization of currencies, however, would interfere with FDR's hopes of raising American prices, and he criticized the efforts, arguing that domestic economic recovery was more important. He subordinated international considerations to pressing domestic problems.

In 1934, Roosevelt brushed aside an opportunity to veto an important piece of isolationist legislation. This was the Johnson Act, sponsored by Senator Hiram Johnson of California, and it prohibited Americans from making loans to or buying the securities of European governments that had not paid their debts to the United States. The list included most major powers.

The administration in its early years also developed a good neighbor policy for Latin America that was ambiguous in its meaning for America's role in the world. The essence of the policy was rejection of military intervention in Latin America. Roosevelt rejected this in his speeches; his administration accepted a nonintervention pact at the Pan-American Conference in Montevideo in 1933 and reaffirmed the principle at the

Inter-American Conference in Buenos Aires in 1936, and Washington abrogated the treaty sanctioning American intervention in Cuba and removed troops from Haiti in 1934.

The good neighbor policy did not end attempts by the United States to exert influence in Latin America. The State Department and American businessmen remained very interested in obtaining raw materials, selling American products and investing American dollars south of the border, promoting political stability there, and checking efforts by other nations to penetrate the region. Concern about the ambitions of Germany and Italy in Latin America grew increasingly important and led to an agreement at Buenos Aires in 1936 that American nations would cooperate to keep others out of the hemisphere. Washington policy makers assumed now that the United States could be more influential in its own hemisphere if it would operate more tactfully there than it had in the past. Marines would be kept home, while diplomats and businessmen went abroad.

The good-neighbor policy involved both a retreat from military activism and a new effort to cooperate with and influence other nations, and a somewhat similar move at the same time promised independence for the Philippine Islands. Congress passed and Roosevelt accepted the Tydings-McDuffie Act in 1934 that promised full independence in 1946 and dominion status during the intervening period. The measure was influenced by a desire to demonstrate that the United States was discarding imperialism and also by desires to protect American producers against Philippine competitors and to free the United States from the cost of defending the islands.

Several other policies and proposals of the early Roosevelt years clearly assumed that other parts of the world were important to the United States. One was recognition of the Soviet Union in 1933. This break with the past was influenced by a desire for trade between the two countries, a hope that Russia would check Germany and Japan, and a belief that the two large nations should have more contact, but the results were disappointing. And the administration was also disappointed with the fate of its proposal in 1935 for American membership in the World Court. The Senate, pressured by Coughlin, William Randolph Hearst, and other isolationists, rejected this even though two-thirds of the senators were Democrats.

The critics of isolationism enjoyed their most important victory with the establishment of the Reciprocal Trade Agreements program. This was largely the work of the Secretary of State, Cordell Hull. A former congressman and senator from Tennessee and a disciple of Woodrow Wilson, Hull emphasized the importance of world trade and investment, viewing them as significant for both economic and political reasons. American prosperity, he argued, depended upon vigorous trade with other nations, and the alternatives to economic internationalism were authoritarianism and war, as well as depression. If nations could not trade with one another, they would be forced to control their economies rigidly and to fight for the resources they needed.

To Hull, Germany and Japan seemed, if not a threat to American existence, at least a threat to American hopes for recovery from the Depression. The nationalistic and imperialistic policies of those nations seemed likely to close significant parts of Europe and Asia to American business and to drive American businessmen out of Latin America.

After failing to persuade Roosevelt to press for trade legislation in 1933, Hull obtained the powers he desired the following year. He wanted to move away from the high tariff levels of the Hawley-Smoot law and to persuade other nations to lower their tariff walls, and he obtained legislation authorizing the executive branch to cut tariffs as much as 50 percent in exchange for reductions by other nations.

Hull's brand of thought was the most influential form of internationalism in the administration during Roosevelt's first term. This form was economic in character. It did not involve political action by the major nations or the use of military power.

The Reciprocal Trade program was hardly the major American policy during these years. Almost all members of the administration and almost all members of Congress had more interest in programs designed to change life at home. To most active participants in American politics at the time, Hull's policies were of no more than supplemental importance.

Furthermore, at the same time that the trade agreements program was taking shape, the isolationists were able to establish another policy designed to reduce rather than enlarge the American role in the international economy. This was the neutrality policy that was involved in a series of laws passed in 1935, 1936, and 1937 and that constituted the major illustration of isolationist strength in the period. The laws were designed to keep the United States out of future wars by blocking actions of the type that, according to many, had led the nation into World War I. The legislation, in its final form, would prevent Americans from selling arms or making loans to belligerents and would force nations at war to pay cash for other commodities and transport them in their own vessels. Also, Americans could not travel on belligerent ships and could not arm their own merchant vessels. And since Wilson was seen as the focal point of economic pressure in 1917 and the man who finally made the decision for war, future presidents had restrictions placed on them. Once a president acknowledged the existence of a war, including a civil war, he would not be free to decide how his country would behave. He would be forced to impose the restrictions on American economic operations. The legislation, in other words, severely restricted the use of American economic power to influence the behavior of other nations.

Roosevelt did not use the veto to defeat this effort to place restrictions on his activities and the nation's. He wanted to be able to discriminate among belligerents and impose arms embargoes against aggressors, but he did not battle strenuously against these congressional efforts to tie his hands. He liked some features of the legislation, including its expression of the desire to stay out of war and its efforts to prevent businessmen from risking national involvement in war as they pursued profit; he respected the strength of the isolationists, and he wanted their cooperation in his efforts to grapple with problems at home. Thus, he only cautiously expressed his disagreements with the isolationists on this issue.

The neutrality legislation was dominated by the desire to stay out of war. It was not designed to remove the United States from the international economy. In fact, it would not sever all economic ties with belligerents. Munitions manufacturers and bankers would not be able to deal with them, but other groups, such as farmers, could if the belligerents had both ships and dollars.

The legislation would, however, reduce the ability of the United States to use its economic power for political purposes. Forces beyond American control, such as the size of another nation's navy, the health of its economy, or the state of its military preparations, would influence its relations with the American economy. The proponents of the legislation feared that the conscious use of American economic power by the American President would lead the nation into "foreign wars."

The most significant consequence of American foreign policy from 1931 to 1937 was that Japan, Germany, and Italy made their moves without substantial opposition from the United States. Hoover's Secretary of State, Henry L. Stimson, tried to use the threat of military force as a means of influencing the outcome of the Manchurian crisis. He threatened to strengthen the American Navy and American fortifications in the Philippine Islands and Guam, but the President called upon another State Department official to give a speech saying that the United States would always employ peaceful means in international affairs. Hoover would tolerate use of only the feeble "Stimson Doctrine" that declared the United States would not recognize the regime that had been established in Manchuria by force of arms. The United States, in other words, tried to rely on words to restrain the Japanese, and they were not restrained. They attacked Shanghai after the doctrine was promulgated.

Roosevelt refused to commit his country to the use of force against aggressors and did not offer significant opposition to the moves by Germany, Italy, and Japan from 1933 to 1937. Troubled by Japanese expansionism and anti-Americanism, he tried to avoid a serious clash with Japan and to keep the American role in the conflict between Japan and China as small as possible. While refusing to endorse Japanese expansion, the administration did not actively oppose it and relied almost entirely on words—and very mild ones—to persuade the Japanese to reduce their demands.

If Roosevelt had been inclined to deal forcefully with the expanding nations, he could not have done so. He had only a small amount of military power available to him. The administration did enlarge the Navy, but Congress refused to appropriate enough money to bring it up to the strength agreed upon earlier in the naval conferences and rejected a request to expand the regular Army to 165,000 troops and the National Guard to 210,000. And the nation did not strengthen its outposts in the Pacific substantially.

Thus, the international situation deteriorated in the early and middle 1930s, and the United States did not make a major effort to check the deterioration. Some Americans believed that developments abroad were very important to them and to the nation, but not many advocated the use of military force to influence those developments. And many Americans assumed that the United States must turn away from other nations, especially when they became involved in war. The fear of involvement abroad, especially military involvement, and the desire to concentrate upon tasks at home were very strong. Consequently, the United States did not play a large role in international affairs during the period. Instead, the nation was dominated by the domestic problems associated with the Depression and was busily building a New Deal.

SUGGESTIONS FOR ADDITIONAL READING

For an excellent guide to the literature on American foreign policy in this period see John E. Wiltz, *From Isolation to War, 1933–1941*, Thomas Y. Crowell, New York, 1968. Wiltz skillfully weaves a discussion of historical writing into his narrative. For a useful survey, see Selig Adler, *The Uncertain Giant: 1929–1941, American Foreign Policy between the Wars*, Macmillan, New York, 1965. Adler represents the point of view that dominated writing on American diplomatic history in the early 1960s, a point of view that was very critical of isolationism. He should be compared with a representative of a revisionist position then emerging, Lloyd C. Gardner, *Economic Aspects of New Deal Diplomacy*, The University of Wisconsin Press, Madison, 1964. On the economic dimension, one should also consult Julius W. Pratt, *Cordell Hull, 1933–44,* 2 vols., Cooper Square, New York,

1964. C. Vann Woodward, *The Age of Reinterpretation*, American Historical Association, Washington, 1961, and Robert E. Osgood, *Ideals and Self-Interest in America's Foreign Relations*, The University of Chicago Press, Chicago, 1953, are valuable on the ideas involved.

Isolationism in the 1930s is the subject of several important works. Selig Adler, *The Isolationist Impulse: Its Twentieth-Century Reaction*, Abelard-Schuman, London and New York, 1957, is a substantial survey. Manfred Jonas, *Isolationism in America 1935–1941*, Cornell University Press, Ithaca, N.Y., 1966, analyzes the ideas involved. Wayne S. Cole, *Senator Gerald P. Nye and American Foreign Relations*, The University of Minnesota Press, Minneapolis, 1962, and John E. Wiltz, *In Search of Peace: The Senate Munitions Inquiry, 1934–36*, Louisiana State University Press, Baton Rouge, 1963, look at some of the most important people. Robert A. Divine, *The Illusion of Neutrality: Franklin D. Roosevelt and the Struggle over the Arms Embargo*, The University of Chicago Press, Chicago, 1962, focuses on the neutrality legislation, and Fred L. Israel, *Nevada's Key Pittman*, University of Nebraska Press, Lincoln, 1963, takes a critical look at one of the weak reeds that FDR had to lean on in this period.

On Hoover, Robert H. Ferrell has made very important contributions. See especially *American Diplomacy in the Great Depression: Hoover-Stimson Foreign Policy, 1929–1933*, Yale, New Haven, Conn., 1957. Elting E. Morison, *Turmoil and Tradition: A Study of the Life and Times of Henry L. Stimson*, Houghton Mifflin, Boston, 1960, provides the most thorough study of Hoover's Secretary of State. James MacGregor Burns, *Roosevelt: the Lion and the Fox*, Harcourt, Brace, New York, 1956, and Robert A. Divine, *Roosevelt & World War II*, Johns Hopkins, Baltimore, 1969, argue, not always persuasively, that FDR could and should have acted more boldly. For excellent specialized studies of his early foreign policies, see Dorothy Borg, *The United States and the Far Eastern Crisis of 1933–1938*, Harvard, Cambridge, Mass., 1964, and Arnold A. Offner, *American Appeasement: United States Foreign Policy and Germany, 1933–1938*, Harvard, Cambridge, Mass., 1969.

Chapter 15

Toward War
with Hitler's Germany

By the end of the 1930s, the Depression in the United States was in retreat, and the opportunities to build a New Deal were in decline. Americans could, if they wished, pay more attention to developments outside the United States. And they were becoming increasingly alarming. Germany and Japan were stepping up their efforts to change the world, and they weakened the hold of isolationism on the American mind for they seemed to a growing number of Americans to threaten their nation's security and interests. The United States now tried to restrain the expanding nations but found itself incapable of doing so. American leaders succeeded only in provoking Germany and Japan into attacks on American forces. One result was a limited war on the North Atlantic between the United States and Hitler's Germany by the fall of 1941.

The deterioration of the international situation accelerated in the late 1930s. The army had gained predominance in Japanese politics in 1936, and its program of expansion had become the official policy of the government. The goals were the conquest of China and expansion into

Southeast Asia to gain bases and raw materials, especially oil, a scarce commodity in Japan. To accomplish their objectives, the Japanese enlarged their armed forces, developed their war industries, and improved their air and sea transportation. In July 1937, their clash with China became a major war, and Japan soon gained control of the coastal section of that vast country.

At the same time, Hitler began to enlarge his territory in Europe. His ambitions were even larger than those of the expansionists in Japan. He thought not only of conquests in his neighborhood and the reestablishment of Germany's "normal" position, which had been destroyed by World War I. His aspirations reached most of Europe and beyond.

With help from Hitler and also Mussolini, Franco moved toward victory in the civil war in Spain. In 1939, he gained control and substituted a Fascist regime for the republican government.

Well before the end of the 1930s, Roosevelt's fears about developments abroad began to grow rapidly. He feared that they would emerge into a world war that would engulf the United States. He expressed his concern in his refusal to recognize the clash between Japan and China as a war. Neither had declared war; he did not want to provoke Japan by cutting off trade, and he recognized that China had greater need for arms from the United States and that Japan had the funds and ships needed to obtain other supplies from the United States while China did not and thus would suffer if the arms embargo and the cash-and-carry provisions were applied to the conflict. To reduce the risks to the United States, Roosevelt warned that American ships carrying arms to the belligerents would travel "at their own risk."

Roosevelt tried to stabilize the international situation. His "Quarantine Speech" in Chicago in October 1937 was a prominent part of this effort. In that speech and subsequent statements, he expressed alarm about developments abroad and a desire to exert a restraining influence, and he indicated that he viewed the expanding nations as threats to America and did not regard security as a built-in feature of American life.

Other moves at the time also testified to Roosevelt's growing concern. He worked successfully in early 1938 against a popular isolationist proposal for a constitutional amendment, sponsored by Congressman Louis Ludlow of Indiana, that would require a referendum before Congress could declare war. The proposal assumed that only special-interest groups would press for American intervention in "foreign wars." The "people" would not.

Roosevelt also promoted the expansion of the Navy. He was determined to build a two-ocean fleet strong enough to match the combined fleets of Japan, Italy, and Germany, and he triumphed over isolationists who opposed the move. Congress passed the Vinson Naval Expansion Act of 1938.

At the same time, the President worked for greater solidarity in the Western Hemisphere. Fearing Fascist penetration, he obtained the Declaration of Lima in December 1938. Adopted by twenty-one American nations attending the Pan-American Conference, it promised consultation and joint action by the nations when one or more was faced with subversion of invasion. He also promised Canada that the United States would help her defend herself against attack.

Throughout this period, however, Roosevelt moved cautiously. He was restrained by respect for the strength of the isolationists and also by fear of provoking Japan. Thus, he did not take strong actions against Japan as she swept through eastern China. He was not willing to use military or economic pressure.

Fortunately for Roosevelt's peace of mind, he had confidence that Britain and France would ultimately defeat the aggressors in their neighborhoods. Most Americans shared this confidence. Britain and France were, after all, two of the largest and most productive nations in Europe; they controlled significant parts of South and Southeast Asia, the Middle East, and Africa, and they were superior to the expanding nations in control of vital raw materials.

Roosevelt certainly did not have the strength in his own hands to defeat the expanding nations. He was limited by the restrictions that had been placed upon the use of American economic power, and he could call upon only a small military force to support his foreign policy objectives. Spending on national defense had remained below $1 billion per year throughout his first term and was below $2 billion in 1939. By then, the Navy was being enlarged, but little development was taking place in other parts of the armed forces, even though the Army had fewer than 175,000 men. Sixteen nations had larger armies, and Germany had four times as many men under arms as the United States did. Also, the American forces were poorly trained and armed. The Army, in fact, had spent much of its time during the 1930s in civilian activities, such as the CCC. The nation did have bases in such important parts of the world as Hawaii and the Philippine Islands, but only small forces were stationed in them.

Although he held only a small amount of power, Roosevelt felt compelled to try to influence the situation in Europe. His goal was to prevent the outbreak of war, which seemed to be a strong possibility and likely to lead to American involvement.

Words were the major instrument available to the President, and words were the instrument he used. When Hitler seized Austria in March 1938, the United States refused to recognize the new regime. When he demanded in September that Czechoslovakia cede her German-populated territories to him, Roosevelt appealed to European leaders for a peaceful, fair, and constructive settlement while making it clear that "the United States has no political involvements in Europe" and would not get involved in the negotiations. The result was the Munich agreement in which Hitler received the land he sought and promised not to seek additional territory. The agreement was in line with the appeasement policy advocated by the British Prime Minister, Neville Chamberlain, and reflected the unwillingness of the European powers to resort to arms.

In March 1939, Hitler seized the rest of Czechoslovakia, and Roosevelt, in response, tried without success to augment American power and move beyond reliance on words. He struggled for repeal of the arms-embargo feature of the Neutrality Act, seeking to place all trade with belligerents on a cash-and-carry basis and hoping that the possibility of American aid to victims of aggression would restrain potential aggressors. The measure would favor England in a war with Germany, owing to the naval superiority of the former, and would keep the risks of American involvement in the fighting quite low. But the isolationists, doubting that war was imminent and that it would endanger the United States if it came and unwilling to give the President the discretion his proposal called for, defeated him.

Thus, Roosevelt was forced to rely upon words again in the crisis of the late summer of 1939, and they were ineffective. In August, Hitler and Stalin signed a nonaggression pact that opened the door to war by assuring Hitler that he could move without fear of attack by Russia. Roosevelt then appealed to the King of Italy, the President of Poland, and Hitler to avoid violence, but Hitler attacked Poland on September 1 and quickly gained control of much of that country. Stalin seized the rest and all of Finland.

In this situation, Roosevelt obtained the substitution of the cash-and-carry principle for the embargo on the sale of weapons and ammunition. Although the opposition remained strong, it had declined substantially in a short period, largely in response to events in Europe. Roosevelt also brought his charm to bear and made concessions on domestic policy. The desire for sales abroad also exerted an influence.

Roosevelt hoped that this use of American economic power could prevent a Germany victory and enable the United States to avoid war. His public statements on the issue stressed only the desire to stay out of war, not the desire to aid Great Britain and France, but he recognized that their need for weapons and ammunition was greater than Germany's and that Britain's ability to obtain supplies from the United States was greater.

At the same time, Roosevelt promoted a military buildup in the

Western Hemisphere, including the expansion of the American armed forces. The two policies, however, were not fully harmonious. They competed for scarce supplies. The American economy had not been converted to war production, and the output of planes, tanks, guns, and ammunition was now far behind the demand for them from the armed forces of the United States, Great Britain, France, Canada, and Latin America. The small American defense industry grew as war orders came in, but it could not catch up with the demands upon it. The situation severely restricted the strengthening of American forces in late 1939 and early 1940.

After a lull in the war, Hitler resumed his program of expansion. From April to June, he seized control of Denmark, Norway, Belgium, and Holland, pushed British forces off the Continent, and seized the valuable supplies they left behind. His most important accomplishment in this period was the defeat of France, long one of the world's major nations.

As France fell, Roosevelt announced his determination to supply "the material resources of this nation" to Hitler's foes, but he rejected French appeals for American military intervention. Germany seemed a more serious threat than ever before, but Roosevelt remained determined to stay out of the fighting. He hoped that economic intervention would be enough.

Recognizing that the situation had become more dangerous, Roosevelt called for a strengthening of American defenses. He again rejected the theory that American security was a gift from God, guaranteed by the oceans, and insisted that the United States must spend substantial sums to obtain it. Congress responded with an appropriation that would finance a doubling of the Army.

While these events marched forward, a great debate raged in the United States, and the course of it revealed growing American concern about developments overseas. The isolationists maintained substantial strength and, in September 1940, formed a new pressure group, the America First Committee, chaired by Robert E. Wood of Sears, Roebuck and Company. Some isolationists found justifications for Germany's behavior; many denied that the conflict was a struggle between good and evil, and many stressed British and French vices, especially their imperialism. Some also denied that the United States had the power needed to promote desirable results in Europe, such as peace and democracy.

The isolationists denied that German and Japanese expansion threatened America. American security depended, they continued to insist, on the broad oceans and American defensive power, not upon a balance of power abroad or the British Navy. The American nation could survive no matter what happened in the Eastern Hemisphere, could not be attacked effectively, and would not be attacked by Hitler. The isolationists battled against efforts to weaken the neutrality legislation and to supply aid to the belligerents. They argued that economic aid would weaken national defense by depriving American forces of weapons they needed and would lead to unnecessary involvement in the fighting. Arms would be followed by dollars and dollars by troops.

The need for military power was now more frequently emphasized by isolationists than it had been earlier, but they continued to see dangers in it. It seemed to be needed for defense, but it could lead the nation into war. Thus, the solution lay in providing no more military power than the national defense required and developing only the kinds of forces that were required for defensive purposes. Consequently, the isolationists supported military appropriations bills that seemed to be focused on defense but opposed those that seemed to be designed for offensive operations and participation in "foreign wars."

Although most isolationists were not pacifists, all of them continued to warn of the domestic consequences of involvement in war and to advise that the United States must concentrate on domestic affairs. The nation, they insisted, would damage itself rather than promote desirable developments if it tried to manage affairs elsewhere. It would not only suffer the loss of life and property. War would destroy American institutions, such as private enterprise, democracy, and civil liberties, and establish an authoritarian government, even a totalitarian regime. Brushing aside the future feared by the interventionists, the isolationists projected a black picture of the America that would result from intervention.

Some of the isolationists continued to employ economic interpretations. For example, they blamed international bankers and munitions makers for the growing sentiment in the country for American involvement. They also argued that the United States could prosper no matter what happened in Europe. The Western Hemisphere, some argued, provided all the economic opportunities that the United States needed, while others insisted that the United States could do business with a victorious Hitler, for he would be forced by economic necessity to trade with the United States and could not compete more effectively than Americans.

Isolationists also supplied noneconomic interpretations of the forces that were working for intervention. Some blamed Jews who were influenced by concern for their coreligionists in Europe. Many emphasized political rather than economic motives and the dangers of presidential, not economic, power. According to this version, Roosevelt was leading the American people into war in order to maintain and enlarge his power and conceal his failures at home.

The isolationist movement remained very broad and complex. It was not confined to one party, one region, or one occupational, ethnic, or ideological group. It contained Republicans such as Senators Arthur Vandenberg of Michigan and Hiram Johnson of California and Democrats such as Senator Bennett Champ Clark of Missouri. It contained conservatives such as Herbert Hoover and Senator Robert A. Taft of Ohio and many anti-New Deal businessmen, but reformers and radicals such as Charles A. Beard, Gerald Nye, Burton K. Wheeler, and William E. Borah also participated. A genuine national hero, Charles A. Lindbergh, was in the movement, and so was a leading national critic, Norman Thomas. Both Fascists and Communists in the United States insisted that the nation should stay out of war, but only a few isolationists, such as these groups and Father Coughlin, were influenced significantly by strong sympathy for a foreign power. Conceptions of the national interest dominated the movement.

More and more Americans, however, deserted isolationism. The conversion of former isolationists occurred frequently in 1940 and 1941, and changes in groups as remote from one another as the *New Republic* and the American Legion illustrated the movement of opinion. Some of the anti-isolationists joined an interventionist pressure group, the Committee to Defend America by Aiding the Allies, which was organized in May 1940, headed by William Allen White, a Kansas newspaperman, and designed to shape public opinion.

The critics of isolationism emphasized the threat to American security that they saw in the expanding nations. Germany seemed much stronger and Great Britain and France much weaker than had been assumed by most Americans earlier, and consequently the world seemed much more dangerous. The Atlantic, in the interventionist view, had ceased to be a barrier against an aggressive nation in Europe, for the Fascists were employing new techniques and technologies, including fast, long-range bombers, that enabled them to leap the ocean, and thus American security called for struggle as never before. Americans had to discard their negative attitude toward power, including military power, for they needed it to meet the threat. They also needed to recognize the importance of Great Britain to American security. The advocates of aid to Britain argued that if Germany gained control of Britain and her Navy, then Hitler could easily move into the Americas. Most Americans came to believe that Germany planned to invade the Western Hemisphere.

The interventionists also saw a moral dimension to the European war. To most Americans by the 1940s, Germany's behavior, which involved the persecution of Jews as well as the seizure of other countries, seemed clearly immoral. Thus, contrary to predictions that isolationists had made earlier, the outcome of the European war seemed very important. Most Americans could not be indifferent, nor could they favor Germany. Democracy's future seemed to be at stake. The United States would be forced to change its political system in order to survive if Germany became the dominant nation in the world.

Although the German threat to American security and American political institutions was now the dominant consideration in the shaping of American attitudes and American policy, the German threat to American economic life also exerted an influence. Her use of various devices to strengthen herself at the expense of American business alarmed the State Department and many businessmen who believed that the United States could not permit herself to be cut off by Germany from the rest of the world. "We do not eat all the food we can produce; and we do not burn all the oil we can pump; we do not use all the goods we can manufacture," Roosevelt reminded the nation.

Like isolationism, interventionism was a broad, multigroup movement. It contained anti-New Deal Democrats as well as New Deal Democrats, and it was bipartisan. In fact, two Republicans, Henry Stimson and Frank Knox, joined FDR's Cabinet in June 1940 to help him deal with the crisis. Stimson became Secretary of War, and Knox became Secretary of the Navy.

By the fall of 1940, interest in foreign policy had reached a high point, and it figured prominently in the presidential campaign. Roosevelt's foe, Wendell Willkie, was an interventionist. Nevertheless, he often criticized Roosevelt's foreign and military policies, and he charged that a Roosevelt victory would mean war for the American people. The pollsters had revealed that, while most people favored aid to Britain and viewed a German victory as a possibility and a threat to the United States, most hoped to avoid military intervention and did not believe that helping Britain was more important than staying out of war. Thus, Roosevelt felt compelled to promise that "your boys are not going to be sent into any foreign war."

Roosevelt's handling of the international crisis, his cautious use of American power, apparently helped him more than it hurt him with the voters. His actions did cause many German-Americans, Irish-Americans, and Italian-Americans to desert him, but Yankees in the East who sympathized with Great Britain gave him more support than they had in the past, and Polish-Americans and Jewish-Americans backed him even more strongly than they had in 1932 and 1936. Democrats argued that Roosevelt's experience was needed to deal with the new crisis and that the Republican record on foreign affairs and defense was very bad. The situation also enabled the President to make dramatic and popular decisions in the midst of the campaign.

By then, the crisis was very serious. Britain stood alone and was enduring a savage pounding from the German air force, facing a threat of invasion, and encountering difficulties in obtaining badly needed supplies from the United States. In this alarming situation, Roosevelt and the American government took several major steps.

Some American moves were designed to improve relations with Latin American countries. The aim was to strengthen their resistance to German efforts to gain greater influence in the hemisphere, and the moves included a refusal to back American oil companies in their clash with Mexico over payment for oil lands that had been nationalized. Roosevelt and his aides were determined that clashes such as these would not provide opportunities for Germany.

Washington also stepped up the preparedness program. The government increased military spending, called units of the National Guard and the Organized Reserve to active duty, and established a selective service system. It permitted the federal government to draft men into military service for a year.

Several other moves were made to guarantee that Britain received supplies. The complicating factors here were the German submarine and the British dollar shortage. To help Britain deal with the submarine menace, Roosevelt in September 1940 gave her fifty destroyers in exchange for bases in the Western Hemisphere. Winston Churchill, the new British Prime Minister, had requested the destroyers in May and had been supported by Morgenthau, Stimson, Knox and the White Committee, and Willkie had promised not to make an issue of it. Roosevelt's action, however, had been delayed by fears of his opposition, doubts about his power to give the ships away, and concern about Germany's response. And after he moved, his explanation stressed the benefits to American defense.

To deal with Britain's financial crisis, Roosevelt decided upon a program of large-scale economic aid. The decision was made after the election and in response to appeals from Churchill, who pointed out that Britain did not have the dollars needed to pay for essential goods. The President persuaded the Congress to pass the Lend-Lease Act in March 1941. It bypassed the ban on loans of *money* to belligerents and permitted the nation to lend or lease *supplies* to any country whose defense the President deemed vital to the defense of the United States. Although it amounted to a declaration of economic war, the act was defended as a means of guaranteeing British survival and avoiding American participation in the fighting.

Lend-lease quickly became a giant program. Congress appropriated $7 billion to get it started and added $6 billion more in October.

Germany continued to enlarge her area of control, and as she did, she added to the complexities that Roosevelt faced. German forces moved toward victory in Libya and Egypt and seized control of the Balkans, and then, in June of 1941, invaded the Soviet Union. Hitler hoped that he would defeat Russia quickly, thereby strengthening himself substantially, and then destroy Great Britain.

In hopes of frustrating Hitler's plans, the United States soon began to send supplies to Russia. The decision was made in spite of strong hostility to communism. Some Americans wished to sit back and allow Germany and Russia to destroy each other, and some regarded Russia as the greater threat. Roosevelt disliked the Russian regime, but his decision was dictated by his overriding desire to prevent a German victory. He regarded Hitler's armies as "the chief danger" that the United States faced, and he believed that aid to Russia would strengthen the opposition to them, thereby increasing the possibility that the United States could stay out of the war. And he did not believe that any long-term problems would be created by American aid for, unlike Germany, Russia used no weapon outside its boundaries except propaganda.

Thus, the American decision to aid Russia was made rather quickly. Supplies began to move from the United States in August; Roosevelt pressed for an enlargement of the program, determined that "all reasonable munitions help be provided for Russia . . . as long as she continues to fight the Axis powers effectively," and Russia was brought into the Lend-Lease program in November and promised $1 billion in supplies during the next nine months. Roosevelt had ignored the warnings that Russia's defeat and Russian-American conflict were inevitable and made his decision as German troops moved rapidly toward Moscow.

By then, the United States was involved in a limited, undeclared naval war with Germany on the North Atlantic. The large and effective German submarine fleet had hampered efforts to supply Hitler's foes, and the British Navy had not been able to do all that was required to guarantee that those supplies reached their destination. Thus, Roosevelt had felt compelled to increase American action in the Atlantic, and the German Navy had responded to his moves.

Roosevelt's moves began in the spring and continued through the summer and into the fall. In April, the American naval patrol of the waters of the Western Hemisphere was extended much farther out into the Atlantic; American ships began to help the British detect German submarines, and American troops occupied Greenland. The next month, a portion of the Pacific fleet was shifted to the Atlantic to join in the American patrol, and shortly thereafter, the United States occupied Iceland and began convoying ships supplying American forces there. Late in the summer, the American Navy began escorting convoys composed of ships of any nation, not just American ships, from the United States to Iceland. Roosevelt also ordered his commanders to destroy German and Italian forces when necessary to protect the shipping. As a consequence of this enlargement of American operations, Great Britain was able to shift ships into waters close to home.

By now, the United States was involved in the fighting. On September 4, the first American naval ship, the U.S.S. *Greer*, a destroyer, was fired upon by a German submarine. The *Greer* had been assisting a British patrol plane and responded to the sub's torpedoes by dropping several depth charges. On October 17, another destroyer, the U.S.S. *Kearny*, which was defending a convoy south of Iceland, became the first American ship to be hit by enemy fire and to suffer casualties. And on October 30, the U.S.S. *Reuben James* was sent to the bottom of the Atlantic, the first American naval vessel sunk in World War II.

Shortly thereafter, Roosevelt attacked the Neutrality law once again. In spite of strong opposition, he obtained repeal of the provisions that prevented American merchant ships from carrying arms for their defense and carrying supplies to Great Britain. Almost nothing now remained of the restrictions that had been imposed on the use of American economic power.

The United States was fighting a limited war against a nation that controlled almost all of Europe and a large part of North Africa. Roosevelt may have believed that the United States would be forced to declare war against Germany. He surely hoped, however, to keep the American military role very small and to avoid sending troops to Europe. He even gave some consideration in the fall of 1941 to proposals to cut the size of the Army and rely for American defense on economic aid, the Navy, and air power.

The United States was not ready to fight a large war in Europe. The Army had been enlarged. By July 1941, it had grown to nearly 1,500,000 men. It was, Stimson pointed out to newsmen on October 1, almost equal in strength to the Belgian and Dutch armies when they were crushed by Germany.

In addition to its small size, the American Army was not designed for overseas action. It was designed for hemispheric defense. By the fall of 1941, only one infantry division was ready for combat in Europe.

The Army was also an inexperienced force. Most members had joined only a short time before, and many leaders were new to their jobs. Many experienced men were being passed over for high positions because they were not qualified for the new demands. Younger officers, like Colonel Dwight D. Eisenhower, were being advanced rapidly. Giant maneuvers late in the summer and fall of 1941 revealed the progress that had been made and the weaknesses and defects that remained, and provided Eisenhower with the opportunity he needed to prove that he should be advanced to Brigadier General.

American forces had supply as well as manpower problems. Still not converted to war, the economy could not keep pace with the many demands upon it. It was hampered by strikes by labor, resistance to conversion to war production by business, and ineffective administration by government. And there was intense competition between the needs of American forces and those of other nations whose defense seemed vital to the United States. Roosevelt placed higher value on aid to others than his military advisers believed was desirable. Pessimistic about British and Russian prospects and eager to develop their own forces, American officers criticized aid proposals. They were convinced that the United States would have to move into the fighting before Germany could be defeated, and Army leaders, such as General George C. Marshall, the Chief of Staff, were also convinced that the nation could not rely only on air and sea power and would need to invade Europe with a large army. Thus they were distressed by the size and condition of the force that they commanded. It was not prepared for large operations.

To Roosevelt, it also seemed that Congress and the people were not ready for a declaration of war. In fact, as late as August, his opponents in Congress had nearly defeated his efforts to extend the Selective Service Act and the terms of service of the men already drafted. Yet, the polls suggested that 70 percent of the people now believed that defeat of Germany was more important than staying out of war. Although most still hoped to stay out, involvement no longer seemed to most people to be the worst development that could take place. And some interventionists, like the new pressure group, the Century Group, had moved beyond economic intervention and had come out for military intervention. The widely syndicated columnist Walter Lippmann argued that the nation had intervened in World War I when Germany threatened to wrest control of the east side of the Atlantic from Great Britain and thus endangered American security and that the same reason for intervention existed now. And Stimson believed that American military intervention was the only way to prevent a German victory, and thus he urged the President to be a more forceful leader and to prepare the American people for this. Morgenthau agreed.

The United States was not ready for a large war, but it was already fighting a limited one. Alarmed by German expansion because it seemed to threaten American security and American economic interests, the United States had taken steps to check it, but the steps had failed.

Germany continued to expand, gaining control of much of Europe and reaching into Africa, and hit American forces on the Atlantic as a consequence of the American threat to her ambitions. The United States possessed enough power to worry Hitler but not enough to intimidate him.

SUGGESTIONS FOR ADDITIONAL READING

Almost all the books cited in Chapter 14 remain valuable for the subjects discussed in this chapter. Valuable guides to the literature, in addition to Wiltz's book, include Wayne S. Cole, "American Entry into World War II: A Historiographical Appraisal," *Mississippi Valley Historical Review*, vol. 43, pp. 595–617, March 1957; Ernest R. May, *American Intervention: 1917 and 1941*, American Historical Association, Washington, 1969; Robert A. Divine, ed., *Causes and Consequences of World War II*, Quadrangle, Chicago, 1969; and Arnold A. Offner, ed., *America and the Origins of World War II, 1933–1941*, Houghton Mifflin, Boston, 1971. Divine, one of the most prolific writers in this area, has also contributed a valuable survey of American intervention: *The Reluctant Belligerent*, Wiley, New York, 1965. On the controversy between the isolationists and the interventionists, one should also consult Wayne S. Cole, *America First: The Battle against Intervention, 1940–1941*, The University of Wisconsin Press, Madison, 1953 and Mark Lincoln Chadwin, *The Warhawks: American Interventionists before Pearl Harbor*, The University of North Carolina Press, Chapel Hill, 1968. The second volume of Burns's biography of Roosevelt, subtitled *The Soldier of Freedom* and published by Harcourt Brace Jovanovich, New York, in 1970, is very valuable, as is John M. Blum, *From the Morgenthau Diaries: Years of Urgency, 1938–1941*, Houghton Mifflin, Boston, 1964. James V. Compton, *The Swastika and the Eagle: Hitler, the United States, and the Origins of World War II*, Houghton Mifflin, Boston, 1967, is important on German-American relations. To gain an appreciation of the military factors, see A. Russell Buchanan, *The United States in World War II*, Harper & Row, New York, 1964, and Forrest C. Pogue, *George C. Marshall: Ordeal and Hope, 1939–1942*, Viking, New York, 1966. On the establishment of Lend-Lease, see Warren F. Kimball, *The Most Unsordid Act: Lend-Lease, 1939–1941*, Johns Hopkins, Baltimore, 1969.

Chapter 16

Toward War
with Imperial Japan

In early December 1941, the United States remained unprepared for
large-scale war but found itself unable to avoid one. Developments
abroad forced the nation to make a formal declaration of war and to move
into the largest war in its history. These developments took place in the
Pacific, not the Atlantic, and were promoted by Japan, not Germany. In
Asia as in Europe, the United States could not stop an expanding nation
and succeeded only in provoking an attack upon American forces.

By the summer of 1940, the impact of the European war on the Far
Eastern situation had created a problem for the United States. Japan had
established a puppet regime for eastern China, and now war was
dominating and weakening European nations and reducing their ability to
resist Japanese efforts to gain control of resource-rich Southeast Asia, a
region that could solve Japan's oil problem and strengthen her in other
ways. Excited by the prospects, the military forced a change in the
Japanese government that placed two expansionists in key positions,
Matsuoka as Foreign Minister and General Tojo as War Minister. And the

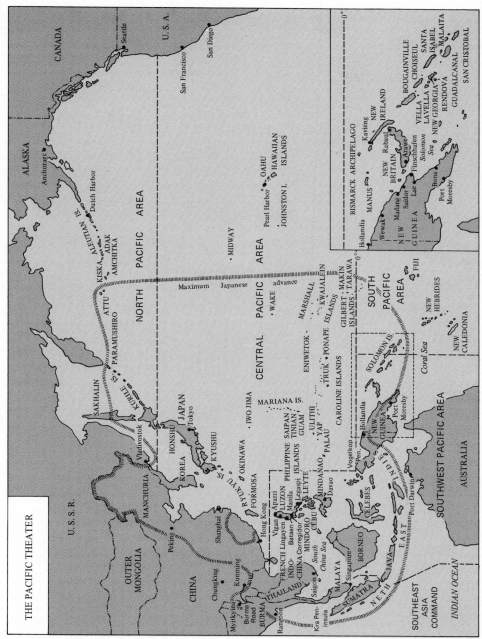

Figure 15 The Pacific Theater (*From George C. Marshall: Ordeal and Hope by Forrest Pogue. Copyright © 1965, 1966 by George C. Marshall Research Foundation. Reprinted by permission of The Viking Press, Inc.*)

Japanese reached an agreement with Russia that reduced their worry that the Russians would intervene in China. Thus, in July, Japan decided to move beyond China and began to make serious preparations to do so.

German ambitions remained a matter of some concern to the Japanese, but actually those ambitions harmonized with Japan's hopes. Japanese leaders feared that Germany would herself seek to move into Asia, and so they sought to gain German approval for their plans. Hitler was quite willing to approve, for he was concerned about American aid to Great Britain and convinced that Japanese expansion would distract the United States as well as deprive Great Britain of resources from Southeast Asia. Thus, in September 1940, Japan and Germany and also Italy signed a Tripartite Pact that divided the world into spheres of influence with Europe reserved for Germany and Italy, and Asia for Japan. The pact also promised help in case of attack on any one of the three by the United States. Both Germany and Japan hoped that the pact would restrain the United States from interfering with their plans for expansion.

With her prospects very bright, Japan moved into Southeast Asia. In September 1940, she invaded Indochina, and by July of the following year, she controlled that French colony and its important air and naval bases. They were close to British, Dutch, and American possessions.

Throughout 1941, Germany encouraged Japan to expand. The Germans assured their ally that the United States would not intervene or at least would not do so effectively, owing to American weaknesses. Japan needed these assurances, for she was disturbed by U.S. opposition to her plans and very concerned about American intentions, convinced that the American position in the Phillippines would enable the United States to interfere significantly. To strengthen Japan's determination, Germany promised that American action against Japan would produce a German response.

These developments in Asia alarmed the Roosevelt administration and strengthened its hostility to Japan, but the situation in Europe seemed even more alarming. While Japan appeared to threaten American interests, Germany seemed an even greater threat. American military advisers recommended that the administration should adopt a Europe-first policy, and early in 1941, American and British officials agreed that if the United States were drawn into the war, the first objective would be the defeat of Hitler.

Thus Washington attempted to check Japanese expansion and yet prevent Japan from taking steps that would force the United States to fight. As Hull explained, "The point is how we can maneuver the situation until the military matter in Europe is brought to a conclusion." The

Europe-first policy and the state of American preparations made war in the Far East highly undesirable. " . . . It is terribly important for the control of the Atlantic for us to help to keep peace in the Pacific," Roosevelt advised Ickes in July 1941. "I simply have not got enough Navy to go around—and every episode in the Pacific means fewer ships in the Atlantic."

To accomplish its objectives, the administration cautiously applied pressure on the Japanese. In April 1940, the American naval force at Pearl Harbor had been enlarged in hopes that its presence would have a restraining influence. Then, beginning in July and continuing for over a year, the administration steadily increased the number of items that Americans could not sell to Japan. The sharpest and longest debate preceded the addition of all types of oil to the list after Japan overran Indochina in July 1941, and the decision at the same time to freeze Japanese assets in the United States soon stopped all trade between the two countries by depriving Japan of dollars. Washington also supplied economic assistance, including Lend-Lease aid, to Japan's foes in China, led by Generalissimo Chiang Kai-shek.

The President hoped to avoid provocation as well as appeasement. As late as August 1941, he rejected an appeal from Churchill for a strong warning to Japan against an attack upon British Malaya and the Dutch East Indies. FDR continued to believe that the United States could stay out of the fighting or at least participate in only a small way.

While applying pressure, the administration also engaged in negotiations, with Secretary Hull as the chief American negotiator and Ambassador Nomura, an admiral with only limited diplomatic experience, speaking for the Japanese. In these negotiations, which began in March 1941 and continued to December, the United States had several objectives. Hull hoped to discover Japanese intentions and limit Japanese expansion. He also hoped to gain time in order to develop American power.

American military leaders were especially zealous advocates of negotiations. Secretaries Stimson and Knox, General Marshall, and Admiral Harold R. Stark, the Chief of Naval Operations, hoped to avoid war with Japan, for they believed very strongly in the Europe-first policy and they were deeply troubled by American weaknesses. They did not want the United States to be drawn into a war that it was not prepared to fight. Struggling to enlarge the United States Navy, they pointed out that the American fleet in the Pacific was inferior to the Japanese fleet and could not undertake "an unlimited strategic offensive in the Western Pacific." To do so, most of the Navy and much of the merchant tonnage would have to be withdrawn from the Atlantic, and the withdrawal "might well cause the United Kingdom to lose the battle of the Atlantic in the near future." Fearful of possibilities in Southeast Asia, they strengthened the forces in the Philippine Islands commanded by General Douglas MacArthur. They were especially interested in stationing there a fleet of B-l7s, the new long-range bomber, hoping that by February 1942, American air strength would be "a deciding factor in deterring operations in the area south and west of the Philippines."

The military leaders advocated negotiations and counseled against efforts to force Japan to evacuate China, for they wanted time to develop their forces. As late as November 17, 1941, Marshall and Stark advised that "the most essential thing now, from the United States viewpoint, is to gain time." The "desirable strength" had not yet been reached in the Philippines. "The longer the delay, the more positive becomes the assurance of retention of these Islands as a naval and air base," the top military people suggested. "Japanese action to the south of Formosa will be hindered and perhaps seriously blocked as long as we hold the Philippine Islands."

In their negotiating efforts, the Japanese had ambitions of their own. They did hope to avoid war with the United States, but they also wanted to restore normal trade relations between the countries and to gain American support for their efforts to control China.

The American Secretary of State, however, sought endorsement by Japan of several principles that seemed very important to him. They involved respect for the territorial integrity and sovereignty of all nations, noninterference in the internal affairs of other countries, equality, including equality of commercial opportunity, and nondisturbance of the status quo in the Pacific, except as it might be altered by peaceful means. These principles clashed with Japanese ambitions.

While negotiating on a lower level, Washington rejected appeals for a summit conference with the Japanese. In August 1941, the Japanese Prime Minister, Prince Konoye, who had dismissed his militant Foreign Minister, Matsuoka, in July, called for a conference with Roosevelt in hopes of finding a peaceful solution to the conflict, and the American Ambassador in Tokyo, Joseph Grew, endorsed the suggestion arguing that the conference would help advocates of reliance on diplomacy, represented by Konoye, defeat the champions of military action, spearheaded by the Army leaders. Leaders in the American State Department, however, argued against the conference, maintaining that Japan was weak and needed to be persuaded that the United States would resist further expansion with force and that the United States should not believe Japan's promises that she would withdraw her troops from Indochina and not attack elsewhere in Southeast Asia. Other advocates of firmness, including Secretary Morgenthau, supported Hull and his aides.

Actually, only the willingness of one of the nations to scuttle its basic Asia policy could have produced a successful conference. Japan hoped to build a "New Order" or a "Greater East Asia Co-Prosperity Sphere," and this meant domination of the area by Japan so that she could obtain space for her surplus population, essential raw materials and markets, and a buffer zone against Europeans. She sought by negotiations to get the United States to accept rather than resist her plans, and Konoye promised the military that he would use the conference for this purpose. They doubted that he would be successful, but they were not yet prepared to move beyond Indochina. Thus, they pushed forward with their military preparations while Konoye made his diplomatic moves.

Washington, on the other hand, believed in the "Open Door," which meant freedom for a nation from domination by an outside power and opportunities in Asia for all countries. The United States demanded that Japan accept American principles in advance of the meeting and hoped by negotiation to obtain the withdrawal of Japanese troops from China and Indochina. The United States demanded that Japan give up the gains of a decade as well as her ambitions in exchange for American trade and friendship.

China was the focal point of controversy. Japan was determined to maintain her position there, while the liberation of China was the chief American objective. Hull and other American leaders believed that the United States had a moral duty to promote the principles of territorial integrity and equal opportunity. America must uphold the principles, supporting them with economic pressure and diplomacy, even at the risk of war with Japan over China. Japan's commitment to principle was equally strong. Neither side was willing to discard its China policy, even temporarily.

The conflict included a clash over economic policy. As Hull and others saw the situation, the United States needed to sell some of her surplus products in Asia and to obtain raw materials there, such as rubber, and could not tolerate Japan's forceful efforts to dominate the region and destroy, or at least reduce, the American presence. As Japan had advanced, she had imposed restrictions on the business firms of other nations. "The United States has its rights and interests there just as Japan," Hull insisted. "American opinion believes it to be incompatible with the establishment and maintenance of American and world prosperity that any nation should endeavor to establish a preferred position for itself in another country."

Beyond concern about China and economic policy, Washington was influenced by a theory about the behavior of aggressors. It reflected recent experiences in Europe, especially the events following Munich. Concessions to Japan on the control of China, American policy makers assumed, would only encourage her to move further, perhaps eventually to the Philippines. Consequently, America must resist, not appease, Japan.

Thus, Roosevelt and Konoye did not go to the summit, and Japan completed plans for futher expansion. On October 16, Konoye resigned, forced to do so by his failure and his inability to persuade General Tojo, the War Minister, to give him more time for negotiations. Tojo became Prime Minister as the military, firmly opposed to compromise, increased still more its strength in the government. Early in November, the government decided that the dwindling supply of oil would force Japan to go to war in December in order to create the New Order if the United States did not agree to resume trade and accept Japan's terms on China. As they accelerated their military preparations, Japanese leaders made plans to move against Burma, Thailand, Java, Sumatra, Borneo, Malaya, the Philippines, and a number of Pacific islands, thereby gaining control of an area rich in oil and other resources and securing the New Order against British and American forces. The moves would involve war with the Netherlands, Great Britain, and the United States. American military action seemed to be the greatest danger, but Japan's German allies continued to assure her that she need not worry about that, should be uncompromising in pursuit of her objectives, and could count on Germany to declare war on the United States if Japan attacked the latter. Germany made this promise even though Hitler apparently hoped that Japan would expand without attacking the United States.

Clearly, American pressure had not worked as expected. The advocates of embargo, including Stimson, Morgenthau, and Ickes, had emphasized Japan's dependence on the United States for oil and had pictured it as providing Washington with a way of stopping Japanese expansion and producing a negotiated settlement. Opponents, such as Admiral Stark, had warned that the embargo might force Japan to move farther in order to get the oil needed by the war machine and to protect the advance. As the resources were only a short distance beyond the line that the Japanese had reached, these calculations, rather than those that had controlled the American decision, proved to be correct.

Although American officials still hoped to avoid war in the Far East, the administration did not believe that it could tolerate an attack upon British, Dutch, and American possessions in Southeast Asia. Tied down in the Atlantic, the United States had to tolerate, militarily, what was taking place in China and Indochina, but additional expansion would, among other consequences, deprive the British of resources, such as rubber, that they needed to fight Hitler. The developments in different parts of the world were linked together, and the United States could not allow Japan to deprive Britain of materials at the same time that the United States was trying to supply her with the means of war. Thus, by the beginning of December, Roosevelt planned to offer some armed resistance to further Japanese moves in Southeast Asia.

Hull recognized before the end of November that the United States had failed to restrain the Japanese. He knew that Nomura had been advised on November 22 that the twenty-ninth was the deadline for negotiations and that after that "things" were "automatically going to happen." On the twenty-sixth, the Secretary defined American demands once again, insisting that Japan must withdraw her troops from China as well as Indochina and accept American trade as a substitute for the New Order. Japan, however, preferred to depend upon her own power and quickly made the final decision for war, with the progress of American preparations and the weather dictating that the move should be made on December 7. On the twenty-seventh, the American Secretary of State wrote to Stimson: "I have washed my hands of it and it is now in the hands of you and Knox—the Army and the Navy." "These fellows mean to fight and you will have to watch out," Hull advised General Marshall. The general did not need the advice; the evidence available to him suggested that Hull was right.

On November 27, Navy and War sent war warnings to their commanders in the Pacific, including Admiral Kimmel and General Short in Hawaii and General MacArthur in the Philippines. Short was advised that negotiations seemed over and that hostile Japanese action was possible at any moment. As to his course of action:

> If hostilities cannot, repeat cannot, be avoided the United States desires that Japan commit the first overt act. This policy should not, repeat not, be construed as restricting you to a course of action that might jeopardize your defense. Prior to Japanese action you are directed to undertake such reconnaissance and other measures as you deem necessary but these measures should be carried out so as not, repeat not, to alarm civil population or disclose intent . . . Undertake no offensive action until Japan has committed an overt act.

Kimmel was advised that the most likely targets of "an amphibious expedition" were Thailand, the Kra Peninsula, and Borneo. Seemingly in the most dangerous position of all the American commanders, MacArthur was not cautioned against alarming civilians or disclosing intent.

Washington failed to anticipate some of Japan's moves. For several reasons, American leaders assumed that the attack would take place close to Indochina, with British and Dutch possessions and neutral Thailand as the most likely targets. The United States had substantial but not complete information on Japanese activities for it had broken their diplomatic code and was well supplied with observers in China and Southeast Asia. All positive intelligence reports indicated that Japanese ships and troops were moving south and west. On the other hand, the United States was not well supplied with observers between Japan and Hawaii for, to avoid incidents, the government had been keeping American merchant ships out of that area. Also, the decoded messages did not provide information on such important matters as the location of the carrier fleet and its target. Furthermore, a thrust south and west would be in line with the pattern of Japanese movement since 1931, would give Japan the resources she needed, and could not be resisted effectively by Western power.

When it came, however, the attack was not limited to the expected areas. In addition to Thailand and Malaya, American forces in the Philippines, Wake Island, and Guam were attacked on Sunday, December 7 (Washington time). Most surprising, the American naval base on Pearl Harbor was also hit.

The Japanese had concluded that they must destroy the American fleet there in order to succeed. It seemed to be the strongest force opposing them. The Japanese assumed, apparently, that the destruction of the American force in the Pacific would compel the United States to come to terms with Japan so as to concentrate its remaining power on Germany and avoid a long and costly war. There was no plan to invade the United States or force it to surrender. The Japanese intended to fight a limited war that would enable them to expand and then defend their holdings and thereby establish themselves as a great power controlling all the resources needed for greatness. They assumed that they could not run the risks involved in ignoring the American forces and attacking only British and Dutch possessions.

In hitting American territory, Japan solved a political problem that Roosevelt had faced. Shortly before the attack, he had concluded that he must resist further expansion, and he had given the British assurances of armed support if Japan attacked British or Dutch territory or Thailand and had decided to ask Congress for a declaration of war if Japan moved against British Malaya or the Dutch East Indies. But he believed that Japan would be canny enough to avoid action that would arouse the American people and thus he would have difficulty obtaining adequate support for steps that seemed essential. Consequently, he had talked about maneuvering the Japanese "into the position of firing the first shot without allowing too much danger to ourselves." Now, Japan had fired that shot, and Roosevelt had the popular support he needed. Only one member of Congress voted against his appeal on December 8 for a declaration of war against Japan.

While solving his political problem, however, Japan enlarged Roosevelt's military problem. She had seriously damaged the small forces available to him in the Pacific, killing more than 2,300 people in Hawaii, destroying or disabling nearly every plane at Pearl Harbor, and sinking or seriously damaging eight battleships, three cruisers, and three destroyers. He placed a high value on his Navy and had planned that it would play an essential role if the United States were drawn into the war. Fortunately, three American aircraft carriers, plus accompanying cruisers and destroyers, were not in Pearl Harbor on the morning of the attack, and many of the ships that were damaged could be repaired. But the American armed forces were much weaker on December 8 than they had been on December 6.

Japan's attack upon Pearl Harbor succeeded militarily because of the limited resources available and the assumption concerning the direction in which Japan would move. The possibility of an attack had been recognized months earlier, defenses against an air attack had been strengthened, and a defense plan had been developed. It included special precautions on Sunday and continuous air search. The plan, however, was not in operation on December 7. American intelligence experts had concluded several months before that an attack on Pearl Harbor was not a strong possibility. Bits and pieces of evidence pointing to such an attack had been discounted for they conflicted with dominant assumptions, and responsible officials had not probed the significance of the fact that they did not know the location of the Japanese carrier fleet. Furthermore, the plan placed a heavy drain on airplanes and fuel oil, commodities that were in short supply. The chief danger at Pearl Harbor seemed to be subversive activities, and thus when the war warnings had been received, steps to prevent sabotage had been taken. In Washington, officials such as Marshall assumed that more was being done, did not worry about Hawaii, and were more concerned about the Philippines, where an attack seemed more likely. These officials did not know that the defense plan was not in operation.

Washington learned on the night of December 6 and the morning of December 7 that Japan had rejected Hull's proposals of November 26, war was imminent, and something was likely to happen at 1 P.M. Washington time. But the evidence had not indicated what was to happen and had not pointed clearly to Pearl Harbor. As an attack somewhere seemed possible, Marshall at the end of the morning sent a message to the Army and Navy commanders in the Pacific that the Japanese would present "an ultimatum" at 1 P.M. and were "under orders to destroy their code machine immediately" and that the "significance of the hour set" was not known but that they should "be on the alert accordingly." The message to Pearl Harbor failed to arrive before the attack because of defects in communication facilities.

The attack on the Philippine Islands was also successful militarily even though the warnings there were adequate. MacArthur received the last message plus news of the Japanese attack at Pearl Harbor and a telephone call from Washington before the Japanese attacked his forces. Nevertheless that attack succeeded in destroying half of his planes on the ground and left the islands vulnerable to further attacks. That air force had been counted upon to play a crucial role in the Far East, but its effectiveness was destroyed.

Thus, the United States was drawn into a formal declaration of war and full-scale involvement in it as a consequence of developments in the Pacific. They, in turn, resulted from developments in Asia that had alarmed Americans but that they could not control. The United States possessed only enough power to worry Japan, not enough to intimidate her, and thus she had concluded that she must shatter American power in the Pacific in order to succeed with her program of expansion.

The developments in Asia were linked with even more alarming ones in Europe, and, while the United States declared war only on Japan on December 8, the nation was formally involved in war with Germany before the end of the week. Germany had promised to declare war on the United States after Japan attacked, and on December 11, Hitler did so.

Japan had only accelerated the process whereby Germany and the United States moved to full-scale war with one another. Busy with the Russian campaign, Hitler had hoped to avoid incidents of the type that had drawn the United States into World War I, but the two countries had been on a collision course. As soon as the situation in Europe justified the risks, Hitler would surely have made a major move against the commerce that was hampering his efforts to defeat Britain and Russia, and the United States would surely have declared war when sinkings had become numerous. American power hurt Hitler but did not force him to retreat from his ambitions. Now that the United States had to contend with the might of the Japanese Empire, Germany seemingly could afford to move more forcefully against the United States.

Thus Hitler seized the opportunity for boldness that Japan had supplied. Japan, he assumed, would weaken the United States while he completed the conquest of Europe. Then, he could move on to establish a strong position in the Western Hemisphere.

The United States had made efforts to restrain the expanding nations but had found itself incapable of doing so. American leaders had succeeded only in provoking Germany and Japan into attacks on American forces. Now, the nation found itself in a global war and not yet ready to fight one.

SUGGESTIONS FOR ADDITIONAL READING

American involvement in war with Japan is one of the most controversial subjects in recent United States history. Shortly after the war, revisionists such as Charles A. Beard, *President Roosevelt and the Coming of the War*, Yale, New Haven, Conn., 1948, and Charles C. Tansill, *Back Door to War*, Regnery, Chicago, 1952, challenged the official explanation and placed much of the blame upon the American President, rather than the Japanese. This interpretation was rejected by Herbert Feis, *The Road to Pearl Harbor*, Princeton University Press, Princeton, N.J., 1950, and William L. Langer and S. Everett Gleason, *The Challenge to Isolation, 1937–1940* and *The Undeclared War, 1940–1941*, Harper, New York, 1952–1953, who, when critical of Roosevelt, criticized him for not being sufficiently bold in a serious situation, not for plotting to bring the United States into a war it should have avoided. Paul W. Schroeder in *The Axis Alliance and Japanese-American Relations, 1941*, Cornell University Press, Ithaca, N.Y., 1958, developed the most careful and sophisticated revisionist account. Rejecting the "plot thesis," he appraised American policy from a "realist" point of view and argued that the administration should have been more willing to compromise with the Japanese. He should be compared with Robert J. C. Butow, "The Hull-Nomura Conversations: A Fundamental Misconception," *American Historical Review*, vol. 65, pp. 822–836, July 1960. Roberta Wohlstetter, *Pearl Harbor: Warning and Decision*, Stanford University Press, Stanford, Calif., 1962, provides the best account of American intelligence and the Japanese attack. On Japanese politics, see Butow, *Tojo and the Coming of the War*, Princeton University Press, Princeton, N.J., 1961, and Louis Morton, "Japan's Decision for War (1941)," in Kent Roberts Greenfield, ed., *Command Decisions*, Harcourt, Brace, New York, 1959. And on the American Ambassador in Tokyo, consult Waldo H. Heinrichs, Jr., *American Ambassador: Joseph C. Grew and the Development of the United States Diplomatic Tradition*, Little, Brown, Boston, 1966.

Chapter 17

The Persistence
of National Weakness

The weaknesses that plagued the nation during 1941 continued to cause serious troubles for the United States for many months after Pearl Harbor. The nation could not move quickly and effectively against Germany and Japan, but their continued expansion was not the only development affected by American weaknesses in 1942. They also limited the ability of the United States to strengthen its ally in China and damaged relations between the United States and the Soviet Union. And the weaknesses of 1942 limited America's ability to influence events in Europe—then and later.

The United States did strengthen itself after the Japanese attack but continued to be hampered by internal difficulties and many demands. Government spending increased rapidly, stimulated war production, and accelerated the growth of the armed forces. At the same time, however, conversion to war production remained in an early stage; progress was restricted by ineffective direction from Washington and by labor-management conflict, and Washington's allies continued to compete with America's armed forces for the output of America's industry.

Very soon after Pearl Harbor, Washington made a decision of basic importance concerning that output. The decision was that the United States would make a giant economic contribution to the war effort and thus would expand the American Army to only ninety divisions. The United States could have built a much larger force but only by shifting manpower and other resources out of the economy. There were, of course, some obvious benefits for the United States from this decision. It would keep American losses low and would stimulate American economic growth. On the other hand, the decision would limit what the United States could accomplish with military power.

The decision meant that the United States would continue to supply Lend-Lease aid for its allies. The program was now enlarged. Eventually, it would cost more than $50 billion and would deliver substantial portions of American production to Great Britain, Russia, China, and other allies. This large program of economic aid was one of the powerful instruments that the United States used to accomplish its wartime objectives.

Russia was one of the chief beneficiaries. Roosevelt was very eager to help the Soviet Union in this way. If he did not share the enthusiasm for her that some Americans developed during the war, neither did he share the very negative views of a few. He doubted that Russia was trying to impose communism on the rest of the world; he stressed her importance for the accomplishment of his major objective, the defeat of the Axis Powers, and he tried to find ways for Russia and the United States to work together, convinced that their cooperation was necessary and possible. Recognizing the seriousness of her plight in 1942 and the importance of the battle she was waging against Germany, which had reached the outskirts of Moscow, he insisted that Russia must receive a large amount of aid, and he hoped that this would would help her win her war and would improve relations between the two countries.

Washington was linked even more closely, however, with Great Britain and the British Commonwealth. Eventually, they would receive three-fifths of the aid delivered under Lend-Lease. The British future was uncertain in late 1941 and early 1942. British forces were in combat in North Africa with German forces led by General Erwin Rommel, and he was moving close to Alexandria. Churchill came to the United States soon after Pearl Harbor, and the meeting resulted in the formation of the Combined Chiefs of Staff composed of American and British officers. There was not a meeting of this kind at the time between Roosevelt and Stalin or an institution of this type involving American and Russian officers.

The Washington meeting also reaffirmed the Europe-first policy. Churchill had feared that the United States would now give first attention to the war against Japan. Thus, he sought reaffirmation of the policy that had been agreed upon earlier, as well as support for a larger British effort in Africa and a greater American effort to supply and defend Great Britain. The American President did not disappoint the British Prime Minister.

The Europe-first policy meant the Americans and British would take the offensive against Germany as soon as possible and fight only a defensive war now against Japan. Men and supplies would be sent to Great Britain as they became available, and they would not be diverted to other combat areas. The policy assumed that Hitler was the most dangerous enemy, Europe was more important than Asia, and it was easier to get American troops into action against Hitler than against Japan. The problem of shipping war resources across the Atlantic was a smaller problem than the one created by the great size of the Pacific.

The problem of the Atlantic, however, was not a small one in 1942. Following the declaration of war, Hitler removed the restrictions that he had imposed upon his submarine commanders, and they became very bold and effective, operating close to American shores and on the route to Russia that ran close to German-controlled Norway. American and British naval and air forces could not cope successfully with the problem; American shipbuilders stepped up their output in a desperate effort to replace the losses, but losses exceeded construction during the year. The American Navy needed more training and experience in antisubmarine warfare and new equipment to detect and destroy the undersea craft.

The problems in the Pacific were also very large. The Japanese pushed forward rapidly in the early months following December 7. By May, they had gained control of a vast, rich area stretching from Burma, Thailand, Malaya, and Sumatra on the west to Wake Island and the Solomon Islands on the east and including Hong Kong, Guam, Borneo, Java, Timor, and New Guinea, among other places. In addition to rich resources, the Japanese gained control of major bases, including Singapore, which fell in February, and many in the Philippines, which surrendered in May. By then, the Japanese had accomplished their objectives of December 7 and had moved close to India and Australia.

As the Japanese moved forward from December to May, they encountered only weak opposition from American and other forces. The nation had few reinforcements to send to the Philippine Islands and other places, and efforts to send the few that were available were hampered by the shortage of ships, the great distances that had to be traveled, and strong opposition from Japanese planes and ships in the combat zone. Efforts to strengthen American forces in the Pacific were also limited by the Europe-first policy.

American commanders in the Pacific battled against the limitations imposed upon them by that policy. Its leading champion in the armed forces was General Marshall, who was convinced that the main battles of the war would be fought in Europe. Admiral Ernest J. King, the new Chief of Naval Operations, favored greater attention to the Pacific than Marshall advocated, as did Admiral Chester Nimitz, the commander of Allied forces in much of the Pacific.

The chief critic of the Europe-first policy was General MacArthur. He had been forced to leave the Philippines in March, ordered to move to Australia so as to be able to supply leadership for Allied operations in that region. Bitter that he had not been given what he wanted for the defense of the Philippines, he now insisted that the war against Japan be given top priority and that a major buildup be made in Australia.

MacArthur and other commanders in the Pacific received more resources than had been planned but not nearly as much as they desired. Some men and supplies that had been planned for Europe were sent to the Pacific in 1942, but the Europe-first policy was only modified, not discarded, as a consequence of the spectacular Japanese advance.

American weaknesses in the early months of the war also prevented the United States from providing much support for China in her war against Japan. The situation there was grave, and the United States did send some Lend-Lease aid, a small number of American soldiers and fliers, and two American generals, Claire Chennault, who became the American air commander in the China-Burma-India theater, and Joseph Stilwell, who became the commander of American ground forces there and chief of staff to Chiang Kai-shek. Chiang appealed for even more help, but Roosevelt had to turn him down even though he regarded China as one of the "Big Four" and hoped that it would become a major democratic power after the war. Aid to Chiang did not seem as important as most other American needs in 1942; the difficulties of getting aid to him were very large, for the Japanese controlled China's coast, and the difficulties became even greater after the Japanese conquered Burma in May. After that, the only supply routes were by air over very high mountains. The British also operated in the theater, but Churchill did not give a large amount of help to Chiang, for the Prime Minister had a low opinion of the Generalissimo and of China's prospects as a great power.

It seems unlikely that Chiang would have used American aid effectively against Japan. His army was inefficient and corrupt, and he was eager to save it for use against his other enemies, the Chinese Communists. Stilwell pressed for more aid from the United States, reform of the Chinese forces, and more action by them, but the United States could not increase the supplies and troops that it provided, Chiang resisted Stilwell's pressure, and FDR did not impose pressures of his own upon the Chinese leader.

Thus, Japan moved forward during the early months of 1942 without encountering strong resistance. At the same time, American weaknesses also contributed significantly to the development of a conflict within the anti-Axis alliance over the ways in which the war should be fought. The conflict involved Russia, Great Britain, and the United States, and it concerned the timing of the invasion of Europe by American and British forces.

As soon as the United States moved into the war, Russia began to press for the opening of a second front in Western Europe. The Russians hoped that the move would be made before the end of 1942. It would compel Germany to move much of her army out of Russia and into Western Europe.

Most of Roosevelt's top military advisers advocated an invasion of Western Europe as the major military effort by American and British forces. This was the type of advice that the President received from Secretary Stimson, General Marshall, and General Eisenhower, who, in June, became the Army's commander for the European Theater of Operations. They assumed that attack across the Channel, preceded by a massive buildup in the British Isles and heavy bombing of German-controlled Europe, and then large-scale action on the ground and a steady advance toward Germany would be the most efficient and effective way of using Western forces. And they counseled against wasting resources in less important areas. The war against Germany was, in their view, the crucial war, and the defeat of Hitler was the key to victory.

In April 1942, these military advisers suggested a timetable for invasion. The massive assault would come in April 1943, and it might be preceded by a limited operation in Western Europe in the fall of 1942. A very ambitious proposal, it assumed that the American buildup would be rapid and American resources would not be diverted away from Europe.

Roosevelt liked the advice. It made sense militarily, and it seemed capable of accomplishing valuable political objectives, including improvement in relations between Russia and the West. He hoped to satisfy Stalin as quickly as possible, believing that he would gain more confidence in the West and conclude that Russia need not expand her boundaries in order to gain security. World peace, the President assumed, demanded that he reduce Russian distrust of the capitalistic nations. He was influenced also by Russia's grim situation, a fear that she would collapse, and a desire to keep her in the war. Thus, in conversations with a Russian diplomat, Molotov, in May and June, Roosevelt gave a rather vague and ambiguous promise that the invasion would come before the end of 1942.

Churchill and his military advisers, however, opposed a quick move

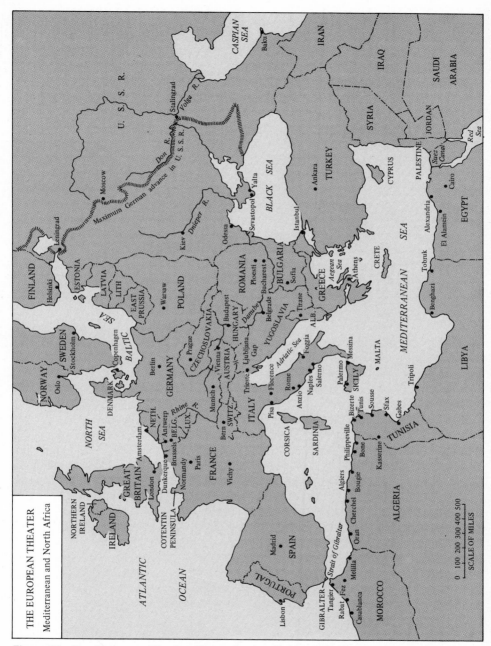

Figure 16 The European Theater (*From George C. Marshall: Ordeal and Hope by Forrest Pogue. Copyright © 1965, 1966 by George C. Marshall Research Foundation. Reprinted by permission of The Viking Press, Inc.*)

on to the Continent. They recalled the bitter trench warfare of World War I and the more recent episode at Dunkirk in 1940 when British forces had been driven off the Continent, and they wanted to wait until Germany was very weak and the Allies were very strong. Also, they were interested in military operations elsewhere, for they feared that Germany and Japan would gain control of India, the Middle East, North Africa, and the Suez Canal. In addition, the British assumed that the Russians could hold out without the opening of a second front in 1942.

Although restrained by their desire for American aid, the British battled against an early attack across the English Channel, and their arguments were backed up by the realities of power. The United States still had only a small army; essential supplies, such as landing craft, were scarce, and the war in the Pacific and Asia was imposing heavy demands. Any operation on the Continent in 1942 would be largely a British operation.

Early in the summer, Churchill persuaded Roosevelt that the invasion of 1942 should be made in North Africa, not Western Europe. In addition to the weight that the Prime Minister could exert, the President was influenced by a desire to get American forces into action against Germany somewhere in 1942. Such a move would enable him to resist the pressure to concentrate upon the war against Japan and permit him to maintain the Europe-first policy. A desire to develop good relations with the British also influenced FDR. And an invasion of North Africa could be managed by the limited forces that were available.

Stimson and Marshall were unhappy with the decision. They believed that an invasion of North Africa would not contribute significantly to victory, would delay the invasion of Europe, and would postpone the large-scale operation against Japan. Distressed that they were not having a larger influence upon Allied policy making, the Army leaders believed that the British were using Roosevelt to further their imperial ambitions.

The failure to move quickly on to the Continent harmed relations between Russia and the West. Stalin was angered by it and felt betrayed. It seemed to him that Great Britain and the United States wanted the Russians to do most of the fighting and most of the dying in the war against Germany so that Russia would be very weak at the end of the war.

The decision did mean that Russia would suffer much more than her allies. It also meant that much of Central Europe as well as almost all of Eastern Europe would be liberated from German control by Russian rather than Western armies. And the decision strengthened Russia's determination to insist that she must be permitted to enlarge the territory that she influenced and controlled.

The question of Russia's boundaries emerged in 1942 and added to the tension within the anti-German alliance. While her back was to the wall, Russia demanded that her allies must recognize the western boundary that she had established before Hitler attacked. That is, they must recognize her claim to the territories that she had seized in 1939 and 1940. The British were ready to accept this demand, but Washington officials insisted that the demand must be rejected, for it violated the principle of national self-determination. Roosevelt argued that such questions must be postponed and attention now must be concentrated upon the defeat of Germany. In the end, Russian power and influence would reach far beyond the 1941 boundaries.

The United States was trying to fight a global war with only a limited amount of power. The nation had not been forced to do nearly as much in World War I. Then, the United States had been able to limit its naval and military operations to the North Atlantic and Western Europe. Now, American resources were needed in China, Southeast Asia, the South Pacific, the North Atlantic, Great Britain, Western Europe, North Africa, and the Soviet Union, and the United States did not have the military manpower or military supplies needed for effective operations in so many places. The continued expansion of Germany and Japan was but the most obvious result. American weaknesses had long-term as well as immediate consequences.

SUGGESTIONS FOR ADDITIONAL READING

For valuable guides to the literature on wartime diplomacy and military operations see Divine, ed., *Causes and Consequences of World War II*; Louis Morton, *Writings on World War II*, American Historical Association, Washington, 1967; and Morton, "World War II: A Survey of Recent Writings," *American Historical Review*, vol. 75, pp. 1987–2008, 1970.

The basic books are William H. McNeil, *America, Britain and Russia: Their Cooperation and Conflict, 1941–1946*, Royal Institute of International Affairs, London, 1953, and Herbert Feis, *Churchill, Roosevelt, Stalin: The War They Waged and the Peace They Sought*, Princeton University Press, Princeton, N.J., 1957. Both view Roosevelt as ignorant of the political implications of military operations and naïve about postwar prospects. For a briefer treatment written from a similar point of view, see Gaddis Smith, *American Diplomacy during the Second World War, 1941–1945*, Wiley, New York, 1965. Such interpretations have been challenged by John L. Snell, *Illusion and Necessity: The Diplomacy of Global War, 1939–1945*, Houghton Mifflin, Boston, 1963, and William R. Emerson, "F.D.R. (1941–1945)," in Ernest R. May, ed., *The Ultimate Decision: The President as Commander in Chief*, George Braziller, New York,

1960. In these accounts, Roosevelt appears as pragmatic and realistic and alive to the political implications of military operations.

In recent years, a revisionist interpretation of American-Russian relations has developed. Represented by D. F. Fleming, *The Cold War and Its Origins, 1917–1960*, 2 vols., Doubleday, Garden City, N.Y., 1961, and William Appleman Williams, *The Tragedy of American Diplomacy*, World Publishing, Cleveland, 1959, among others, the distinguishing characteristic of this revisionism is the tendency to place much of the blame upon the United States for the beginning of the cold war. For the war period, the most important revisionist account is Gabriel Kolko, *The Politics of War: The World and United States Foreign Policy, 1943–1945*, Random House, New York, 1968. Unlike much of the earlier work, Kolko focuses on Hull and the State Department, rather than Roosevelt, and although the author lacks enthusiasm for American policy, he does not regard American policy makers as politically unsophisticated. One weakness of his work is his neglect of 1942. Another work on wartime diplomacy, *After Victory: Churchill, Roosevelt, Stalin and the Making of the Peace*, Harper & Row, New York, 1967, by William Neuman, stands between the revisionists and the earlier writers, picturing Roosevelt as naïve and unsophisticated but objecting to the "conventional" American view of Russian behavior.

One characteristic of the earlier work that the revisionists have challenged is the neglect of economic factors in foreign relations. On this theme, two books by Lloyd C. Gardner, *Economic Aspects of New Deal Diplomacy* and *Architects of Illusion: Men and Ideas in American Foreign Policy, 1941–1949*, Quadrangle, Chicago, 1970, are especially important.

Two of the most recent and most valuable books are the second volume of Burns's biography of Roosevelt and John Gaddis's study of *The United States and the Origins of the Cold War 1941–1947*, Columbia University Press, New York, 1972. Burns supplies a large and quite critical account of FDR as war leader, while Gaddis gives us our best survey of American-Russian relations during the war. Moving beyond revisionism, he emphasizes the complexity of the influences at work and the limits on American power.

For a valuable survey of the military history of the war, see the book by Buchanan cited in Chapter 15. He draws heavily on the massive and impressive work on the war by military historians, especially those employed by the American armed forces. One of the leaders in this work, Kent Roberts Greenfield, has summarized his findings in *American Strategy in World War II: A Reconsideration*, Johns Hopkins, Baltimore, 1963. Biography provides an interesting and helpful way of gaining understanding of these very important matters. In addition to the excellent work by Pogue on Marshall already cited, see the substantial and exciting study by Stephen E. Ambrose, *The Supreme Commander: The War Years of General Dwight D. Eisenhower*, Doubleday, Garden City, N. Y., 1970. A recent and useful article on subjects with which this chapter is concerned is Richard W. Steele, "Political Aspects of American Military Planning, 1941–1942," *Military Affairs*, vol. 35, pp. 68–74, 1971.

Chapter 18

The War and American Capitalism

The United States was weak in 1942, but the nation became strong. To a significant degree, it did so because the war stimulated rather than retarded American economic growth. This was one of many significant ways in which World War II changed American life.

The war forced changes in both the structure and the performance of American capitalism. In some ways, the war continued the work of the New Deal, enlarging government and labor and completing the process of recovery from the Depression. The war, however, also strengthened anti-New Deal groups, and the economic system did not evolve precisely as New Dealers desired. Yet, they could find much to applaud in the performance of the system during the war and the potential that it revealed. Although it did not function perfectly, American capitalism became an unusually effective economic system.

The war weakened Roosevelt's support for social and economic liberalism of the New Deal variety. It diverted his attention away from the kinds of issues that had interested him in the 1930s, left him little time to support those who still advocated New Deal-type programs, and forced him to seek the cooperation of anti-New Dealers who were important in the economy and the Congress. At one point, he announced that "Dr. Win-the-War" had replaced "Dr. New Deal."

Wartime conditions also weakened popular support for New Deal liberalism. The New Deal's appeal to many voters declined as war brought prosperity; the party that had given the nation the New Deal suffered from discontent with economic controls, high taxes, deficit spending, and strikes during the war, and the Democrats were hurt also by a drop in voter turnout among the young people and the workers who moved away from home to serve in the armed forces or take jobs in war plants and shipyards.

These developments encouraged critics of the New Deal. The Farm Bureau, for example, pressed its campaigns against the Bureau of Agricultural Economics and the Farm Security Administration, seeing them as threats to the farmers that the organization represented and to the organization itself. The American Medical Association behaved in a similar way, challenging proposals to add national health insurance to the Social Security program.

In this situation, the conservative coalition in Congress enjoyed a substantial increase in its strength. The Republicans gained victories at the expense of Northern Democrats in the 1942 congressional elections, adding forty-four seats in the House and nine in the Senate. The losers were mostly Roosevelt supporters, and they went down to defeat without help from him as he remained aloof from partisan politics during the election. As a higher percentage of Southern Democrats also now voted with the Republicans, the coalition that had been apparent for several years became larger than ever before. It also was more active, appearing on a higher number of roll calls, and more effective, usually winning when it functioned.

Thus strengthened, conservatives frustrated liberals frequently. Conservative congressmen were chiefly responsible for the destruction of the CCC, the WPA, the NYA, the BAE's program of state and local planning, and the National Resources Planning Board, a bold agency that had proposed a substantial enlargement of the welfare state, and these congressmen also slashed the appropriations for FSA. And liberals such as Senator Wagner also suffered defeats in battles for changes in the Social Security program that would add more people and a health insurance feature and pay higher unemployment benefits. Congress also rebuffed liberal efforts to raise wages for workers at lower income levels and to impose a $25,000 ceiling on salaries.

There was one major exception to the wartime decline of the

welfare part of the American economic system. This was the G.I. Bill of Rights, which Congress passed and the President signed in 1944. It promised to help veterans make the transition to civilian life, obtain an education, and purchase a house. This legislation, however, was not evidence of liberal power. The measure had strong support from the American Legion, no opposition from other pressure groups, and little from conservative congressmen. They did block efforts by New Dealers to link social insurance, educational assistance, and other benefits to many groups with these benefits to veterans.

As the war weakened liberals, it strengthened business leaders. It restored the effort at cooperation between the federal government and big business that had characterized the National Recovery Administration. Just as Roosevelt had believed in 1933 that he must have help from business leaders in order to combat the Depression, so now he concluded that he must have their help in order to win the war. The appointment of prominent businessmen to high office symbolized the change. Many, including William Knudsen and Charles Wilson of General Motors, Edward Stettinius of United States Steel, Ralph Budd of the Great Northern Railroad, William Jeffers of the Union Pacific, and Donald Nelson of Sears, Roebuck, moved into key positions in wartime agencies like the War Production Board.

Business leaders welcomed the change in their relations with the national administration. They were convinced that they had the abilities needed for successful government service. And they believed that the administration had behaved unwisely in the 1930s in not relying more heavily on successful businessmen and in allowing people with other backgrounds to exert a large influence on the operations of government.

The administration used many other devices to gain the confidence and cooperation of business leaders. The government helped to finance the costs of industrial expansion and guaranteed that war contracts would be profitable. Also, the antitrust campaign of the late New Deal became a casualty of war. Most officials involved in the economic programs, including Secretary Stimson, recommended such a move, arguing that antitrust efforts had to be dropped in order to encourage business leaders to cooperate with the government and to promote greater efficiency in the business system. Thurman Arnold opposed the recommendation but failed to carry the administration with him. Firms were permitted to form cooperative schemes if they could demonstrate to the satisfaction of the War Production Board that the schemes would serve the national interest, and then, in March 1942, the President postponed all antitrust activity that the Justice, War, and Navy Departments believed might harm essential production. If the departments could not agree on a specific issue,

Stimson's opinion would be decisive. A discouraged Arnold resigned the following year.

The wartime experiences also helped business leaders develop cooperative relations with military leaders. In the past, there had been some ties between these groups, but they had not been very large, for then both the military establishment and the defense industry had been very small. And conflict rather than cooperation had dominated their relations just before Pearl Harbor, for the military had pressed for conversion of the economy to military production and many corporation executives had resisted the pressure. Even now the two groups did not agree on all issues, such as the degree of control that government should have over the work force, but they were drawn together by the economic demands of war, their service together on wartime agencies, and the convergence of their interests. They agreed about the ways in which contracts should be distributed, and both, for their own reasons, opposed plans for reconversion that would have increased production for civilian purposes in 1944 and early 1945 and enlarged opportunities for companies that did not have military contracts.

Some officials with business backgrounds, including James V. Forrestal, Knox's successor as Secretary of the Navy, and Charles Wilson, tried to guarantee that the two groups would remain close after the war and serve the nation's need for military power. These men assumed that the United States would always need such power, and they feared a return to prewar relations between big business and the military.

The war not only substituted cooperation for conflict in the relations between big government and big business; it also promoted the growth of the latter. The distribution of war contracts was the decisive influence, for government procurement officers granted most of the contracts to the larger firms. The men who dominated procurement had confidence in the larger firms and found it more convenient to deal with a small number of giants than a multitude of small operators. "This defense business is big business," Wilson insisted. " . . . Small plants can't make tanks, airplanes, or other complex armaments."

Small business had its friends, such as Senator Harry S. Truman and his Special Committee to Investigate the National Defense Program, but they did not dominate policy. Concerned about the concentration of defense contracts, he had established the committee early in 1941, and for three years, he criticized business leaders and the government officials cooperating with them and the tendency to favor the large firms and ignore the small ones. He failed to check the tendency, however, and he complained bitterly about the increasing centralization of American industry. "I am hammering all I can to help the little businessman," he informed a Chamber of Commerce official in 1943. "We seem to be fighting a losing fight, however . . . "

One of the most significant parts of the New Deal was not damaged by the war. This was government promotion of the labor movement. It persisted in spite of the continued hostility to it from many businessmen. Hoping that the growth of the labor movement would come to an end, they proposed that New Deal labor legislation should be discarded for the duration of the war or at least not imposed on government contractors. Roosevelt, however, backed by a labor movement that had new strength, resisted the pressure. There were limits on his willingness to court business leaders, for he believed that he must have the cooperation of labor leaders and workers as well as businessmen. And the new War Labor Board, in addition to the New Deal's National Labor Relations Board, protected and promoted the organizing process and collective bargaining. To many government officials and an increasing number of business leaders, unions seemed valuable institutions, helpful in keeping workers on the job, rather than a threat to management and the economic system. Unions seemed to be institutions capable of serving an interest that united government officials and business leaders during the war: an interest in expanding industrial production.

In this favorable climate, the labor movement flourished. Unions added more than 4 million members, rising above 12 million by the end of the war, and collective bargaining became more widely established and effective. Although many Americans remained critical of organized labor and called for antiunion legislation, unions had become a large and important part of American life. Symbolizing recent developments, labor chiefs like Sidney Hillman joined business leaders on the new government agencies concerned with economic mobilization and stabilization.

The federal government also grew tremendously during the war. This was the most obvious and spectacular change in the structure of American capitalism that came with the war. The government grew to gigantic size in order to bring economic activities under control and point them in directions that now seemed desirable and essential. Federal expenditures jumped from only slightly above $9 billion in 1940 to nearly $100 billion five years later, and the government became the purchaser of about half of the output of the economy and controlled most of it. The New Deal had not had such a large impact on the size of government.

The growth of the federal government involved the creation of many new federal agencies as well as the explosive growth of government spending. The list of agencies included the Office of Price Administration, the War Manpower Commission, the Office of Economic Stabilization, the War Labor Board, and the Food Administration. These were only some of the most prominent, and their names suggest the large range of the government's activities and the scope of its ambitions.

It was the executive branch of the national government that enjoyed most of this growth in the government's role in American economic life. The President and his appointees made many of the big decisions about the operations of the economy just as he and his aides made most of the big decisions concerning America's military operations and the nation's relations with other countries. Some congressmen harassed the executive branch by making many investigations of it, but they could not halt its growth.

In creating new governmental institutions, the President was dominated by desires to increase the effectiveness of the government's operations in the economy but also to avoid the creation of a body that he could not dominate. In 1941, the major economic agency was the Office of Production Management; early in 1942, it was replaced by a stronger agency, the War Production Board, and in 1943 an Office of War Mobilization was established and empowered to coordinate the activities of the economic agencies. OWM had broad powers, but it was subordinate to the President. Its position was directly under him.

The war also promoted a vast increase in the economic importance of another part of government—the military. The influence of military officers in American economic life grew tremendously as they held on to control of military procurement while that task expanded rapidly. They awarded the contracts for production of ammunition, planes, tanks, ships, and the like, and they inspected the finished products. Direct control of these activities was not transferred to the civilian-controlled WPB.

Military men did not become quite as powerful in the economy as they desired. The administration hoped to produce a rapid expansion in production along lines dictated by the needs of war and gave top priority to the requirements of the armed forces, but the morale of civilians was also an important consideration in wartime Washington. The government sought a balance between "guns and butter." Throughout the war, officers such as Lieutenant General Brehon B. Somervell, the chief of the Army Service Forces, battled over economic policies with some civilian officials, especially Donald Nelson of the War Production Board. The two men clashed over the rate at which production should be expanded, the ways in which it should be distributed between military and civilian needs, and the size of the armed forces as compared with the civilian work force. Nelson and his allies suffered many failures, and power shifted away from him to James Byrnes of the Office of War Mobilization, a man with greater sympathy for the military's point of view, but military leaders and their civilian allies, such as Secretary Stimson, were seldom fully satisfied with economic decisions.

The expansion of production was the federal government's major economic objective, but there were others. One was to limit inflation. Another was to prevent the rich from profiting from the war at the expense of other groups.

To accomplish its objectives, the administration employed a large battery of weapons. The most important was massive purchasing of the products of American industry and agriculture. The administration also developed an antistrike agreement, regulated the workweek and the place of employment, and settled labor disputes. Controls were imposed on wages and prices, and the distribution of important commodities was regulated by systems of priorities and rationing. The government invested in defense plants and other essential facilities, altered tax laws to guide private investment, and imposed a new system of central control on the railroads. It employed appeals to patriotism, subsidies, and draft exemptions to encourage farmers to increase their production, ordered industrialists to convert to war production, ordered workers to "work or fight," exempted essential employees from the draft, and linked contract distribution with labor supply. Taxes were increased sharply, producing $5 billion in 1940 and nearly nine times as much in 1945, and they hit all income levels harder than ever before. While the federal income tax was raised on upper-income levels, it was also extended to many low- and middle-income people who had never before been called upon to pay it. In addition, elaborate war bond drives, involving patriotic slogans and Hollywood stars, encouraged people to save money.

Washington also recruited American higher education and American science. The war pulled boys and men of college age out of schools, forcing them to operate without the normal supply of male students and creating serious financial difficulties for the institutions, but the federal government solved the problems of some by calling upon and paying them to assist the war effort by providing the training needed by some members of the armed forces and the war economy, thereby linking the schools more closely than ever before with the federal government and the military. Many educators welcomed the new opportunities, reshaped the schools so as to make them more useful, and hoped that the federal government would supply even more funds after the war and that higher education would gain additional opportunities to serve national interests. Scientists made especially large contributions. Recruited for military purposes, they produced major results, including napalm, radar, and the atomic bomb.

The structure of the economy remained essentially what it had become by the end of the 1930s, but it was modified in important ways. It continued to be dominated by large public and private organizations, but each sector became larger. The conflict over the shape of the business sector was resolved in favor of bigness, helping the larger firms to grow once again, and their growth was matched by the growth of government and labor. The public sector was enlarged by the development of a large military establishment as well as by the creation of many new civilian agencies, and the relations among the different parts of the system became more harmonious.

This modified system performed quite successfully during the war. It performed better than the system had in the 1930s. It functioned more successfully than the American system had in any earlier period.

The economy did not expand as rapidly as desired nor along all of the desired lines. Before the Japanese attack, some business groups, including the producers of steel, aluminum, and automobiles, resisted plans to convert to wartime production and to expand beyond peacetime needs. They feared that established profitable arrangements would be disturbed and that competitors who did not convert would be able to enlarge their share of the markets. The new costs also troubled the reluctant businessmen, and the bitter experiences of the 1930s restrained them. They feared that they would develop productive capacity that could not be used after the war. As many of the government officials had come out of the business world, they sympathized with this resistance to change and were reluctant to apply pressure. As a consequence, there was not much economic conversion before 1942.

Some economic problems persisted well beyond Pearl Harbor. Rubber production was one. Rubber was an essential commodity during the war, but the Japanese advance in Southeast Asia gave them control of almost all of the American supply of crude rubber, and the production of synthetic rubber in the United States had not developed significantly before the war. To deal with the problem, scrap drives were conducted, and gasoline was rationed. Finally, a government-financed program produced synthetic rubber and solved the problem.

Labor problems also interfered with the war effort. The success of efforts to channel workers into essential jobs was limited by congressional provisions designed to protect fathers and farm workers and by workers who left important jobs. And the use of the strike weapon by some unions in spite of the no-strike pledge also kept output behind plans. Strikes increased sharply in 1943 and included especially important walkouts by John L. Lewis's coal miners. Workers believed they were being hurt by the rising cost of living and not receiving a fair share of the benefits of economic expansion.

The government on both state and national levels responded quite ineffectively to the strikes. A dozen states passed laws imposing restrictions on unions, and Congress passed, over the President's veto, the

Smith-Connally War Labor Disputes Act that imposed restrictions on the use of the strike and on political action by labor unions. The law failed to produce a settlement of the mine dispute or to end strikes that affected the war effort. In fact, the most significant use of the act was against an antiunion employer, Sewell Avery of Montgomery Ward, rather than against a union.

Labor problems also stimulated interest in a national service law. It would enable the government to assign any citizen to any job that seemed essential, but, although supported by Stimson and Roosevelt, it was not enacted. It encountered especially strong opposition from organized labor and additional opposition from many businessmen.

In addition to the defects in the production record, inflation ex-

Figure 17   Building the B-17s (*Office of War Information, Library of Congress*)

ceeded Washington's hopes. Business, farm, and labor organizations had power that they used to hamper efforts by government to control prices and wages; consumer goods were scarce relative to purchasing power, and Congress refused to push taxes as high as Roosevelt recommended as he attempted to reduce the number of dollars chasing those goods. He suffered an especially dramatic defeat on the tax issue in 1944 when Congress rejected his request for an increase of more than $10 billion, increased taxes by only about $2 billion, and passed its measure over his veto. In the end, only about 44 percent of federal income came from taxes during the war.

Inflation, however, was not as great as it had been in World War I. While prices had jumped 63 percent from 1914 to 1918, they rose only 29 percent from 1939 to 1945, and almost all of the increase came before FDR's hold-the-line order of April 1943.

Most important, the nation obtained the economic expansion needed to outproduce its enemies and accomplished this while increasing production of consumer goods. The economy supplied both "guns" and "butter." The war consumed more than 40 percent of the national product from 1942 to 1945, but the production of consumer goods, although below demand in many lines, moved above the prewar level. America made its giant economic contribution to the war—the largest of any nation—without economic sacrifice by the American people. They were not mobilized as completely as other belligerents.

The war moved the American economy from depression to boom. More accurately, the fiscal policies encouraged by the war accomplished what the New Deal had been unable to produce and completed the task of recovery. The massive increase in federal spending was accompanied by large-scale deficits in the federal budget, reaching a peak of more than $57 billion in 1943 and raising the national debt from $43 billion in 1940 to $259 billion in 1945. And as the government indulged in large-scale deficit financing, the gross national product increased by more than 75 percent, industrial production nearly doubled, unemployment dropped close to 1 percent of the labor force, and employment jumped from 46 million to 63 million as the unemployed found jobs, women and children moved into the labor force, and older workers delayed retirement.

As the economy zoomed upwards, American society changed rapidly. People moved; nearly 30 million did so. More than 14 million moved into the armed forces while a slightly larger number left home for civilian jobs elsewhere or to be close to husbands in uniform. People left the rural areas and the towns that could not get defense contracts or a military base and crowded into old industrial centers in the Northeast and the Middle West, new ones in the South and West, and areas surrounding

Army and Navy bases. Negro migration out of the rural South, which had been slowed by the Depression, was accelerated by the war.

Under the impact of large-scale migration, communities decayed or grew. In either case, they experienced disruption as some found their facilities, such as their schools, no longer needed while others found theirs too small for the new burdens. Often housing and other facilities had to be constructed hastily and could not be built fast enough to keep up with demand. Overcrowding, inadequate sanitation, and other problems were common, as was conflict between social groups thrown together by the war.

Women and children took advantage of the rapidly expanding job market. The ranks of working women jumped from 12 million to well over 16 million, and heavy industries such as steel and shipbuilding opened their doors to females for the first time. Women also moved into special branches of the armed forces. The increase in the employment of married women was especially large, and the employment of teen-agers nearly tripled, reversing a twenty-year trend and often violating laws that social reformers had championed in a different situation.

Migration and employment patterns created major problems in the lives of families. The war meant separation of sons and daughters from parents, husbands from wives, and fathers from children, often for long periods, and it also reduced the time that many mothers could devote to their children. It encouraged some lovers to postpone marriage and others to hurry into it. Premarital and extramarital intercourse, venereal disease, and illegitimate births increased; the divorce rate jumped, and juvenile delinquency rose sharply, especially among girls. The birthrate also increased.

The war also affected class relations. Here, the administration achieved an objective. Upper-income groups did not benefit at the expense of others. In fact, the upper classes experienced a drop in their share of the national income. The share held by the top 5 percent dropped from 26 percent in 1940 to 16 percent in 1945 while the top 1 percent's share dropped from 12 to 7. On the other end of the scale, millions of people emerged from poverty. Nearly half of the population remained below the poverty line at the beginning of the 1940s, but only about one-third remained there by the end of the war. The middle class, on the other hand, nearly doubled in size, so that nearly one-third of the people were in that income range by the end of the war.

Clearly, the war, although a time of many social problems, was a period of great economic progress for millions of Americans. Salaried workers, such as engineers and technicians, enjoyed a great improvement in their opportunities. For wage earners, jobs became easy to find for the first time since the 1920s. They were, in fact, much more abundant than they had been then. Wages, especially in the war plants, increased impressively. Real weekly earnings in manufacturing moved from $24 in 1939 to $36.72 in 1944. Many who had been unemployed or who had worked as tenant farmers or agricultural laborers took advantage of the new economic opportunities. The migration of these rural groups dropped farm population by 17 percent, but the remaining farmers increased agricultural production more than 3 percent each year by increasing their use of tractors and fertilizer and enlarging their farms. Many who remained on the farm achieved prosperity for the first time since World War I as farm prices rose above parity and farm income jumped more than 400 percent. Wage earners and farmers were able to enjoy a spending spree or pay debts and save. These groups and others saved about $250 billion during the war.

The wartime experience strengthened confidence in the American economic system. Advertising men promised a new abundance once war stopped consuming a large portion of American production. So did liberals.

Liberal confidence was largely a consequence of the war's lessons about government fiscal policy. Some liberals were worried about the political recovery and enlargement of big business, and many were distressed by the strong opposition to the welfare state. Nevertheless, they were convinced that the system that had taken shape and that they had helped to construct could function successfully. It seemed capable of producing full employment. Viewing fascism as the greatest threat in the world, liberals feared that it might develop inside the United States. An explosive combination of mass unemployment, demagogues, and corporate power could produce a fascist America after the war. Demagogues had to be tolerated, and corporate power now seemed a permanent feature of American life. Unemployment, however, could be avoided. Thrilled by existing employment conditions and worried about a postwar depression, liberals saw full employment as the fundamental requirement for a healthy America and viewed Keynesian economics, with its emphasis on government spending, as providing the intellectual tools capable of maintaining the full employment that had come with the war. By compensating for defects in private enterprise, government fiscal policy could guarantee that the country obtained the required purchasing power and investment. The war years provided significant evidence; they suggested that the American economic system could provide permanent prosperity. It could do so if one part of the system—the federal government—functioned wisely.

Thus, the war was a significant period in American economic

history. In a fundamental sense, the structure of the system was not changed by the war. The economy continued to be dominated by big business, big government, and big labor. But each one of these components grew rapidly, and two functions of government—the fiscal and the military—made especially large advances and became much more important in the economy. And American capitalism, while not free of serious defects, performed in spectacular ways, wiping out unemployment, reducing poverty, and enlarging the middle class. The system still had critics, but its wartime performance enlarged admiration of it. And that performance included the production of the tools needed to make the nation strong and able to accomplish ambitious objectives in many parts of the world.

SUGGESTIONS FOR ADDITIONAL READING

This chapter deals with an underdeveloped theme in American historical writing: the impact of the Second World War on American life. As early as the 1940s, historians recognized that the war changed American life significantly, but the subject had to compete for attention against the exciting and important military and diplomatic aspects of the conflict and the attractions of New Deal historiography. Military history received substantial financial support from the federal government and dominated World War II historiography. Historical writing seemed to suggest that the meaning of the war was to be found chiefly in the operations of the Army and the Navy.

Recently, several historians have called attention to the large impact of World War II on American life and the small amount of historical writing on the subject. See especially Barton J. Bernstein, "Economic Policies," in Richard S. Kirkendall, ed., *The Truman Period as a Research Field*, University of Missouri Press, Columbia, 1967, and Jim F. Heath, "Domestic America during World War II: Research Opportunities for Historians," *Journal of American History*, vol. 58, pp. 384–414, 1971.

In the past few years, several historians, including James MacGregor Burns in the second volume of his biography of Roosevelt, have made important contributions on the domestic history of the war. Burns's volume contains "subthemes" on the great significance of the war in the history of the American presidency and the large impact of the war on American society.

Richard Polenberg, a professor of history at Cornell University, has become the leading historian of the domestic aspects of the war. He moved into the war period in 1968 with a reader, *America at War: The Home Front, 1941–1945*, Prentice-Hall, Englewood Cliffs, N.J. Here, he assumed that the subject had not yet received a "fair share" of historical attention, and he attempted to help students understand the war's "profound" impact upon American society and to encourage further research in this area. Four years later, he published a book-length essay on the subject entitled *War and Society: The United States*

1941–1945 and published by Lippincott. The book demonstrates that the war was a powerful force and supplies an outstanding overall treatment of the subject.

Another essay by Bernstein, "America in War and Peace: The Test of Liberalism," in Bernstein, ed., *Towards a New Past*, Pantheon, New York, 1968, includes an overall interpretation of the domestic history of the war period, and John M. Blum's small essay in C. Vann Woodward, ed., *The Comparative Approach to American History*, Basic Books, New York, 1968, is packed with insights. The books by Lekachman and Stein to which attention was called in Chapters 2 and 10 are valuable on a major subject: the war and fiscal policy. David Brody's essay on "Mass Production Unionism," cited in Chapter 9, helps one understand the significance of the war in American labor history; the item by Douglas North (cited in Chapter 10) should be seen by those interested in the war and poverty. On the struggle between liberals and conservatives, see, in addition to the books by Tugwell on FDR, Huthmacher on Wagner, Baldwin on the Farm Security Administration, and Kirkendall on farm politics, Alonzo L. Hamby, "Sixty Million Jobs and the People's Revolution: The Liberals, the New Deal, and World War II," *Historian*, vol. 30, pp. 578–598, 1968, and John Robert Moore, "The Conservative Coalition in the United States Senate, 1942–1945," *Journal of Southern History*, vol. 33, pp. 368–376, 1967. Davis R. B. Ross, *Preparing for Ulysses: Politics and Veterans during World War II*, Columbia University Press, New York, 1969, is the major book on the passage of the G.I. Bill of Rights.

Chapter 19

The War and American
Race Relations

The war's impact was not restricted to the economic system and its performance. World War II also affected many other aspects of American life, including race relations. It was a time of suffering and loss for one racial group, the Japanese-Americans. For a much larger group, the black Americans, the war had a different meaning. It was a progressive force in their lives. Thus, World War II was very significant in the history of American race relations.

Almost alone among social groups in the United States, the Japanese-Americans were regarded as security risks and deprived of basic rights. German-Americans and Italian-Americans were treated very differently. In fact, a proposal to move Italian and German aliens from their homes was rejected. Anti-German feeling differed significantly from sentiment that had prevailed during the First World War. Now, it was not expressed in hostility toward Americans with a German background. It was focused instead on the German government, its leaders, and its ideology. Italian-Americans enjoyed a similar status and did not suffer

219

discrimination. The loyalty of both groups was taken for granted. Americans seemed now to assume that a cohesive nation could be composed of people of many different cultural backgrounds. And Americans certainly did not feel threatened by radicals as they had in World War I. The left was a weaker force now, and much of it supported rather than opposed the war.

Almost all people in the United States regarded the American war effort as justified and tried to make some contributions to it. Japanese and German behavior produced a high degree of unity and wartime enthusiasm, and the nation's leaders and publicists, including the Office of War Information, which was dominated by men skilled in the arts of the advertising industry, worked to influence attitudes and behavior. A militant nationalism, rarely restrained by social criticism, dominated American thought. Few regarded themselves as heroic crusaders serving and remaking the world. They were satisfied instead to see themselves as defenders of their nation, doing what had to be done to end the war as quickly as possible. Although not expecting as much as Americans had in 1917–1918, they had a very positive attitude toward their nation, regarding it as clearly superior to others.

If not everyone was caught up in the wartime spirit, many were. Some did buy and sell on the black market and looked after only their own material interests, but many felt a spirit of self-sacrifice that was stimulated by the appeals of spokesmen to buy war bonds, participate in war-related community activities, collect scrap metals, do without commodities needed by the war machine, and contribute to the war effort in a variety of other ways. Less than 10 percent of the people entered military service, but the others were called upon to contribute to the war effort, both on and off their jobs. For many, the chance to contribute, however small, gave great satisfaction.

The dissenter was a rare species during the war. Some people remained critical of Roosevelt and blamed him for American intervention. A few, such as Father Coughlin, appeared to have Fascist sympathies and criticized America's role in the war. And many Catholics, as well as some others, protested against America's ally, the Soviet Union, convinced that it was an evil force in the world, eager to spread communism everywhere.

Most Americans, however, approved of the alliance, and few provided the kind of criticism of American involvement in the war that had been made by the left during World War I. Many expressed very positive views of Russia and doubted that she was eager to export revolution, a view that was strengthened when Moscow dissolved the international organization of Communist parties, the Comintern, in 1943. American anticommunism during the war focused largely on domestic

Communists, but they were not a threat to the war effort. Linked as it was with the beleaguered Soviet Union, the American Communist party supported the war. Some religious groups had opposed intervention, but now most of them backed the war and supplied chaplains for the armed forces. And the Socialist party lacked the strength needed to be the troublesome critic that it had been a generation earlier.

With little dissent, there was little suppression by government and private action of the type America had experienced in World War I. Some of the small number of extreme critics were silenced by various methods. Father Coughlin was quieted by his archbishop, acting in response to suggestions from the administration, and the administration developed a loyalty program for federal employees that led to the dismissal of a few and the refusal to hire a few others regarded as dangerously disloyal. Efforts to prosecute a group of "Native Fascists" failed, however; the Supreme Court overturned the convictions of several people who favored Germany, and the Jehovah's Witnesses gained freedom from the obligation to salute the American flag. In 1940, the Supreme Court had ruled in a case involving this religious sect that schoolchildren could be forced to salute even though this violated their religious convictions. In 1943, however, the Court declared that a compulsory flag salute was unconstitutional.

Thus, it seemed to some civil libertarians that progress had taken place since World War I. The leaders of the American Civil Liberties Union found the record "generally encouraging," and the watchdog of academic freedom reported that the war had not "aroused the unjustified passions and baseless suspicion characteristic of so much campus hysteria twenty-five years ago."

Yet, the civil liberties record of the American people during the war was mixed. The treatment of conscientious objectors demonstrated this. They were tolerated but only if their objections were based on religious belief and they could persuade the selective service system that their objections were genuine and they were willing to perform noncombat service without pay. Most of them either served as noncombatants in the armed forces or worked in civilian public service camps controlled by the military and operated by the peace churches. "Their time and energy belongs to the Government and their services should be utilized in performing such projects as will best aid the Government in the emergency . . . ," Roosevelt insisted. Many in the camps were unhappy, for they resented the controls, doubted the value of the work, or believed that they had compromised their principles by serving the war machine in this way; more than 5,000 COs from several religious groups, including the Jehovah's Witnesses, failed or refused to conform to the government's requirements and suffered imprisonment, and the Supreme Court upheld this feature of the selective service system. Clearly, there were limits on the government's recognition of a right not to serve the nation in wartime.

The most shocking violation of liberal principles directly affected many more people than had been harmed by the antiradical hysteria of World War I. Both experiences revealed weaknesses in the Bill of Rights as an institutional safeguard for minorities, and the experience of the 1940s suggested that respect for it depends upon self-confidence as well as confidence in others. The victims in World War II were the Japanese-Americans, a group of slightly more than 100,000 people. They seemed to many frightened people in 1942 to be a threat to the nation even though most were American citizens and intensely patriotic. Racist assumptions influenced decisively the way in which these people were viewed. They were regarded as an "enemy race," incapable of being trusted; they were interpreted by a special set of old ideas that were given new life by the circumstances of late 1941 and early 1942.

Since their arrival in the United States late in the nineteenth century, the Japanese had encountered militant racism. It was especially strong in California, the state in which most of these immigrants settled. Many people there had long hated and feared them and had worked to stop their immigration and to drive them out of the country. And for half a century, agitators and prophets had warned of a war with Japan in which the United States would be invaded by hordes of yellow soldiers aided by yellow residents of the United States.

To many Americans, the events of late 1941 and early 1942 seemed to confirm the wisdom of the prophets. The Japanese had attacked American territory, were seizing Southeast Asia, and seemed capable of and interested in attacking the West Coast. And alarming "reports" of the activities and plans of Japanese-Americans began to appear in the press and to be heard on the radio.

Actually, the Japanese Army and Navy were thousands of miles away and incapable of invading the United States; many Japanese-Americans were trying desperately to demonstrate their loyalty, and none of them was involved in espionage or sabotage. The United States was weak but not as weak as it appeared to those whose thinking was affected by one of the parts of the American racist tradition.

Two forces were interacting to produce pressure against one group of people. The forces were a sense of national weakness and a well-established set of ideas about the Japanese. The combination resulted in an exaggeration of Japan's strength relative to the strength of the United States. Japan seemed not only to possess a very strong Army and Navy and an unusual willingness and ability to use them, but the Oriental nation seemed also to have effective allies inside the United States.

Thus, pressure for evacuation of these people from the West Coast mounted rapidly after December 7. It came from the media and the politicians in the region, including Governor Culbert Olson and Attorney General Earl Warren of California and Mayor Fletcher Bowron of Los Angeles. "We cannot run the risk of another Pearl Harbor in Southern California," Bowron warned, and Warren issued a similar warning and insisted that "in time of war every citizen must give up some of his normal rights."

One important individual who shared the alarm was General John L. De Witt, the commander of the Western Defense Command and the Fourth Army with headquarters in San Francisco. He interpreted the lack of sabotage as evidence that the Japanese-Americans were effectively controlled and would strike when the situation was right, and he was especially suspicious of those who were proclaiming their loyalty. Persuaded that a Japanese attack upon the West Coast was a possibility, he was troubled that the Japanese-Americans lived close to defense plants and military bases. Thus, he concluded that these people must be moved.

Roosevelt offered no resistance and on February 10 signed an executive order authorizing evacuation on grounds of military necessity. Facing a bad situation in the world and eager to unite the country behind him, Roosevelt did not want to take an unpopular stand or alienate men like Stimson who favored evacuation. Furthermore, he personally distrusted the Japanese.

The decision was popular. It was applauded not only on the West Coast but in the nation at large. Most people believed that the decision was justified by the war, and Congress approved on March 21.

The decision meant the removal of Japanese-Americans from their homes on the Pacific Coast and their confinement in remote, fenced, and guarded camps. By June, evacuation was nearly complete, and by November, close to 120,000 people were living in ten camps located from eastern California to Arkansas. Nearly two-thirds of these people had been born in the United States!

Most of the Japanese-Americans remained in the camps until 1945. A few officials pressed for the opening of large opportunities for the people to move out of the camps, but the pressure was resisted by Army and Navy officers, including De Witt, many Californians, including Warren, who was elected governor in 1942, and many congressmen. The influence of anti-Japanese sentiments beyond the Coast also clashed with hopes of permitting large numbers of the people to leave the camps and enter communities in the interior. Some were able to leave to attend college, accept jobs, or serve in the Army, and some of the Japanese-American soldiers served with great distinction. Most of the evacuees, however, did not leave the camps.

For many of these people, the experience involved serious economic losses. They lost property that they left behind or were forced to sell it at low prices. And they worked for low wages in the camps and missed the opportunities for economic advance that were open to many others during the war.

To a few Americans, it seemed that their nation was behaving much like the German enemy. The leader of the American Socialist party, Norman Thomas, charged that the episode was "evidence of a drift toward totalitarianism" in America, and Justice Frank Murphy, among others, compared the program with the treatment of the Jews by the Nazis. The analogy was not perfect. The men who administered the American relocation process and the camps did not brutalize or execute the people who lived in them. The two experiences were, however, linked by racist assumptions.

A few victims of the government program challenged their treatment in the courts, but the challenges failed. The judges, including most of the justices of the United States Supreme Court, accepted the program

Figure 18 Patriots in Concentration Camps (*Franklin D. Roosevelt Library*)

as justified by the "military dangers" that existed in 1942. Only a minority of the high court emphasized the constitutional limits on the power of the military and the constitutional rights of American citizens.

Black Americans also had to contend against racial theories, but World War II had very different consequences for these people. Racial theories concerning blacks did not cause others to see them as a threat to the nation's security. Instead, the war stimulated the growth of a challenge to the Jim Crow system that had been built upon those theories long before, and the war moved the issue of the rights of black Americans into new prominence.

In 1940, the Jim Crow system still governed the lives of the 13 million blacks in the United States. Segregation in the schools was common everywhere and required by law in seventeen states and the District of Columbia. Segregation in trains, buses, and public facilities was also widespread and dictated by law in many places. In the South, Negroes had to contend with obstacles against voting, such as the system of white primaries, and only 5 percent of the adult blacks were registered voters. Public housing projects were segregated; provisions in real estate contracts prevented blacks from buying homes in many neighborhoods, and no government body had an ordinance prohibiting racial discrimination in employment.

The war supplied blacks with new evidence of their second-class status. They were discriminated against by the expanding defense industries. Almost no blacks obtained jobs in defense plants at the beginning of the 1940s, and almost all who did obtained only very lowly ones. Even skilled Negroes could not get jobs, and those lacking skills were discriminated against in the training programs. Blacks also encountered discrimination in the unions, especially those in the AFL.

These Americans also encountered discrimination and segregation in the armed forces. The Air Corps and the Marines were closed to blacks at the beginning of the 1940s, and the Navy offered them positions only as messmen. The Army provided more opportunities than the other services but restricted Negroes to black units, usually limited to noncombatant service and commanded by white officers, and draft boards that drafted blacks often excluded them from membership. The racial practices of the armed forces assumed that blacks were inferior to whites and that the military must conform to the practices of the larger society in order to be effective.

In this situation, black determination to protest gained strength rapidly. Although they hated Hitler's racism and authoritarianism and feared the possibility of a German victory, black leaders refused to subordinate the battle at home to the battle abroad. As whites of different nations maimed and killed one another and had difficulty checking the yellow men of Japan, blacks obtained new reasons to doubt the superiority of the white race. Many criticized the treatment of Japanese-Americans, and a few hoped for a Japanese victory.

As white Americans proclaimed that they were fighting for democracy against totalitarianism and that they hated the racist policies of Hitler's Germany, blacks saw that the war provided opportunities to prick the conscience of white America. They called attention to the contrast between American democratic ideals and the realities of American race relations and similarities between race practices in the United States and in Germany. For this racial group, the war created new opportunities, and many spokesmen seized them.

The racial practices of the armed forces were especially galling and vulnerable. The rapidly expanding Negro press publicized the facts of life in the armed forces; some young blacks refused induction into armed forces that practiced racial discrimination; and many called for greater opportunities to serve. Some were embittered by their experience.

One of the most important illustrations of the rising black militancy was the March on Washington movement. Organized early in 1941 by a Negro labor leader, A. Philip Randolph, the movement excluded whites and sought to employ direct action by the black masses. Concerned chiefly with the economic problems of blacks in the urban ghettos, it protested against discrimination by the defense industries and the armed forces. For a time, it seemed capable of becoming a permanent and large direct-action movement, using mass marches, protest rallies, and civil disobedience, but many blacks regarded Randolph as too radical and his movement went into decline in 1943. Before then, however, it had both represented change in black America and, as we shall see, promoted change in government policy.

The formation of the Congress of Racial Equality in 1942 was another sign of change. It was organized in Chicago by a small biracial group, chiefly students and members of the Fellowship of Reconciliation, a Christian pacifist organization. Although most members of CORE were white, blacks such as James Farmer and Bayard Rustin played major roles. The new organization sought to apply nonviolent techniques to the solution of racial problems, believing that nonviolent, direct action, such as a sit-in in a restaurant that refused service to blacks, was the only practical way to produce change. With Farmer and Rustin providing much of the leadership, CORE spread beyond Chicago to other Northern cities and became a national federation in 1943 with Farmer as chairman. It dealt chiefly with public accommodations, such as restaurants and theaters, but also paid some attention to housing, employment, hospitals, and transportation. Its aim was to wipe out segregation and discrimination and establish equal treatment in an integrated society.

An old civil rights organization, the National Association for the Advancement of Colored People, grew rapidly during the war, moving from 50,000 members to 450,000. In a rapidly changing situation, it maintained its position as the leading black protest group. Fearing violence, the NAACP counseled Negroes to rely upon their votes and the judicial system, rather than mass action in the streets. The organization fought in the courts against Jim Crow and tried to use Negro political power to force Congress to pass an anti-poll tax bill and other measures that would help black Americans.

Just before the end of the war, the NAACP gained a significant victory. In 1944, the Supreme Court declared that the white primary was unconstitutional. It had effectively disenfranchised Negroes in eight Southern states, and it had been upheld by the Court in 1935 when the justices had accepted the argument that a political party was a private organization and thus was not affected by the Fifteenth Amendment. But now the Court ruled that political parties were agents of the state and thus were barred by the Constitution from depriving a citizen of his right to vote. As a consequence, additional Southern blacks moved into politics as voters, although many more were barred by surviving devices, such as literacy tests and the poll tax.

Black America was becoming more militant. Black leaders and many others were working for economic, political, and social equality; they hoped that the government would become a promoter of change in race relations, and they tried to take advantage of the opportunities provided by the war to promote change at home.

Many white liberals did develop a stronger concern about the plight of Negro Americans. And the war stimulated this development. "The nation cannot expect colored people to feel that the United States is worth defending if the Negro continues to be treated as he is now," Eleanor Roosevelt advised. "The Negro lives in our midst," Wendell Willkie suggested, "under discriminations which differ from the racial discrimination practiced by our enemies, the Nazis, only in that ours are illegal and we are free—if we wish— to fight against them." At the same time, many liberals, including Mrs. Roosevelt, feared racial conflict, a white backlash, and disruption of the war effort, and thus urged blacks to press their demands cautiously.

Other forces countered the militant blacks and the liberals. Most whites, Northern as well as Southern, believed that Negroes were treated fairly and were responsible for their second-class status. These whites favored segregation and resisted demands for change in race relations.

White Southerners were very unhappy with, even fearful of, the demands for change that black Southerners were making, blamed them on "outside agitators," defended the Jim Crow system as the best way of managing race relations, and insisted that the white people of the South must be allowed to manage race relations there.

The changes that were taking place, the pressures for more, and the resistance to change resulted in violence in several places. Whites sought to defend the status quo and expressed resentment of the new competition from blacks for jobs and for places in which to live and play, and Negroes voiced resentment of their treatment. The results were racial conflict and riots in military posts, defense plants, and the communities into which whites and blacks were drawn by the war and also in other places.

Two of the largest explosions occurred in Detroit and Harlem in 1943. A major industrial center, Detroit had experienced an influx of both whites and blacks. Living conditions for the black immigrants were deplorable, and several white groups resented the black presence and pressure. A riot erupted in June, required intervention by federal troops, left twenty-five Negroes and nine whites dead, wounded many more, and destroyed a large amount of property. Two months later, blacks in Harlem expressed their frustrations by destroying property and looting stores. Whites were not involved directly in this riot, except as law enforcement officers; all the people killed and wounded were black, and most blacks were very critical of the uprising, although they recognized the social sources of it.

The pressures of the period forced the President to become more actively concerned with race relations than he had been earlier. Faced with the threat of a march on Washington, he issued an executive order in June 1941 establishing a Committee on Fair Employment Practices. It was the first federal civil rights agency since the days of Reconstruction; and it helped to enlarge job opportunities for blacks even though the agency was hampered by the lack of enforcement powers, a shortage of funds, and cautious leadership and was faced with strong opposition from Southern Democrats, many white workers and their unions, employers, and those who feared disruption of war production. The racial policies of the CIO also helped to enlarge job opportunities for black workers, and the labor shortage that had developed by 1943 helped even more. Although discrimination persisted, blacks found many more jobs in the defense plants than had been available to them at the beginning of the war, and the jobs that they found included some on the skilled and semiskilled levels.

An episode in Philadelphia in 1944 illustrated Roosevelt's efforts and the efforts of others to improve job opportunities for blacks during the war. In the City of Brotherly Love, black employees of the Public Transit Company pressed for better jobs but were rebuffed by the company and the union. The black workers then received support from the NAACP and the FEPC, from a CIO union that successfully sought to replace the established union as the bargaining agent for the transit workers, and from the War Manpower Commission, and the company surrendered to the pressure and to the shortage of manpower and announced a decision to train blacks as streetcar operators. White workers, however, with encouragement from the defeated union leaders, went on strike in spite of the opposition to a strike from the new union leaders. The strike severely harmed war work in the city; fears of racial violence mounted; the NAACP, other black groups, and the city's police force worked to prevent an outbreak, and Roosevelt ordered the Army to take control of the company. Troops moved into the city, and workers were threatened with stiff penalties if they did not return to their jobs. Soon the workers, including the black trainees, returned, and the company regained control of its property. Upgrading of black workers resumed and encountered no further opposition.

In this case, Roosevelt gave strong support to the FEPC and black demands. His action was influenced chiefly by the need to resume war production in a major city.

Roosevelt also promoted a few improvements in race relations in the armed forces. Military leaders, including Secretary Stimson, had little sympathy for Negro demands in this area, but the administration made some concessions to them. Before the end of the war, some black sailors were serving outside the mess corps and in integrated crews; some black soldiers were serving in combat units, and a few platoons were integrated into largely white companies. The armed forces, however, remained essentially segregated at the end of the war, and almost all blacks served in noncombat roles.

Although he gave some encouragement and help to advocates of change in race relations, Roosevelt believed that major efforts should be postponed until after the war. Thus, he urged black militants to proceed cautiously, warning that militance would strengthen the foes of change, and he tried to stay out of racial problems. His attention was dominated by the war, and his ties with Southern Democrats, his fears of a Southern revolt against his administration and the Democratic party, and his limited contact with militant blacks also influenced his behavior in this area. He refused to support efforts to repeal the poll tax, and his administration made no effort to enforce the Supreme Court's decision on primary elections.

Nevertheless, the war had promoted progress for black Americans.

The contrast with the experience of Japanese-Americans was especially striking. They had to struggle to recover the ground they lost in 1942. Some of them protested against the loss of their rights as Americans, refused to volunteer for or to be drafted into the Army, and expressed anti-American and pro-Japanese sentiments. Some even renounced their American citizenship and requested expatriation or repatriation to Japan. Most, however, accepted their fate, and many worked strenuously to demonstrate their loyalty, refusing to protest, cooperating with the administration, and serving in the Army, convinced that these were the only ways to gain acceptance in American society.

The chance to regain lost ground began before the end of the war. As the nation gained strength and self-confidence and moved toward victory, the Japanese-Americans came to seem less dangerous and more worthy of freedom. Roosevelt continued to regard the restrictions that had been imposed upon them as justified by "military necessity," but he began to defend the loyalty of some of them and to advocate resettlement out of the camps. During 1944, top men in the Army considered relaxing the ban against settlement on the West Coast, believing that military considerations no longer necessitated mass exclusion and fearing court rulings against the program now that Japan was in retreat.

In January 1945, the Japanese-Americans were permitted to leave the camps and return to the West Coast. While many settled elsewhere, most returned to the region in which they had lived before the war. The returnees did encounter opposition, but many political leaders, including Governor Warren, and several liberal and religious groups helped these people. They had to work to regain the status they had lost through the action of their government, and they struggled to enter the middle class and obtain recognition as loyal Americans.

Thus, the war was a significant, if ambiguous, period and force in the history of American race relations. It produced another ugly episode in the history of this aspect of American life. One variety of racism, plus a sense of national weakness, forced a decision to single out one group for harsh treatment. At the same time, however, the war challenged the established order in another area of race relations. The war did not destroy the Jim Crow system, but one feature of it, the white primary, was destroyed in the war period, thereby enlarging political opportunities for black Americans. The war also enlarged economic opportunities for them. Most important, it stimulated a strong challenge from both blacks and whites to the established order in this area. The opponents of change in race relations remained very strong, but they were functioning in a new situation. Race relations and civil rights had become one of the major issues in American life.

SUGGESTIONS FOR ADDITIONAL READING

Polenberg's and Burns's books are valuable for the subjects discussed in this chapter as is another broad book in this new historiographical field: Keith L. Nelson, ed., *The Impact of War on American Life: The Twentieth Century Experience*, Holt, New York, 1971. The most recent and most valuable book on a major subject considered in this chapter is Roger Daniels, *Concentration Camps USA: Japanese Americans and World War II*, Holt, New York, 1971.

Richard M. Dalfiume has published work of basic importance in this area. See his frequently reprinted essay "The 'Forgotten Years' of the Negro Revolution," *Journal of American History*, vol. 55, pp. 90–106, 1968, and his larger study, *Desegregation of the U.S. Armed Forces: Fighting on Two Fronts 1939–1953*, University of Missouri Press, Columbia, 1969. Also very important are Ulysses G. Lee, Jr., *The United States Army in World War II: Special Studies: The Employment of Negro Troops*, U.S. Government Printing Office, Washington, 1966; August Meier and Elliott Rudwick, "How CORE Began," *Social Science Quarterly*, vol. 49, pp. 789–799, 1969; Harvard Sitkoff, "Racial Militancy and Interracial Violence in the Second World War," *Journal of American History*, vol. 58, pp. 661–681, 1971; and Allen M. Winkler, "The Philadelphia Transit Strike of 1944," *Journal of American History*, vol. 59, pp. 73–89, 1972.

Chapter 20

The Rise
of a Global Power

As American life changed under the impact of war, American power also increased substantially. The weak nation of 1941–1942 was replaced by a powerful nation capable of offensive operations in both Europe and the Pacific and substantial contributions to a series of defeats for Germany, Italy, and Japan. The change from frustration and defeat to repeated victories was highly significant. So was the range of American activities. From 1942 to 1944, the United States became a global power, capable of exerting a major influence on events and developments in many parts of the world.

Improvements in American fortunes were obvious before the end of 1942 and reflected the impressive expansion of American war production and of the American armed forces. By the end of the year, the Army had grown to 5.4 million men, and more than 1 million of them were stationed outside the United States. The Army still suffered from inexperience and needed to grow even more to deal with all the tasks that lay before it, and it did not have all the supplies it needed. Yet, the American armed forces were much larger than they had been only a short time before, and

American industry was supplying their needs more fully than the industrial systems of Germany, Italy, and Japan could supply their forces.

The American Navy in the Pacific checked the Japanese advance well before the end of 1942. A carrier-based air raid over Tokyo in April, commanded by General James Doolittle, had diverted Japan from plans to hit India and Australia and persuaded her that she must complete the destruction of the American Navy and seize additional American bases. Thus, late in May, Japanese forces moved against Midway and the Aleutians; although they gained footholds in the latter, they were repulsed at Midway in a major victory for American forces that demonstrated the effectiveness of naval air power and inflicted heavy losses on Japan. Another American naval force operating in the Coral Sea frustrated Japanese efforts to gain control of Port Moresby in New Guinea. These accomplishments for American naval power secured Midway, Hawaii, and Australia, caused Japan to cancel plans for the invasion of New Caledonia, Fiji, and Samoa, and persuaded her that she should turn her attention to the strengthening of the places she had already conquered.

The Allies in the Pacific, including Australia, now began to move forward. In August, forces commanded by Admiral Nimitz moved against Guadalcanal in the Solomon Islands while others commanded by General MacArthur attacked Japanese positions on the northeast coast of New Guinea. The battles were very difficult, inflicting heavy losses on both sides, and forced the United States to divert bombers, soldiers, and other resources to the Pacific that had been planned for use elsewhere. As a result, the number of American troops there by the end of 1942 equaled those in England and North Africa. MacArthur remained dissatisfied with the support he received, but he moved to victory in New Guinea by late January 1943, and victory in Guadalcanal came the following month. The victories secured the communication line between the United States and Australia and dashed Japanese hopes for a renewal of their drive into the South Pacific.

Similar accomplishments were made on the other side of the world. The Russians stopped the German drive in the bloody battle of Stalingrad, and the British moved successfully against the Germans in Egypt, driving them into Libya, a country controlled by Italy. And in November, American forces, commanded by General Eisenhower, invaded Morocco and Algeria and moved toward Tunisia from the west as British forces moved toward that country from the east. To speed the move toward victory, the United States made a highly controversial deal with a German collaborator, Admiral Darlan, the commander of the French forces in Morocco, Algeria, and Tunisia. The deal helped to end resistance from those forces.

Progress was being made. By May 1943, the United States and Great Britain had gained control of North Africa. German and Italian forces there had been seriously damaged; the Mediterranean had been opened to the Allies, and the Middle East and the Suez Canal had been freed from the German threat.

The victory, however, was not followed by a decision to cross the Channel. In the Casablanca Conference in January, that invasion had been placed fairly low on the priority list in spite of Marshall's insistence that it must be made as soon as North Africa was secure and the buildup was adequate. The British had continued to resist and had advocated an invasion of Southern Europe, and Churchill and Roosevelt had agreed that the cross-channel attack would be made "as soon as practicable," possibly as early as August but more likely in 1944. Marshall now pressed for a more definite commitment, but Churchill battled for his strategy. The British and Americans agreed that Western Europe would be invaded in May 1944, emphasis would be placed on preparations for this, and the bombing campaign would be escalated. They also agreed that Italy would be invaded in 1943.

Stalin remained unhappy. His war remained very destructive, and, while aid to him remained high on the American priority list, the German Navy continued to destroy supplies headed for Russia. The decision on strategy meant that Russian losses would continue to be very high. To him, it seemed that his allies had broken their promises and hoped that his losses would be very heavy. His anger and cynicism mounted.

In July, the Western Allies began to implement the British strategy. With Eisenhower in command, they invaded Sicily and moved quickly toward victory, although they were not able to block the escape of German forces. The Allies also pounded Italy heavily from the air. Their successes stimulated the growth of opposition to Mussolini, and his opponents removed him from office and established a new government that surrendered in September and joined the anti-German alliance.

Churchill now pressed for even larger operations in Southern Europe. In addition to a major move into Italy, he advocated operations in the eastern Mediterranean designed in part to enable Great Britain to gain control of much of the Balkans, including Greece. Stimson and Marshall opposed the plan, and Churchill and Roosevelt agreed to emphasize preparations for the attack across the English Channel but also to knock Italy out of the war. The operation in the Balkans was rejected as costly and diversionary.

The Allies did invade Italy, again with Eisenhower in command. It was now an occupied country with Germany in control, and it was not the "soft underbelly" that Churchill had suggested. The Allies had to fight against a large, strong, well-led German Army on very difficult terrain. The Allied effort was hampered by shortages of bombers, landing craft, men, and other resources as the campaign had to compete for them with other efforts and did not occupy the top position on the priority scale. As a consequence of the great difficulties, the Allies did not gain control of Rome until June 1944.

The value of the Italian campaign is debatable. It did tie down some German forces that could have been used elsewhere, and it made the United States and Great Britain major influences in Italian politics. They were interested in more than the destruction of Mussolini's regime. They were interested also in shaping the government that emerged in its place. Thus, they turned down a Russian request to participate in the occupation, arguing that Russia had not participated in the liberation of Italy and thus had not earned such an opportunity, and they worked successfully against the anticapitalist left in Italian politics. On the other hand, however, the troops that dominated Italy's political evolution might have moved more effectively against Germany in Western and Northern Europe and might have given the Western Allies greater influence in those parts of Europe.

In the meantime, progress was being made in the war against Japan. Having been attacked by the Japanese, Americans were much more interested in the Asian enemy than Britain and Russia were, and the United States assumed primary responsibility for this war and steadily enlarged it during 1943 and 1944. By February 1943, there were nearly 400,000 American troops in the Pacific, and in the next seven months, more than 200,000 were added. The American force also included a large part of the American Navy, and it, especially the fast aircraft carriers, played a very large role in the Pacific war.

Although King and other champions of the Pacific war did enjoy a substantial enlargement of the resources available to them, they continued to receive less than they desired. While the number of American troops in the Pacific increased by 50 percent from February to September 1943, the number in Europe and Africa grew from just slightly above 400,000 to approximately a million. To MacArthur, the disparity was especially distressing. He believed in the great importance of Asia and insisted that the United States must gain control of the islands near that continent in order to exert a large influence there. At Casablanca, however, Roosevelt and Churchill had placed the war against Japan in a low position on the priority list.

In December 1943, Roosevelt and Churchill endorsed plans for the completion of the war against Japan. MacArthur, the commander in the Southwest Pacific, would be in charge of a predominantly military opera-

Figure 19 The Fast Carriers (*Wide World Photos*)

tion, supported by naval forces, that would use Australia as its base, move north toward Japan, and include the Philippines as a major objective. Admiral Nimitz, who was responsible for a vast area stretching from Hawaii to China and from New Zealand to Alaska, would use Hawaii for his headquarters for the command of an operation that would rely heavily on naval forces and move across the Central Pacific toward Japan. The combined operation would, when fully developed, be very large, comparable in size to the invasion of Western Europe. Unlike that move, however, this one would not involve large operations on the continent. The Allies did not have the resources, including the immense transportation facilities, needed for a war in China.

By the time Roosevelt and Churchill reached this agreement about the war against Japan, Allied forces in the Pacific were moving forward successfully. In 1943 and early 1944, they gained control of much of the Solomon Islands, the Admiralty Islands, and New Britain, reduced the effectiveness of the major base at Rabaul in New Britain, and regained possession of Attu and Kiska in the Aleutians. They attacked Makin and Tarawa in the Gilbert Islands and, while suffering heavy losses, gained possession of them and their important air bases. In February 1944, the Allies seized control of Kwajalein and Eniwetok in the Marshall Islands and raided and seriously damaged the major air and naval base at Truk in the Carolines.

By now, Nimitz's forces had become dominant in the Central Pacific, and soon they moved closer to Japan. During the summer, they seized Saipan, Guam, and Tinian in the Marianas. This was a highly significant accomplishment, for Tokyo could be reached from these islands by the B-29s, the new long-range bomber built by Boeing. Southern Japan was already being hit from bases in China, but they were too far from Tokyo and were also more difficult to supply than these bases in the Marianas.

At the same time, the war against the Philippine Islands moved forward. From May to September, MacArthur advanced toward them from the south while Admiral William Halsey closed in from the east. The invasion came in October; late in the month, Halsey won a great victory in Leyte Gulf, and the anti-Japanese forces then pushed north toward Manila.

Only in China was the war against Japan going badly. There, Japan

Figure 20   War in the Pacific (*Wide World Photos*)

Figure 21   MacArthur Returns—October 1944 (*Wide World Photos*)

continued to make progress in the south against Chiang's forces. Part of
the explanation was Chiang's ineffectiveness. He remained reluctant to go
into action on the ground and preferred Chennault's emphasis on air
power over Stilwell's ideas about ground operations. In response to
pressure from Roosevelt and other American leaders, Chiang did attack in
Burma and eastern China but quite ineffectively. Stilwell's pressure for
reform produced only friction between himself and the Chinese leader
and led to the American's removal in October 1944. Chiang's Chinese
rivals for control of the country, the Communists, demonstrated greater
effectiveness in their operations against the Japanese in northern China.

China's low position on the American scale of priorities also
continued to contribute to the difficulties on the mainland. The decision of
November 1943 about the ways in which the war against Japan should be
fought meant that American leaders did not regard the Chinese Army as
very important, and the victories in the Marianas in the summer of 1944
meant that the Chinese bases lost much of their importance. The United
States sent fewer than 30,000 military people into China; they devoted
their attention chiefly to air action and the transportation of supplies, not

to combat on the ground, and the air war was hampered by shortages due to needs elsewhere that had higher priorities.

Many more Americans were stationed in India and Burma. Some were engineers involved in a giant effort to build a road from Burma to China so as to obtain an alternative to air transportation; others transported supplies, and some went into combat in the air and on the ground along with Chinese troops in Burma. The Burma campaign, which also involved a large British role, was quite successful in 1943 and 1944.

By June of 1944, the United States and Great Britain at last felt strong enough to move into Western Europe. The subject had been debated again at conferences in Cairo and Teheran in November and December 1943. Churchill continued to push for enlargement of the operations in the south, but he was countered by Stalin, who was present at Teheran, expressed a low opinion of the Italian campaign, and pressed for an invasion of France. Roosevelt still believed in the Italian campaign but had even more interest in the cross-Channel attack and greater interest in it than Churchill had. The outcome was a decision to invade in May. Churchill continued to fear failure and would do so until the eve of the invasion.

Shortly after Teheran, Roosevelt decided that Eisenhower rather than Marshall would be the commander of the great invasion of Europe. Eisenhower had gained valuable military experience during the preceding year and had demonstrated great skill in promoting American-British cooperation. He was eager to carry the war into Germany on the ground and to destroy German forces, and he decided to increase his chances for success by expanding the invading force from three to five divisions, a decision that forced still another delay of the invasion. This, however, would be the final delay.

The essential preparations had been made. Victory in the battle of the Atlantic, which had been given the top position on the priority list at Casablanca, had come during 1943. By then, the United States and its allies had gained the experience needed to use planes and ships more effectively against submarines and were helped by technological developments, such as radar, sonar, and better depth charges. By then also, the United States had many more ships, planes, seamen, and pilots than had been available in 1942 and had obtained help from Latin American countries that gave the United States important air and naval bases. Although German submarines continued to operate until the end of the war, the Allies now dominated the Atlantic. This was an accomplishment of fundamental significance. It meant that the United States and its allies could transport the men and supplies needed in Europe.

By the spring of 1944, the Allies had also gained control of the air over German-controlled Europe. Zealots in the Army Air Force, led by General Henry H. Arnold, believed that air power could win the war and argued that the way to do this was to destroy German industry in high-altitude, daylight raids. Since the summer of 1942, they had been participating significantly in the air war over Europe, cooperating with the British Royal Air Force, which preferred nighttime raids, relying heavily on the B-17, and learning much from the bitter and costly experiences supplied by German fighter planes and antiaircraft guns.

By the spring of 1943, the fliers had developed a Combined Bomber Offensive Plan and obtained approval of it by the Combined Chiefs of Staff. It involved a list of seventy-six targets determined by their industrial and military importance. The plan would enable the air power enthusiasts to demonstrate the importance of strategic air warfare, and it would also help prepare the way for the invasion.

In June, the bombing plan was put into operation. It was implemented by a large and growing supply of planes and airmen, assisted by the introduction of radar, which reduced the importance of weather as an obstacle, and helped also by allied victories in North Africa and Italy, which enabled the air forces to use bases in the south as well as in Britain. The German air force was the chief target until the spring of 1944. The B-17s, B-24s, and other bombers, accompanied by fighter planes whenever possible, hit aircraft factories as well as the planes themselves and seriously weakened enemy air power. Then they switched attention to more fundamental objectives, such as the German oil industry.

Although the air power theorists did not demonstrate that air power could produce victory, their forces made a significant contribution to it. They gained the control of the air needed to reduce significantly the risks involved in the attack across the Channel. And just before the invasion, the planes and airmen made an additional contribution. They put into operation Eisenhower's plan for the destruction of transportation facilities in northern France. Designed to block any German effort to reinforce the area following the invasion, the operation was very successful.

The Russians also made a major contribution to the cross-Channel attack that they desired. After checking the German drive, they turned to the offensive before the end of 1943 and began to liberate Russian territory from German control. This facilitated the invasion, for Hitler was more concerned about the war on his eastern front. He had more than 250 divisions there and only 90 in France, the Low Countries, and Italy in June 1944. Concerned that the Russian offensive would become increasingly effective when summer weather arrived, Hitler did not give his forces in the west the supplies they needed.

By the spring of 1944, the United States was stronger than ever before. The planners had decided in 1943 that the American contribution

Figure 22   Eisenhower and the Invaders—June 1944 (*Wide World Photos*)

to the cross-Channel attack would be twice as large as the British, and now the United States had a military system composed of more than 12 million men supported by military expenditures that had jumped from less than $2 billion in 1940 to more than $85 billion in 1944. The Army, with more than 8 million members, was the largest part of the armed giant, while the Navy and Marine Corps had 4 million people. The American economy now supplied these fighting men with a powerful array of weapons and delivery systems. By 1944, the nation produced about 45 percent of the world's supply of arms and ammunition and had moved far ahead of its enemies. Its production of military planes had jumped from 2,000 in 1939 to nearly 100,000, and its construction of naval and merchant ships, which totaled more than 75,000 during the war, gave the United States about two-thirds of the world's total. The United States, rather than Britain, was now the most powerful nation in the Atlantic community; Roosevelt had become the dominant figure in the British-American alliance; the American Joint Chiefs of Staff dominated the Combined Chiefs of Staff, and Eisenhower dominated the Allied Expeditionary Force.

On June 6, 1944, that force invaded Europe, hitting the Normandy coast from bases in southern England. Eisenhower had more than 2,500,000 men under his command, including 1,500,000 Americans and about 1,000,000 from Great Britain, Canada, France, and other countries. More than 150,000 moved in on the first day, supported by heavy bombardment by planes and ships and by French resistance forces. The German Air Force could not respond; the German Navy made almost no response, and the German leaders had miscalculated the point of attack and thus had not massed men and equipment in the right places.

For the next six weeks, the Allies strengthened their position on the Continent and then moved forward. By July 23, nearly 1,300,000 troops had landed in France, and they faced a much smaller German force that was weakened by conflict between Hitler and his generals. Some of the German officers made an unsuccessful attempt on Hitler's life, hoping to overthrow the government and negotiate an end to the war, and the event resulted in further deterioration in the relations between Hitler and the leaders of the Army that reduced their effectiveness. Late in July, the Allied forces moved out to the east and to the south with the German Army retreating rapidly before them and suffering much heavier losses than the invaders.

As the ground war moved forward, so did the war from the air. In addition to tactical bombing in support of the troops on the ground, the Allied air forces continued their strategic bombing of the German-controlled areas. The primary target was the German oil industry, and the launching sites of the German rockets and missiles also received considerable attention, for they were damaging British morale.

On August 15, the Germans in France were hit from another direction, the south. This was a move favored by the Americans and resisted by the British, who wanted to enlarge efforts farther east. The decision favoring an invasion of southern France had been made in 1943, but conflict had continued. Churchill hoped to move with force through Italy and Yugoslavia into Austria, Hungary, and Germany for he recognized the political significance of the movements of armies and wished to strengthen the British position in this part of Europe and to place limits on the expansion of Russia.

The Russian offensive had begun to alarm Churchill in 1944. Fearful of Soviet ambitions, he now saw that the defeat of Hitler would open new opportunities for the Russians in Eastern and Central Europe, and he concluded that the West should use military power to limit those opportunities. The United States and Great Britain should move military forces into some of the areas now occupied by Germany. His plan for operations in the south would, he believed, supply the best means of accomplishing one of his objectives. It would contain Soviet expansion.

Roosevelt's thinking on this subject ran along different lines. In 1943, he and his State Department had feared that Stalin would make peace with Hitler as soon as his forces had been driven out of Russia, but the War Department had argued that Russia would try to expand beyond her boundaries and dictate the peace in Europe. The military advisers argued that unless the United States crossed the Channel, Russia would be the dominant influence in the reshaping of Europe. Russian successes in 1943 and early 1944 suggested that the War Department was right, but Roosevelt refused to cross the Channel before all the preparations had been made, and he refused to consider other military means of limiting Russian expansion. He did not want to get into positions that he would be forced to defend for extended periods after the war. He and other American leaders concluded that Russia would become the dominant influence in Eastern Europe, but they hoped that region would not become a permanent sphere of Russian influence.

Aware that Roosevelt favored persuasion and conciliation, rather than military pressure, as the means of limiting Russian expansion, Churchill stressed military considerations in advocating his plan. The question was, how should the Allies use the troops that had just produced the fall of Rome? Churchill argued that they should be kept in Italy, not moved to France, and should be reinforced so that they could move forward more rapidly. That, he maintained, was the most effective way of using them in the war against Germany. After all, they were already in Italy.

Marshall and Eisenhower opposed Churchill's plan. They continued to believe that operations in France provided the most efficient way of moving against Germany, and they wanted to avoid being drawn still more into campaigns farther east over very difficult terrain. They stressed the value of the ports of southern France, especially Marseilles. Additional American troops and supplies could be brought into battle in France through those ports. The American generals also pointed out that the completion of the Normandy invasion freed landing craft that could be used in a second invasion of France.

Eisenhower and Marshall now had stronger support from Roosevelt than he had given them earlier in the war. Their advice was in line with his objectives, including total defeat of Germany and improvement in relations with Russia, and so he forced the British to go along.

Thus, a second invasion of France was made. It was a much smaller operation than the first one, involving only two divisions. Limits were placed on it by the demands of the expanding Pacific war, but some landing craft that had been planned for use there were now diverted to this invasion. In addition, landing craft and troops were also moved out of

Italy to participate in it. The invasion was a joint American-French effort; it was assisted by French resistance forces, and the invaders moved north and east against Hitler's army.

The invasion from the south did make an important contribution. It gave the Allies control of important ports at a time when they did not yet control enough ports in the north. Over one-third of the supplies brought into Europe from September to December came through Marseilles and neighboring ports.

Germany continued to fall back before superior Allied forces. On August 25, the German commander in Paris surrendered. Following that spectacular event, the Allied advance was slowed by shortages of supplies, including gasoline, ammunition, and food, by a shortage of riflemen, and by transportation problems that grew as the lines were extended. But quite effective efforts were made to solve the transportation problems, and the Allied ground troops were larger and much better armed than the German forces and had much more support from the air. By September, the Allies had landed more than 2 million troops on the Continent and had suffered only half as many losses as the Germans had in the battle for control of Western Europe, and Allied troops had $2\frac{1}{2}$ times as many guns and 20 times as many tanks. Furthermore, Hitler was no longer able to find adequate replacements for the men that he lost. Thus, by fall, the Allies had liberated France and Belgium, and on October 21, they captured their first important German town, Aachen.

Germany was also forced to retreat in other places. In September, Roosevelt decided that there would be no additional diversions of troops away from Italy, and thereafter the forces that remained there made slow but steady advances, moving north beyond Rome. Hitler also faced guerrilla warfare in Yugoslavia and was forced to pull his troops out of Greece. And Russian armies continued to advance from the east, capturing Romania, Bulgaria, and much of Hungary and Poland before winter.

By the fall of 1944, the United States had become a global power. Once weak, the nation had become very strong. It had contributed significantly to the defeat of Italy and was now making major contributions to successful offensives against once-powerful nations on two sides of the globe.

SUGGESTIONS FOR ADDITIONAL READING

Most of the items cited in Chapter 17 remain useful for this chapter. I find the books by Buchanan, Burns, Ambrose, Kolko, and Gaddis especially helpful in efforts to think about the major developments considered here.

Chapter 21

Politics in Wartime

The fall of 1944 was a time of approaching victory in the war, and it was also election time. Much to the credit of the American people, they held a major and closely contested election in the midst of the war. The contest continued the power of Roosevelt and his party, but it did not enlarge the President's power significantly or increase the likelihood that all his hopes would be fulfilled. The contest also ratified the selection of his successor that had been made by the Democratic party several months earlier. Roosevelt's health was in decline, and thus the selection of the Democratic candidate for the vice-presidency was one of the most significant features of American politics in 1944.

Roosevelt made his decision to run for a fourth term without much debate within the administration or the Democratic party. There was concern about the President's health, but the decision was dictated by the wartime situation. Roosevelt easily persuaded himself that the pressing problems involved in completing the march toward victory, building the peace, and solving domestic problems demanded that he run again; his

245

admirers had no doubts about this, and the polls suggested that he was the only Democrat who could win. Thus, on July 11, he announced his willingness to run.

By 1944, Roosevelt's hopes included a hope for action at home. He was now giving more attention to domestic affairs than he had for several years. He was, of course, still devoting most of his attention to the task of winning the war, and he was also paying some heed to the shape of the postwar world and making plans for the establishment of an international organization. In addition, however, he was also developing plans for the revival of the New Deal.

Roosevelt had expressed his domestic hopes in his State of the Union message in January 1944. In it, he came out for an economic bill of rights. "We have come to a clear realization of the fact that true individual freedom cannot exist without economic security and independence," the President observed. " 'Necessitous men are not free men.' People who are hungry and out of a job are the stuff of which dictatorships are made." This expressed his old assumption about the conservative function of reform, given new meaning by the international crisis. Paraphrasing an old document, he declared that "these economic truths have become accepted as self-evident" and the nation, or at least the administration, had accepted "a second Bill of Rights under which a new basis of security and prosperity can be established for all—regardless of station, race, or creed." Challenging his conservative foes, he insisted that "after this war is won we must be prepared to move forward, in the implementation of these rights, to new goals of human happiness and well-being."

Within the next few months, however, Roosevelt received fresh evidence of strong resistance to social and economic change from members of his own party. The resistance manifested itself in opposition to the renomination of Henry A. Wallace. Since 1940, the Vice President had established himself as one of the nation's leading liberals, and he had strong support for renomination from liberals, minority groups, and labor, including the CIO's new Political Action Committee. Also, most Democratic voters, according to the polls, regarded him as the best of the possible candidates. Most of the powerful and active men in the party, however, opposed him. His opponents included city bosses such as Ed Kelly of Chicago and Ed Flynn of New York, congressional leaders like Sam Rayburn of Texas and John McCormack of Massachusetts, top men in the Democratic National Committee, including Frank Walker of Pennsylvania, and governors, topped by Robert Kerr of Oklahoma. Concerned about Roosevelt's health and Wallace's ideas, they had an unusually strong interest in the selection of the vice-presidential candidate. Some were unhappy about the way that Roosevelt had forced them to accept Wallace in 1940, and all believed that a similar effort in 1944 would produce a fight that would seriously damage the party and might lead to its defeat. Despite the polls, they believed that Wallace would weaken the ticket and that several other possibilities would strengthen it. Wallace was identified with one faction only, the New Dealers, and they had no alternative to support for Roosevelt. Faced with a sharply divided party, these leaders wanted a candidate with some appeal to all factions.

Some of Wallace's critics regarded Senator Harry S. Truman of Missouri as a good alternative. A supporter of the administration, he had gained fame as chairman of his special investigating committee. And he was also a politician who had good relations with the three major parts of the party, the Southern wing, the city machine faction, and the New Dealers.

The leading role in the movement to substitute Truman for Wallace was played by a St. Louis politician, Robert Hannegan. A representative of the urban machine faction, Hannegan had supported Truman in Missouri politics and was, by 1944, the chairman of the Democratic National Committee. He and his top lieutenant, Edwin W. Pauley, a California oil man and the treasurer of the national committee, quickly pushed Truman to the forefront of party affairs in hopes of strengthening the party and developing a replacement for Wallace. They recognized Truman's new prestige and called upon him to address many Democratic meetings during the first half of 1944. At the same time, these party officials tried to keep Wallace away from such meetings. Sharing the concern about Roosevelt's health, Hannegan and Pauley regarded Wallace as unsafe and radical and likely to drive voters away from the party, and they looked upon Truman as an attractive personality. He thought and behaved in ways that seemed sensible to them.

For months before the convention, Roosevelt was subjected to a barrage of criticism of his Vice President with Hannegan and his close associates mobilizing the troops and firing much of the ammunition. They urged local party leaders to suggest to Roosevelt that the ticket would suffer seriously from Wallace's presence on it, and they personally advised him of the widespread opposition to Wallace. They also advised FDR that Truman was the best of the possible alternatives and campaigned openly for him, stressing his new prestige, his loyalty to the New Deal, his acceptability to conservative Democrats, his political shrewdness, and the importance of his border-state background.

The Hannegan group received significant help. Local Democratic leaders warned Roosevelt against Wallace, and important figures in the administration, including Ickes, Forrestal, Hull, and Rosenman, were impressed with the evidence of hostility to Wallace, had doubts about his ability to serve as president, feared that his nomination would split the party and lead to Roosevelt's defeat, and communicated their concerns to FDR. And Sidney Hillman told him that if it became obvious that Wallace could not be nominated, he would do his best to see that the CIO and its friends did not oppose the Missouri senator.

Hannegan and others also worked against other alternatives to Wallace, including Truman's own choice, James F. Byrnes. Byrnes had been a senator and a justice of the United States Supreme Court, and he was now the head of the Office of War Mobilization and widely regarded as the "Assistant President." Entering the race at a late stage, after receiving some encouragement from Roosevelt, Byrnes eagerly sought the nomination and persuaded Truman to help him get it. The Missourian, however, discovered that the man from South Carolina was opposed by organized labor. In discussing the possibilities with Roosevelt, Hannegan and others argued that Byrnes, as a Southerner, a man who had left the Catholic Church, and an official who had taken stands that organized labor did not like, would be opposed by black voters, Catholics, and the unions and thus would hurt the Democrats in the Northern cities. And Hillman told the President that organized labor and blacks opposed Byrnes and that Truman would be a better choice.

All this talk convinced Roosevelt that he should choose the Missourian as his running mate. This was so in spite of the fact that Wallace was the President's personal preference. He had been persuaded that Wallace would hurt the ticket and could not be forced upon the party as he had been four years earlier, and Roosevelt feared and did not have the time or energy to engage in a bitter party battle. Thus, he did no more for Wallace than write a letter to the Democratic national convention saying that if he were a delegate, he would vote for the man from Iowa. FDR wanted a candidate who supported his policies, would not hurt the ticket, and could help him persuade the Senate that the United States should join an international organization, and, although he did not know Truman well, he had come to admire him and to believe that he was popular, especially in the Senate. Roosevelt was not willing to fight for Truman, however, and thus he merely wrote a second letter that pulled the Missourian out of the crowd of potential substitutes by stating that he would be "very glad" to run with either Truman or Justice Douglas and that either "would bring real strength" to the ticket. Finally, Roosevelt persuaded a reluctant Truman to become a candidate, appealing to his sense of party loyalty.

Truman still faced strong opposition. Wallace arrived at the convention in Chicago with more delegates committed to him than to all his competitors combined, and he had the active and militant support of many prominent liberals and of the CIO. At the end of the first ballot, he was far ahead.

Truman's backers, however, were hard at work. He had the active support of many Missouri politicians and of the American Federation of Labor, but the biggest push for him on the convention floor and in the adjoining lobbies came from representatives of the party's urban machine wing, especially Hannegan. He presented himself as the spokesman for the President, argued that Roosevelt preferred Truman, and worked to persuade delegates to switch to him on the second ballot.

Truman's supporters scored their biggest victories in the South. A few Southerners endorsed him at the beginning of the voting; many did so at the end. They had come to the convention determined to defeat Wallace, for they feared him and his supporters, above all the CIO, regarding them as hostile to Southern traditions and beliefs, especially on the race question. Before the balloting began, a delegation of Southerners led by Senator John H. Bankhead of Alabama had called upon Truman to warn him that the South would bolt if Wallace were nominated and to urge Truman to run; at the same time, Byrnes, recognizing that he was not the President's choice and would have little support outside the South, withdrew from the race and told the chairman of the South Carolina delegation that he hoped his friends would vote for Truman rather than Wallace; and after the first ballot, Senator Burnet Maybank of South Carolina explained: "We're going to anybody who can beat Wallace. We may support Truman on the next ballot." As Southerners concluded that no one from their region could get the nomination, they switched their support to the Missourian. Switching took place rapidly as the second ballot proceeded, and by the end, Truman had 1,031 votes while Wallace had only 105.

Truman was the candidate of the old Democracy—the party of the South and the Northern city machines. Yet, he was acceptable to leading New Deal Democrats as well. Wallace announced that he believed Truman would carry on the battle for liberalism, and other New Dealers agreed. "We were for Wallace, but if we hadn't been for him we would have been for Truman," Hillman had announced as he and the CIO swung their weight behind Truman. "We were for Wallace always, but not *against Truman*," the labor leader informed a newsman. The Missourian, Hillman announced, was "eminently qualified" and would make "a splendid running mate for the President." This attitude was particularly significant, for Roosevelt did not want a running mate who was opposed by organized labor. Had Hillman rated Truman with Byrnes, it seems unlikely that Truman would have received the nomination.

Truman had won because he conformed to the demands of the situation within the Democratic party as they were interpreted by influential party leaders. A militant liberal, Wallace had been acceptable to only one faction. The others distrusted and feared him. Much more flexible, Truman had been acceptable to all three and seemed much more capable of uniting the warring factions and preventing the party from falling apart. The biggest push for his nomination had come from the urban machine faction, but the Southerners and the New Dealers, while preferring other men, had regarded him as preferable to the candidates of their rivals.

The Republican party, although it too was divided into factions, did not have such a hot contest raging within it by convention time. The party's leading liberal and internationalist, Wendell Willkie, had failed in his efforts to reorient the Republican party. He had become more critical of the isolationists and conservatives there than he was of the administration, and he had tried to get the party to endorse him and his stand on domestic and international affairs. Yet, he had antagonized rather than persuaded most of the party leaders, and the voters in the Wisconsin primary had dashed his hopes in April. There, he had suffered a shocking defeat, running far behind Governor Thomas E. Dewey of New York. Dewey's victory, which came without a personal campaign, destroyed Willkie's chances for renomination and caused him to withdraw from the race.

The party's right wing had favored General MacArthur. A critic of the New Deal as well as the Europe-first strategy and an advocate of reliance upon military power rather than an international organization, he had been hurt by publicity given his ideas and had announced that he was not a candidate for the presidency, did not "covet" it, and would not accept it.

Thus, the GOP moved rather easily to the nomination of Governor Dewey. He was young for a presidential candidate; he had been born in Michigan in 1902, the son of a newspaperman, and educated at the University of Michigan and Columbia Law School. He had become famous as a "racket buster" in the 1930s and was elected district attorney in New York City in 1937. Failing in bids for the governorship in 1938 and the Republican nomination for the presidency two years later, he won the New York gubernatorial election in 1942 and began to establish a record of efficiency, economy, and moderate liberalism. His moderate stand on national issues placed him in a middle-ground position within his party between Willkie and the conservatives. While Willkie stood for party reorientation, Dewey was a champion of party unity, and his party nominated him on the first ballot with only one vote cast against him.

In spite of his moderation, Dewey waged a hard-hitting, at times angry campaign, and other Republicans also were not restrained by the wartime situation. The campaigners focused much of their attention on Hillman and the CIO, charging that they had a very large influence on the administration and that they were moving it in radical directions. And this was related to the very large use that Republicans, with help from the House Un-American Activities Committee, made of the Communist issue. The Communists, including their leader, Earl Browder, had, according to this theme, infiltrated the Democratic party and the Roosevelt administration.

A widely circulated anti-Truman story was used to sustain these campaign themes. Some critics charged that Hillman was responsible for Truman's nomination and built upon and circulated a story that Roosevelt had ordered Hannegan to clear the nomination with the labor leader. The story, first reported by Arthur Krock in the *New York Times*, was converted into the charge that the chairman had been ordered to "clear everything with Sidney," and Hannegan felt compelled to brand the charge "an unmitigated lie."

Republican campaigners dealt chiefly with domestic matters. They played down international affairs after affirming their own conviction that the United States should become a member of an international organization after the war and focused their attention on defects in the domestic operations of the Roosevelt administration and on their own plans in this area. Dewey promised to maintain New Deal programs but to administer them—and all government programs—more efficiently and in ways that would not harm private enterprise. "The New Deal really believes that we cannot have good social legislation and also good jobs for all," he maintained. "I believe with all my heart and soul that we can have both." He would continue and improve security regulation, bank deposit insurance, price supports for agriculture, unemployment insurance, and old-age pensions, respect the rights of labor to organize and bargain collectively, and develop relief programs when needed. "But," he insisted, "we must also have a Government which believes in enterprise and Government policies which encourage enterprise," and he would "see to it that the man who wants to produce more jobs is not throttled by the Government—but knows that he has a Government as eager for him to succeed as he is himself."

The Democratic campaign was also vigorous and involved a larger role for Roosevelt than had been planned. Spurred on by the attacks upon him, he participated dramatically and effectively, even in the rain, in part to answer charges about his health by demonstrating that he remained a strong man. He also sought to take advantage of his prestige as Commander in Chief. He and others who helped him stressed the success of the war effort, portrayed the Republicans as foes of the New Deal and of internationalism, and promised to enlarge the New Deal and provide full employment after the war and to establish and join an international organization. They also challenged Republican charges concerning Communist influences.

Roosevelt received even more help from organized labor than he had earlier. Much of this came from the CIO's Political Action Committee, which had been established in 1943 because of fears of growing antilabor sentiment and recognition of the great potential of the labor vote and the great importance of the government for labor. Since its formation, the PAC had been working to educate the wage earners on political issues, enlarge labor's political activities, and increase the funds available for its political campaigns, and now the organization contributed well over $1 million to the Democratic campaign fund, stressed economic issues in the election and the importance of a large labor turnout, and worked to bring out the working-class vote, cooperating closely with the Democratic party in the urban industrial areas.

A vigorous sixty-year-old man, Truman was strong enough to carry much of the burden of the campaign. He visited much of the country in an effort to, as he defined it, "help bring the war to a close as quickly as possible by keeping the Democratic party in power." He spoke of the great value of the New Deal to many groups and of the need to expand it and warned of the dangers to it from the Republican party, and he maintained that the foreign policy issue was even more important. Warning against isolationists, he charged that they were still alive and very important in the Republican party and insisted that the country must not repeat the mistakes of 1919–1920. And he emphasized the importance of Roosevelt's reelection, arguing that the President had supplied very successful leadership during the Depression and the war and that the nation needed his experience and wisdom for the tasks that lay ahead at home and abroad.

Truman became one of the campaign issues. To his critics, the evidence against him demonstrated that a Democratic victory would endanger the nation. Raising questions about Roosevelt's health, they suggested that FDR might die in office or resign and Truman would succeed him. "The appalling fact is that Senator Truman, the weak, machine ridden political hack who bargained with thieves for public advancement, may become President of the United States," the *Chicago Tribune* warned. ". . . A vote for Roosevelt is very likely to be a vote for Truman for President." Thus, critics raised doubts about Truman's ability to provide leadership if need arose. One Republican congressman charged that Truman had been dominated by Kansas City's political boss, Tom Pendergast, and would be dominated by "the corrupt machine bosses and the Hillman-Browder gang . . . ," and the Republican National Committee warned that there was "an enormous risk in a fourth term for a palpably tired man in the White House and in the prospect of the elevation to the presidency of Senator Truman, a professional hack weaned in the Pendergast nursery . . ." In response to such criticism,

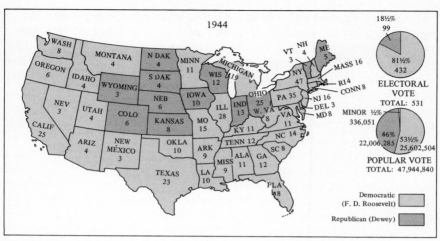

Figure 23 Election Results—1944 (*National Atlas, U.S. Geological Survey, Washington, 1970. Used by permission.*)

Truman reminded the press that he had been nominated by the Senate press gallery as the civilian who knew more about the war effort than anyone except the President.

As Truman expected, he did not drag the ticket to defeat. The voters chose Roosevelt for a fourth term, but they did so by a narrower margin than he had received in the three preceding contests. He received 53.4 percent of the popular vote as compared with 45.9 percent for Dewey and won by a margin of 3,600,000—25,613,000 to 22,018,000. This was the closest presidential election since 1916!

Roosevelt was even more dependent on the urban vote than he had been earlier. He would have lost if he had not received the very strong support of the urban workers for the Democratic vote outside the big cities, which had been dropping for several years, especially in the rural Middle West and Far West, and dropped still farther, except in the South, which remained solidly Democratic. Workers in the war plants voted in larger numbers than they had in 1942, but the war continued to have a negative impact on turnout, in part because Congress had rejected Roosevelt's plan to increase voting opportunities for men and women in the armed forces. Whereas nearly 50 million voters had gone to the polls in 1940, fewer than 48 million did so in 1944. Had the PAC not made its very large effort to counteract the pressures against voting, which were especially strong in Northern industrial states, Roosevelt could have failed to maintain his power.

The election strengthened Roosevelt's position in Congress but only slightly. The Democratic contingent in the House was increased from 218 to 242 while the Republicans dropped from 208 to 190, and the Democrats maintained their control of the Senate, although declining from 58 to 56. Most important, many important isolationists were defeated, including Senator Nye and Congressman Fish. Thus, Roosevelt's chances of Senate acceptance of American membership in an international organization seemed stronger. Chances of success in his efforts to revive the New Deal, however, did not seem very great, for the election had not weakened the conservative coalition in Congress.

Roosevelt had maintained his position at the top of American politics, but he had not enlarged his power substantially. Perhaps he had not accomplished as much as he deserved, given his accomplishments in the war by November 1944. His leadership had not been devoid of success. He could now continue to supply leadership, but he had to move with awareness that his power was limited and that he could not hope to accomplish all that he outlined. And he now knew that his personal physical strength was not as great as it had been in his earlier years as president. What he could not know was just how soon that strength would be gone and the presidential power that he now had would be passed on to the man who had now moved into his circle as vice president.

SUGGESTIONS FOR ADDITIONAL READING

Leon Friedman supplies a valuable survey of the "Election of 1944" in Schlesinger and Israel, *History of American Presidential Elections*. Polenberg also surveys the subject in *War and Society*. The books by Johnson on Willkie and Tugwell and Burns on Roosevelt contain important discussions of the election.

My discussion of Truman draws heavily on my own, largely unpublished research on his career. I have attempted brief discussion of him in "Truman and the Pendergast Machine: A Comment," *Midcontinent American Studies Journal*, vol. 7, pp. 36–39, 1966; "Truman's Path to Power," *Social Science*, vol. 43, pp. 67–73, 1968; and "Harry Truman," in Morton Borden, ed., *America's Eleven Greatest Presidents*, Rand McNally, Chicago, 1971. He published his own *Memoirs*, 2 vols., Doubleday, Garden City, N.Y., 1955–1956, and one of his associates, Jonathan Daniels, wrote an early but still valuable biography, *The Man of Independence*, Lippincott, Philadelphia, 1950.

Much of the evidence on the election is scattered about in memoirs and biographies. Some of the most valuable are Matthew Josephson, *Sidney Hillman: Statesman of American Labor*, Doubleday, Garden City, N. Y., 1952; Samuel E. Rosenman, *Working with Roosevelt*, Harper, New York, 1952; James F. Byrnes, *All in One Lifetime*, Harper, New York, 1958; and John M. Blum, *From the Morgenthau Diaries: Years of War 1941–1945*, Houghton Mifflin, Boston, 1967.

Chapter 22

Building
the Postwar World

Roosevelt had maintained his power in the United States, and now he turned much of his attention to the construction of the postwar world. He still had a war to win; its demands continued to influence his behavior, but its outcome seemed certain, and thus the shape of the world after the war now demanded much of his time and energy. Little of either remained, however, and he would leave major tasks behind when death came in April 1945.

By late 1944, Axis forces could do little more than delay their inevitable defeat. The weather and inadequate supplies of ammunition and riflemen slowed the British-American offensive. The supply problems resulted from the American failure to train enough infantrymen and from the Allied failure to gain control of and begin to use the major port of Antwerp until very late in the year, and the problems encouraged Eisenhower to advise American business and labor that the war was not over and that war production must be maintained. At the same time, Germany strengthened her defensive position on her western boundary, and Hitler decided upon a counteroffensive, overruling his skeptical generals and weakening his forces battling Russia. His move surprised Allied military leaders and created a "bulge" in their line in Luxembourg and Belgium.

Although a serious reversal seemed possible, the Battle of the Bulge only delayed the Allied victory. The battle seriously weakened German forces, and Germany could no longer replace her losses. Thus, the Allies resumed their offensive early in 1945; British, American, and other forces moved into Germany from the west, and Russia gained control of Poland and pushed into Germany and Austria. At the same time, the bombers continued to strike the German oil industry and made major attacks on large German cities, seeking to influence the civilian population and to damage communication facilities. The planes encountered little resistance, inflicted heavy civilian losses, severely damaged the oil industry, and hampered the movements of German troops.

The United States also moved forward on the other side of the globe. By the end of 1944, bombers based in the Marianas were hitting Japan daily, and from November through February, they focused their attention on industries closely connected with the war, especially the aircraft industry. During the same period, MacArthur's forces pushed north toward Manila, and they captured it on February 24. The victory gave the Allies virtually complete control of the Pacific.

The advances against Japan improved the situation in China slightly. Many State Department officials had become very critical of Chiang's government, but Roosevelt continued to funnel American aid to China through Chiang. The administration did try in late 1944 and early 1945 to promote political and military cooperation between Chiang and the Chinese Communists, but the effort failed. General Albert C. Wedemeyer, who had replaced Stilwell, continued to pressure Chiang to reform his army, but though Wedemeyer had better relations with the Generalissimo than Stilwell had, the new military adviser's reform efforts were no more successful than his predecessor's had been. Fortunately, however, the task facing Chiang's army was being reduced by American victories elsewhere, for they forced Japan to shift some of her troops out of China.

Thus, Roosevelt and his aides continued to move toward military victory. They were not, however, simple-minded men who had that as their only aim. They were convinced that major mistakes had been made after World War I that had caused the suffering of World War II, and they were determined to avoid similar mistakes now and in the immediate future. They had a broad vision of the postwar world; they hoped to reshape the world and make it a place in which Americans could enjoy peace and prosperity.

Roosevelt had given some thought to the shape of the postwar world even before the United States entered the war. In their first conference in August 1941, Roosevelt and Churchill had drafted the Atlantic Charter. It envisioned a world of self-governing peoples enjoying economic prosperity and social security through trade and economic collaboration and free of the fear of war. The nations "which threaten, or may threaten, aggression outside of their frontiers" would be disarmed, the "crushing burden of armaments" would be lightened for "peace-loving peoples," and a "wider and permanent system of general security" would be established.

After the United States joined in the fighting, this vision influenced the conduct of the war itself. At Casablanca in January, 1943, Roosevelt announced a policy of "unconditional surrender." Its long-run aim was the prevention of future wars. That was to be accomplished by destruction of the "war makers." The policy meant that the war would go on until total defeat of the enemies had been achieved. There would be no compromises with them. Instead, their political regimes, their empires, and their military forces would be destroyed, and the new political systems in those countries would be shaped with care. The United States had been drawn into the war by the efforts of Germany, Italy, and Japan to create giant empires, but the U.S. used the war to accomplish more than military victory and containment. It worked for a total victory that would transform the enemy nations in fundamental ways. In its extreme form, the American scheme involved a plan to destroy German industry and make Germany into an agricultural nation once again. Such a plan was developed by Henry Morgenthau's Treasury Department and endorsed by Churchill at a conference in Quebec in September 1944. The Allies retreated from this extreme position but maintained their determination to achieve unconditional surrender.

The vision that influenced American leaders assumed that the American people would discard isolationism and participate actively in international affairs. The vision also emphasized the principle of national self-determination, the removal of barriers to the flow of trade and investment among nations, and the establishment of new international institutions.

Both political and economic considerations affected American thinking. Efforts to reduce economic barriers reflected both. Recognizing the great increase in American production during the war, many administration leaders assumed that after it was over, the nation must find large markets for goods and capital and obtain raw materials. Without large economic opportunities abroad, America would return to the depressed conditions of the 1930s once war no longer consumed the output of the

American economy, and depression would generate class conflict and nationalistic and socialistic schemes for economic recovery. Furthermore, nations would fight for markets and materials if they did not have free access to them. Peace, prosperity, and freedom depended on the development of liberal international economic policies—the Open Door—throughout the world. Washington brushed aside suggestions that the United States was now so strong economically that in an open world no other nation could compete successfully with America and that underdeveloped areas needed protective devices in order to industrialize and thereby gain freedom from the already industrialized nations.

Western imperialism conflicted with the American vision, and the conflict generated tension within the British-American alliance. The Japanese exploited this and the discontent with Western rule in Asia. As they had advanced, they had portrayed themselves as liberators, freeing Asians and others from white domination. Displacing Western rulers, they had promised independence for colonial people.

Roosevelt was quite sensitive to the imperialism issue. The practices of his allies seemed to him to conflict with American principles, and he pointed with pride to the American treatment of the Philippines, suggesting that it provided a model that others should follow. They should promise independence for their colonies as the United States had promised independence for the Philippine Islands. He believed that the discontent in India would grow and spread and that imperialism would lead to new wars, and he criticized French rule in Indochina.

Churchill, however, resisted Roosevelt's pressure. Although extravagantly admired as a "realist," the British Prime Minister did not understand or sympathize with the forces that were at work in the colonial world and was determined to preserve the British Empire. "I have not become the King's First Minister to preside over the liquidation of the British Empire," he had announced in 1942.

Washington regarded one feature of the British Empire as especially distasteful. This was the imperial preference system that discriminated against efforts by countries outside the empire to trade inside of it. This seemed harmful to the United States, and American officials pressured the British to abolish the system.

There was tension within the Western alliance on the imperialism issue, but Churchill exerted a restraining influence on Roosevelt's anti-imperialism. Chiang and others urged the President to provide strong leadership on the issue, but he was reluctant to press very hard. He was interested in cooperation with the British in the war effort. Winning the war was his biggest interest, and he recognized that he must have allies to accomplish that purpose.

Roosevelt was a cautious anti-imperalist in another way. Unlike some American critics of imperialism, he called for a transition stage, rather than immediate independence. Again, American treatment of the Philippines provided a model. In 1943, he proposed international trusteeships for Indochina, Korea, and other dependent areas, rather than either restoration of colonial rule or immediate independence.

By 1945, Roosevelt remained interested in ending Western imperialism, but he continued to be restrained by other considerations. He favored a temporary trusteeship for Indochina, administered by the United States, Great Britain, China, and Russia, but, while Stalin and Chiang endorsed the idea, Churchill opposed it. Roosevelt criticized the British Prime Minister on this point but did not press it, and he was also unwilling to press De Gaulle, who advocated the restoration of French rule. The desire for British-American cooperation continued to exert a restraining influence.

Thus, Roosevelt had anti-imperial ideas, but he did not know how to implement them and was not willing to crusade for them. All he could do was reaffirm that the Philippine Islands would be independent as soon as Japan was driven out. He hoped that this would set an example for the other colonial powers, including Great Britain. He could carry out this plan, for American forces were gaining control of the Philippines. In Indochina and India, on the other hand, the American military role was very small. He could only hope that after the war he would be able to push his ideas for those parts of the world.

By 1945, the administration's chief hope for the creation of a world that made sense from an American point of view lay in the establishment of an international organization. Roosevelt himself had moved slowly toward open endorsement of American membership in such an institution. He had been influenced by his reluctance to think in long-run terms, his emphasis upon the pressing problems that surrounded him, and his fears of congressional insolationism. He did not want to endure a Wilsonian defeat. More important, perhaps, was his disillusionment with the League of Nations. To him, it had demonstrated its ineffectiveness. Thus, early in the war, he had concluded that peace in the postwar period would depend upon police action by the big powers. At first, he had thought that the United States and Great Britain would do the job, but in 1942, he had come to think in terms of "Four Policemen." The United States, Great Britain, Russia, and China would have a monopoly on military power; all other nations would be disarmed, and the four nations would use military and economic force quickly in crisis situations.

Pressures inside the United States forced Roosevelt to modify his ideas. Much of the pressure came from outside the administration as groups and individuals began to demand an international organization, public opinion came to favor it by a wide margin, and Congress in the fall of 1943 passed resolutions calling for the establishment of an American membership in such an institution. Inside the administration, the pressure came chiefly from the State Department. As a consequence of the many demands, Roosevelt encouraged State to work on plans for a postwar organization.

The movement for an international organization made progress in late 1943. The foreign ministers of the four leading nations in the anti-Axis alliance met in Moscow in October 1943 and, while refusing to endorse Hull's proposals for freer trade and trusteeships as substitutes for imperialism, the foreign ministers did endorse the American proposal for the establishment of an international organization. A latter-day Wilsonian who viewed such an organization as an extension of American principles to the international scene, a substitute for old-fashioned power politics, and the only way to avoid future wars, Hull was delighted with his accomplishment. As he explained: "There will no longer be need for spheres of influence, for alliances, for balance of power, or any other of the special arrangements through which, in the unhappy past, the nations strove to safeguard their security or to promote their interests." The old approach had not worked and could not work, he assumed.

Progress continued during the following year. By May, the State Department had developed specific plans that involved broad membership in the organization but great power for the leading nations. While most nations would participate, the leading nations would be able to veto proposals for action. During the summer, the Allies met at Bretton Woods, New Hampshire and agreed to establish international economic institutions that would liberalize trade relations, stabilize foreign exchange rates, promote economic reconstruction, and provide relief, and at the same time, representatives of the Big Four meeting at Dumbarton Oaks, an estate in Washington, endorsed most of the State Department's plans, although the United States and Russia disagreed about the scope of the veto power. Russia insisted that it should be absolute, but the United States maintained that the veto should not be used by a party to a dispute.

By now, Roosevelt was committed to the idea of an international organization. He believed, however, that it should be dominated by the Big Four, and he placed heavy emphasis on the importance of Russian-American cooperation. He had moved away from the idea of the Four Policemen, but the veto power would guarantee big-power domination of the organization. And he also held on to his belief that the United States would need military power after the war. Some internationalists criticized his ideas about the role of the big powers.

Roosevelt and State Department officials worked with leading Republicans on the issue, hoping to keep it out of partisan politics. Both parties in their 1944 platforms did endorse proposals for the establishment of and American membership in an international organization, and these ideas were championed not only by long-time internationalists like Wendell Willkie but also by former isolationists, most notably Senator Arthur Vandenberg, a Michigan Republican on the Senate Foreign Affairs Committee.

The administration's plans for the postwar world also included the frustration of the anticapitalist left in the war-torn areas. The hardships of war, the brutality of German and Japanese occupation forces, and the failures of the old order, such as Chiang's regime in China and the French in Indochina, stimulated the growth of the left, and American as well as British officials worried about this development. Left-wing regimes in Europe or Asia seemed certain to seize American property and to close regions to American trade and investment. They also seemed likely to be dominated by the Soviet Union. Americans tended to blame Russians as well as depressed conditions for the threat of revolution. They envisioned Communist parties receiving help from Moscow and exploiting problems such as food shortages and unemployment in their drives toward victory. The United States and Great Britain hoped to contain revolution.

The movement of American troops helped the United States accomplish this objective. As they moved against the enemies and occupied conquered territories, they accomplished more than the destruction of existing regimes. American armies also influenced the development of the new regimes and, in doing so, frustrated the revolutionaries. American officials, backed by military strength, regulated the political activities of radicals, disarming them, giving them rations and jobs, jailing those who refused to cooperate, and controlling their use of the news media, and these officials also helped other politicians, in part by helping them deal with the severe economic problems that they faced. "The chaos and collapse which may result in these countries from starvation, unemployment and inflation can be averted principally by making available essential civilian supplies," the State Department believed. "Political stability and the maintenance of democratic governments which can withstand the pressures of extremist groups depend on the restoration of a minimum of economic stability."

In most of the European countries in which American and British forces were victorious, the left behaved in a nonviolent fashion. They attempted only to win victories at the polls and recognized that the American Army could crush a revolution. And Russia encouraged this tendency to behave cautiously.

The movement of American troops was, in other words, making the United States a major influence in the most productive parts of Europe. Roosevelt had not planned that his troops would remain abroad for a long period after the war. He believed that the American people would not tolerate that, and he personally opposed it. In a crucial period, however, American troops were influencing political developments in important areas.

There were, however, limits on American power in Europe. Although it had played a major role in the liberation of France, it was not able to give French politics the precise shape that American leaders desired. Following the fall of Paris, Charles De Gaulle became the leading figure in French politics in spite of American opposition to him.

Since moving into the French sphere with the invasion of North Africa, the United States had attempted to shape French political development. Fearful that the left would triumph in French politics, American leaders had been hostile to De Gaulle, regarding him as a "man on horseback" type and as a politician who was too friendly to the left. Thus, they had looked for an alternative to him and had tried to work with Vichy France and its representatives, such as Admiral Darlan.

Two factors worked against the American efforts. One was the unattractiveness of the alternatives to De Gaulle. The other was the support for him by the British. They hated Vichy because of its collaboration with Hitler and saw De Gaulle as his leading French opponent and the best hope of realizing the British aim of a strong France to counterbalance a strong Russia.

Thus, in spite of the opposition of Roosevelt and other Americans, De Gaulle established himself in power in France following liberation. In October, the United States and Russia, as well as Great Britain, recognized him. The United States was not the dominant influence in French politics even though American forces had helped to free France from German control.

The American presence in France did help to frustrate the left. This was so even though the United States had felt compelled to supply arms to the French resistance. Although dominated by the left, it was the only anti-German force in German-occupied France. Once the Germans were driven out, however, the left, including the Communist party, did not move into power in France.

The limits on American power were even more important in Eastern Europe. There, Russian, not American, forces displaced the Germans. By February 1945, Russia was dominant in Poland, Romania, Bulgaria, Hungary, and Czechoslovakia and was reaching into Germany and Austria.

The Soviet Union hoped to establish "friendly" governments in the countries that separated her from the West. Considerations of national security, not a desire to communize the globe, dominated her behavior. Often in the past, armies from the West had moved across weak and anti-Russian countries on their way to Russia, and now the war against Germany was costing her the lives of millions of her citizens and fighting men. The German-Russian war was an unusually large and brutal affair that included such horrible events as the siege of Leningrad from October 1941 to January 1944 in which about 1,500,000 Russians died. Russia hoped to guarantee that Eastern Europe would no longer serve as a corridor for aggressors; she was determined to prevent the development of an anti-Soviet bloc there, and she feared that the British were especially eager to develop such a bloc. Thus, with armed force available for the task, she guided the evolution of most of Eastern Europe.

The British were eager to limit Russian expansion. They had long been interested in Poland and had gone to war when that country had been attacked. Their security seemed linked with Poland's fate, and they felt a need for a Poland that could help contain Russia. And the British had additional interests in Southeastern Europe. After failing to gain acceptance for his ideas about the importance of the Italian campaign, Churchill turned to diplomacy and, in spite of American opposition to spheres of influence, worked out an agreement with Russia about spheres in Southeastern Europe that tolerated some Russian expansion into that region but gave the British a sphere there, including a predominant position in Greece. Then, after German troops were withdrawn from that Balkan country, Churchill sent British troops in, fearing that otherwise the Communists would come to power, and those troops helped the Greek monarchy regain power and suppressed the left. Russia, which was establishing a puppet regime in Poland at the same time, did not help the Greek Communists.

Roosevelt also tried to find ways to limit Russian expansion. Advisers in the State and War Departments encouraged him to do so. The American interest was largely ideological. Russian control of the region would conflict with the principle of national self-determination. It would constitute a major violation of the kind of world that the United States was trying to construct, would lead to other violations, and would generate opposition to American plans for the postwar world. This concern was reinforced by economic and political considerations, including a desire to trade and invest there and a need to satisfy the demands of Polish-Americans. A part of the Roosevelt coalition, they were very interested in what happened to Poland, and Democrats made promises to them in the 1944 elections.

Other factors restrained Roosevelt in his dealings with Russia over Eastern Europe. He wanted Russian cooperation in the war against Germany and Japan and in the development of the new international organization, and he certainly did not want to make a move that could lead to war between the United States and the Soviet Union. The principle of national self-determination, he assumed, could not be his dominant principle. Cooperation and avoidance of war with Russia seemed even more important. Thus, as Russia moved into the region in 1944 and began to establish control, FDR felt distressed but helpless.

In hopes of bringing reality into harmony with principle without using military force, Roosevelt pressed for an agreement that "free elections" would be held in Eastern Europe. This was part of a larger effort to rely upon words there. Roosevelt tried to persuade Stalin to be restrained and to rely upon means other than control of the region in his quest for security. And the American leader tried to persuade the Russian that democratically elected governments would be friendly to him. Stalin, however, was convinced that free elections would produce anti-Russian governments, and he would not tolerate such a development.

The issue of who was to rule Poland was sharply defined by the beginning of 1945. The British supported the claims of the Polish government in exile in London, which was dominated by the Church, the officer corps, and the large landowners and was anti-Communist and anti-Russian. The Russians, on the other hand, supported the claims of a group based in Lublin that was dominated by Communists. The defeat of Germany had enabled this group to come to power in Poland.

Some American officials believed that American economic power could be used to influence the situation in Poland and other parts of Eastern Europe. That power was greater now than ever before and was already demonstrating its political effectiveness in the Lend-Lease program. The American Ambassador in Moscow, W. Averell Harriman, among others, suggested that a firmer attitude toward Russia in the handling of Lend-Lease and even a reduction in aid to Russia could encourage Russia to change her ways. Roosevelt's hope for good relations with the Russians influenced his management of Lend-Lease to Russia, and he was reluctant to make changes in the program that could reduce Russia's military contribution, prolong the war, and increase the loss of American lives.

There was an alternative way in which American economic power could be employed. Some American officials and businessmen recognized that Russia faced a huge job of reconstruction while the United States faced the possibility of a postwar depression. In such a situation, American loans and credits to Russia could accomplish two very valuable objectives: a Russian market for American goods, especially industrial equipment, and a change in Russian behavior in Eastern Europe. Harriman stressed the political potential of a reconstruction loan. Washington, however, did not make a major effort to work out a loan agreement, in part because of congressional reluctance to spend money on reconstruction, and Russia, while interested in a loan, would not make concessions to get one. She had alternative ways of financing reconstruction. She could rely upon the exploitation of Eastern Europe and reparations from Germany. The Russians also felt that the United States would be forced by economic necessity—the need to avoid a depression—to sell her the goods she required. Thus, in early 1945, the administration merely held out the possibility of a loan, hoping that the prospect would have a desirable influence on Soviet behavior.

The British wished to use military pressure to influence Russian behavior. They advocated a quick thrust to key places, especially Berlin, with their top general, Montgomery, in command of the move. He and other British leaders, including Churchill, stressed military considerations, arguing that the operation would shorten the war, but they had other considerations in mind. British power was at stake. The British wanted to make a giant contribution to victory and to get themselves into a good position for bargaining with the Russians. Eisenhower, however, favored a steady advance all along the line, regarding it as the most effective way of using Allied power against Germany. It would inflict heavy losses, find and exploit German weaknesses, and reduce risks. Also, it would guarantee that American generals and forces contributed significantly to the final victory. And Eisenhower, backed as he was by Marshall and Roosevelt, was now the dominant figure in the development of strategy for the Western Allies.

Roosevelt preferred diplomacy to economic and military pressure on an ally, and he gained a large diplomatic opportunity in February when he met with Churchill and Stalin at Yalta in the Crimea. Poland was one of the focal points of controversy in this summit conference. For Roosevelt the dominant facts were Russian control of the region, the American need for Russian help against Japan, and the American desire for Russian cooperation in the establishment of an international organization.

The American President participated actively in the discussion of Poland's government. He and Churchill proposed the establishment of a new government composed of representatives of both the London and the Lublin groups. It would rule until elections were held. Stalin opposed this and would permit only a slight broadening of the ruling group. Roosevelt then provided an acceptable formula that called for the reorganization of the government by the addition of Poles from outside the country to those

Figure 24   The Yalta Conference (*Wide World Photos*)

now in power and for "free and unfettered elections as soon as possible on the basis of universal suffrage and secret ballot" and with all "democratic and anti-Nazi parties" free to participate. This agreement was supplemented by a "Declaration on Liberated Europe" in which the Allies promised to help the liberated people "solve by democratic means their pressing political and economic problems."

To influence political developments in Eastern Europe, Roosevelt had worked for and gained acceptance of the principle of national self-determination, but he had not found an effective way of combating the influence of powerful Russian armies. A proposal for international supervision of elections was rejected. The President recognized the weaknesses of the solution he had developed, but he felt it was the best he could get, given the situation.

Roosevelt had other interests to serve at Yalta. He was interested in Germany. Here, the Allies agreed that the Nazi regime and its military power would be destroyed. They also agreed on zones of occupation and on the principles that would govern reparations.

Roosevelt was also interested in reaching an agreement with Russia about her participation in the war against Japan. His military advisers believed that a long war against Japan lay ahead and that an invasion of the country would be required to produce surrender. They recognized the serious weakness of the Chinese forces led by Chiang, worried about the large Japanese army in China and Manchuria, did not want to support the Chinese Communists, and did not want to send a large American army into Asia. Thus, they urged the President to draw the Russians into the war against Japan on the mainland in hopes of shortening the war and saving American lives, and Roosevelt now persuaded the Russians to reaffirm an agreement made earlier that they would enter the war against Japan and do so in strength after the defeat of Germany and before the American invasion. The Russians also agreed to cooperate with Chiang. In return, they would receive territorial concessions at the expense of both China and Japan. The agreement violated the principle of national self-determination and was dictated by desires to shorten the war and save American lives.

Roosevelt's biggest interest at Yalta was the international organization. The Allies had already agreed that it would be established, but disagreements had developed over some of the details, including the scope of the veto power. The conferees now agreed that all conflicts could be discussed but the big powers could use the veto if economic or military action were proposed.

Although Roosevelt had been forced to recognize limits on his power, he had a great sense of accomplishment. "The Crimean Conference was a successful effort by the three leading nations to find a common ground for peace," he informed Congress and the nation on March 1. It "ought to spell the end of the system of unilateral action and exclusive alliances and spheres of influence and balances of power and all the other expedients which have been tried for centuries—and have always failed," he predicted. "We propose to substitute for all these a universal organization in which all the peace-loving Nations will finally have a chance to join." The agreements about elections as well as those about the international organization encouraged him to believe that a new world could take shape. The note of uncertainty in the message related chiefly to his concern about the ways in which Congress would respond.

Most congressmen and most Americans applauded the agreements on elections and the international organization. There were exceptions. Polish-Americans were alarmed, and so was Senator Vandenberg, who represented many of them. He, however, was restrained by his support for the international organization and by his appointment as a delegate to the forthcoming conference in San Francisco that would, it was hoped, reach the final decisions on that new institution.

Developments on the fighting fronts reinforced the optimism that many Americans felt. The bombing of Japan was becoming heavier. On March 9 and 10, a fleet of B-29s moved against Tokyo from the Marianas and dropped their devastating fire bombs, killing more than 80,000 people in the most destructive air raid in history. The Air Force leader in the Marianas, General Curtis LeMay, drove his crews at an exhausting pace, hoping to end the war against Japan without an invasion.

The Army and Navy also moved closer to Japan. In March, American forces gained control of Iwo Jima, an island of major importance in the defense of Japan against air attacks. The Americans as well as the Japanese suffered heavy losses, but the United States was now only 700 miles from Japan and in a position to hit her even more heavily from the air. Then, on April 1, American forces moved into the very tough battle for Okinawa. Only 350 miles from one of the main parts of Japan, Kyushu, it could play a major role in an invasion.

By late March, Germany was very close to collapse. Although the bombing had not accomplished as much as the air power theorists had predicted, it had inflicted very heavy damage and had nearly exhausted the supply of targets. On the ground, German armies were suffering very heavy losses. Hitler, however, refused to allow his commanders to surrender.

The Western Allies disagreed once again about the best way of bringing the European war to an end. Eisenhower now emphasized a quick move against German forces in central Germany and hoped to work out agreements with the Russians about the places in which the armies would halt their advances so as to avoid clashes between Russian and Western forces. The British, on the other hand, continued to press for a quick thrust to Berlin, and Churchill also suggested that Western troops should be moved as far east as possible and kept there until the Russians fulfilled promises made at Yalta and pulled back their troops.

Eisenhower's attention was still focused on Germany, while Churchill's was shifting to Russia. To Eisenhower, Berlin no longer seemed militarily significant. His objective was the destruction of the German Army as quickly as possible, and he feared that if Western forces rushed to Berlin and came into conflict with Russian armies, portions of the German Army might escape into Norway and southern Germany, fight a holding action in mountainous terrain, and thereby extend the length of the war. The British Prime Minister thought that the war against Germany was essentially over and that thus other objectives, such as British security, the shape of postwar Europe, and the threat of Russian power, should now be considered, and he hoped to move into a strong position in relation to the Russians.

In their discussions with American leaders, however, the British still did not press these political considerations. In fact, Eisenhower concluded from the discussions that the British sought glory for Montgomery and other British soldiers. The American general, in turn, wanted his subordinates, especially General Omar Bradley, to contribute significantly in the final stages of the war.

Roosevelt continued to back Eisenhower. The American President still sought ways of working with the Russians and still hoped to avoid military confrontations with them. Thus, he and Marshall did not order their top general in Europe to follow the British advice.

Roosevelt was concerned about Russian behavior in Eastern Europe. It did not conform with American desires. Stalin still did not trust the West; he feared that Roosevelt and Churchill would reach a separate peace with Germany at Russia's expense, and he worked to strengthen his position. He was determined to maintain a Communist-dominated government in Poland rather than to permit the establishment of a broad anti-Fascist one, and the Russians forced a pro-Russian government on Romania.

Distressed by these developments, Roosevelt joined Churchill in criticism of them, but the American President had not lost confidence that the world that he desired could be created. He would not use military pressures in Eastern Europe, but he did agree to a change in Lend-Lease policy that was in line with congressional wishes and would prevent Russia from obtaining significant amounts of heavy industrial equipment under Lend-Lease after the war. This increased the importance of a reconstruction loan, and he continued to dangle that prospect before the Soviet Union.

Roosevelt did not have time to solve the problems that he faced by early April, for he died on the twelfth. He passed on a substantial amount of power. Under his leadership, his nation had become much stronger than ever before, had moved close to victory over Germany and Japan, and had advanced plans for the reconstruction of world affairs. He had not, however, passed on an easily managed situation. The war was going very well, but extended fighting against Japan appeared to be ahead, and conflict between Russia and the West was increasing. A new international organization was taking shape and might improve international affairs, but it was not yet in existence. The United States had become a global power, but even a global power had limits on its strength.

SUGGESTIONS FOR ADDITIONAL READING

Again, attention should be called to the items cited in Chapter 17. Most of them remain very helpful. The debate over military strategy in the late stages of the war in Europe is dealt with most successfully in Ambrose's biography of Eisenhower as well as his smaller book, *Eisenhower and Berlin, 1945: The Decision to Halt at the Elbe*, Norton, New York, 1967. See also his *Rise to Globalism: American Foreign Policy 1938–1970*, Penguin, Baltimore, 1971. The British position on this and related issues, which Ambrose rejects, is developed in Chester Wilmot, *The Struggle for Europe*, Harper & Row, New York, 1952. On economic issues, see Thomas G. Paterson, "The Abortive American Loan to Russia and the Origins of the Cold War, 1943–1946," *Journal of American History*, vol. 56, pp. 70–92, 1969, which is highly critical of the handling of the loan question, and George C. Herring, "Lend-Lease to Russia and the Origins of the Cold War, 1944–1945," ibid., pp. 93–114, which challenges both the official and the revisionist accounts of the handling of Lend-Lease to the Soviet Union. For a sample of the literature on the Yalta Conference, a highly controversial subject, compare William Henry Chamberlain, *America's Second Crusade*, Regnery, Chicago, 1950; Sidney Warren, *The President as World Leader*, Lippincott, Philadelphia, 1964; and Diane Shaver Clemens, *Yalta*, Oxford University Press, New York, 1970. On another controversial subject, the surrender policy, compare Paul Kecskemeti, *Strategic Surrender: The Politics of Victory and Defeat*, Stanford University Press, Stanford, Calif., 1958; John L. Snell, *Wartime Origins of the East-West Dilemma over Germany*, J. G. Hauser, Inc., New Orleans, 1959; and Anne Armstrong, *Unconditional Surrender: The Impact of the Casablanca Policy upon World War II*, Rutgers University Press, New Brunswick, N.J., 1961. Gary R. Hess has taken a close look at FDR's ideas about Indochina in "Franklin Roosevelt and Indochina, " *Journal of American History*, vol. 59, pp. 353–368, 1972.

Chapter 23

Victory—and Frustration

Roosevelt's death did not check the march toward victory or block efforts to establish the United Nations Organization. And it did not lead to abrupt change in America's relations with the Soviet Union. The new President continued his predecessor's policies, avoided Wilson's fate in the effort to bring the United States into an international organization, and brought the war to an end, reaching that goal even more quickly than had been expected. Unhappiness with Russian behavior in Eastern Europe persisted and grew, and President Truman increased American criticism of it. He was restrained, however, by a sense of need for Russian help in some of his projects. American power grew even greater during Truman's early months as president, but the nation continued to suffer frustration as well as to enjoy victory.

International affairs dominated Harry Truman's early months in the White House, but he was not a man of large experience in this area. He had not been trained as a diplomat or as a maker of foreign policy. In fact, Roosevelt had not given him special training for his new responsibilities.

Truman's chief task during his brief vice-presidency had been the rebuilding of cooperation between the Senate and the President. The new Vice President believed that, because of his experience and his personality, he could change their relations by working closely with the senators and FDR and interpreting them to one another. He was especially interested in laying the groundwork for Senate ratification of the administration's program for the postwar world. Truman felt obligated to help his chief avoid Wilson's failure. World peace, he assumed, depended largely on "whether a peace treaty can be written which will be ratified by the Senate."

Truman worked on important matters, but he was not trained for the problems of the presidency in 1945. Talk about the possibility that Roosevelt's health would prevent him from serving to the end of his fourth term persisted after the campaign, and Truman worried that he would be forced to take over. Roosevelt, however, made no effort to train his lieutenant for the job. He did attend meetings of the Cabinet and the congressional leaders with the President, but they were rare. The Vice President spent a larger amount of time as the representative of the White House at social functions. Had Roosevelt been inclined to train a successor, he would have had little time for it because he was out of Washington much of the time, traveling first to Yalta and then to Warm Springs, Georgia, where he died. Thus, the two men had seldom conferred with one another, and now Truman had the responsibilities that had been Roosevelt's.

Truman did bring to the White House a point of view on international affairs. The product of his own experiences as a soldier and the nation's experiences in world affairs since World War I, his point of view stressed political considerations, especially the distribution of power, the importance of the military factor in international affairs, and the need to deal forcefully with aggressive nations.

Truman believed that the United States must play a very significant role in the world in the postwar period. The other side of this basic conviction was fear that the American people would retreat into isolation. That policy had failed in the past and seemed certain to fail in the future. While he hoped that the nation would be able to trade and invest abroad, these economic considerations did not dominate his thinking on foreign policy. While he hoped that the nation would be a member of a new international organization, he did not believe that the United States could function successfully without a substantial military establishment. He regarded military power as very important, believed that military weakness had led to trouble in the past, and was convinced that America must be strong and tough. He did not introduce into the White House an especially negative attitude toward the Soviet Union, but he did bring with him convictions as to how expanding nations should be treated.

Truman's thinking on international affairs was dominated by political considerations. He was determined to avoid what he regarded as the errors of the past: national weakness and a refusal to get involved in international problems. He recognized that the nation now had two very important forms of power—both economic and military strength—but he did not regard American ability as unlimited. An awareness of limits had dictated his support for Lend-Lease and influenced his attitude toward an international organization. And he regarded popular attitudes, such as isolationism, as limiting factors. Thus, he assumed that the United States could not do all that it might wish to do or accomplish all that it might hope to accomplish.

The United States could contribute significantly to the defeat of Hitler's Germany. By April 12, that job was almost done. The German armies were defeated, but Hitler had not yet surrendered. He held back in hope of making a deal with the West and joining with them in an anti-Communist campaign, but Truman accepted Roosevelt's unconditional surrender policy and joined Churchill in insisting upon such a surrender. On April 30, Hitler committed suicide; shortly thereafter, the German commander in Italy surrendered, and on May 8, the new German government did so.

Germany had suffered total defeat, and now the Allies could begin the task of reconstruction. Her once great military force had been destroyed, and now military governments were quickly established by the Allies, replacing the Nazi government, and Nazi leaders were seized and imprisoned. Roosevelt and his War and Treasury Departments had advocated a harsh, repressive peace, believing that the peace after World War I had been too soft and had been a great mistake. The Morgenthau plan had represented the extreme form of this proposal. The State Department, however, had advocated rehabilitation. Leaders there hoped to create the conditions needed to convert Germany into a democracy. Now, the administration moved quickly away from the harsh peace idea, emphasized change in the German political system, and left Germany's economic future somewhat unclear. The State Department's influence was on the rise, while War Department leaders were changing their minds about the treatment of Germany. It was symbolic of the defeat of the harsh peace proposal that Truman asked for and received Morgenthau's resignation in July.

Washington had decided to work for a militarily weak but economically strong and politically stable Germany. Several considerations influenced this decision. One was recognition of Germany's economic importance; another was fear that the weakening of the German economy would force the United States to provide very costly relief programs.

The decision was also influenced by growing concern about Russian ambitions. Administration leaders feared that Russia would exploit economic chaos in Germany and elsewhere in Europe.

The new President was critical of Soviet behavior. Ambassador Harriman, James Forrestal, the Secretary of Navy, and Admiral William Leahy, among others, had concluded well before Truman came to power that cooperation with the Russians was very difficult, that they had great territorial ambitions, and that the United States must be tougher in dealing with them, and they urged him to adopt a firmer line. And he did accept their advice, at least to a degree. On April 23, for example, he criticized Russia's top diplomat, Molotov, for his nation's performance in Poland, which the President regarded as a violation of the Yalta agreements.

Although he was troubled by Russian behavior in Eastern Europe as Roosevelt had been, Truman's efforts to influence it were restrained by the same types of considerations that had restrained his predecessor, including a desire to avoid a military clash with the Soviet Union. In the last weeks of the war against Germany, he had, like Roosevelt before him, rejected Churchill's ideas about the use of military power. Late in April, an American general, George Patton, was close to Prague, and Churchill and his military chiefs argued that he should capture that capital. Churchill believed that the move would have significant political consequences, especially in containing Russian expansion. Eisenhower, however, opposed such an operation as diversionary and likely to produce a clash with the Russians, and Truman accepted the advice of his military commander.

In June, Truman once again rejected a Churchill plan. The British Prime Minister recommended that the American and British armies should not withdraw to their agreed-upon occupation zones until the Western Allies were satisfied with Russian behavior in Eastern Europe. Eisenhower and others, including Stimson and leaders in the State Department, opposed the suggestion, arguing that it would promote conflict rather than cooperation, and Truman vetoed the proposal.

Several considerations influenced Truman's decisions. One was his desire to avoid a delay in the transfer of American troops from Europe to the Far East. The President also did not want to break with policies that had been developed by Roosevelt. Beyond that, he did not want to set a bad example. Breaking the agreement on occupation zones would interfere with his efforts to get the Russians to live up to the agreements that they had made. He was not ready to give up hope that Americans could, without using military force, persuade the Russians to change their behavior in Eastern Europe. Furthermore, he feared that Churchill's suggestions would lead to a dangerous and unwanted military confrontation.

Thus, Western forces retreated to previously defined zones of occupation soon after the German surrender. So did the Russian troops. They had suffered very heavy losses in their efforts to liberate Berlin, but now they allowed the British and the Americans to occupy the zones that had been defined for them in that German city.

Truman was more receptive to Harriman's advice to use economic pressure to accomplish Western political objectives. The President suggested to Molotov in April that Congress would not approve of aid if Russia continued to behave as she was in Eastern Europe; the administration reduced Lend-Lease aid to Russia following the German surrender so that the Russians would get only what they needed to fight Japan, and he continued to delay the decision on a loan even after congressional legislation in July made a $1 billion loan possible without further discussion in Congress. He also delayed discussion of German reparations and opposed amounts that would seriously damage the German economy and force Germany to turn to the United States for relief, and then, at the Potsdam Conference in July, Truman and his Secretary of State, James Byrnes, opposed Russian demands for heavy reparations and forced an agreement on an amount well below the Russian request.

All this did not add up to a very forceful use of economic power. The United States did deprive the Russians of one alternative to a reconstruction loan, Lend-Lease, and cut the size of another alternative, reparations. But the administration did not move beyond suggestions as to how Russia should behave if she wished a loan. Washington did not engage in hard bargaining over a loan before the end of the war. And Lend-Lease was not used to extort concessions.

To change the situation in Eastern Europe, Truman and his aides relied mainly on words. They included Truman's harsh criticism in April and more gentle efforts at persuasion by his representative, Harry Hopkins, in a conference with Stalin late in May and early in June. And Truman tried criticism, appeals, and persuasion at the Potsdam Conference late the following month. The President was actually more optimistic and less critical than most of his advisers. He had not given up hope in the possibility of cooperation, although he and his aides were deeply troubled by Russian behavior in Eastern Europe.

American words did not persuade the Russians to change their ways. They continued to strengthen their political control of the region and to seize industrial machinery and other parts of the economy. They also defended their actions against American criticism, emphasizing the requirements of Russian security. And they criticized American behavior in Italy and British behavior in Greece and suggested that they should be allowed a free hand in Eastern Europe just as they allowed Great Britain and the United States to control the countries they occupied.

Thus, the American administration experienced frustration in Eastern Europe. It was not, however, the administration's largest interest in the summer of 1945. Truman and his lieutenants were also interested in establishing the United Nations Organization and in defeating the Japanese, and those interests affected Washington's handling of the issue of Eastern Europe. For Washington wanted Moscow's cooperation in both of those projects.

Since Roosevelt's death, Truman had been carrying on the battle on behalf of the new international institution and American membership in it. He described it as a battle to build "a new world—a far better world—one in which the eternal dignity of man will be respected," but he did not expect to discard old ways completely. He did not believe that the new institution would enable the United States to destroy all of its military power. He planned to have a strong military establishment after the war and advocated the creation of a program of universal military training for America's young men. And he and his aides did not want to construct an international organization that would destroy American influence in Latin America or prevent the United States from maintaining control of and establishing bases on the islands it had conquered in the Pacific. As American leaders viewed it, the new organization would provide opportunities for the extension of American influence in the world. They hoped that the new international institution would promote international cooperation, but they had quite clearly defined ideas about the arrangements that should be made in the world. They were not naïve, unsophisticated men who assumed that America's interests, as they defined them, could be served by a small American role in world affairs. They believed instead that the United States should be the major power, and they hoped that the United Nations would work effectively to create and maintain the kind of world that they believed the United States needed for prosperity and peace.

In the international conference in San Francisco, the administration enjoyed a high degree of success but did not avoid international conflict, including conflict with Russia. Agreements were reached on the establishment of an international organization, but a new world did not come into existence. Nations clashed, and they clashed over old issues, including spheres of influence. Russian influence in Eastern Europe and American influence in Latin America produced much of the debate. Such strong critics of Russian behavior as Ambassador Harriman and Senator Vandenberg participated prominently in the conference and came away convinced that the United States could not cooperate with the Soviet Union.

The conference did, however, establish an international organization, and Truman now moved on to victory at home. On July 28, the Senate, by a vote of 89 to 2, ratified American participation in the new organization. Truman had avoided Wilson's fate.

Another major task remained unfinished. This was victory over Japan. The United States had continued to move toward that goal since Roosevelt's death. By summer, American forces and their allies had gained control of nearly all of the Philippine Islands and had defeated the Japanese in Okinawa. The victories, however, had been purchased at heavy cost. At Okinawa, the Navy, as well as the Army and the Marine Corps, suffered very heavy losses. Naval losses were due chiefly to suicide—Kamikaze—attacks by Japanese pilots upon American ships.

The very tough battle at Okinawa, plus the earlier bloody battle for control of Iwo Jima, strengthened convictions that the invasion of Japan would be very costly for American forces. Consequently, most American leaders, including General Marshall, continued to regard Russian participation in the war against Japan as highly desirable. There were exceptions to this consensus, including Ambassador Harriman. They had come to doubt that Russia should be drawn into the Far Eastern war, and they urged Truman to reconsider the agreements on the Far East that had been made at Yalta. He was reluctant to break agreements that had been made by his predecessor, however, and he agreed with those who argued that the United States needed Russian help. Thus, at Potsdam, he obtained from Stalin a personal reaffirmation of Russia's determination to fight Japan.

Truman and his aides might have appraised the situation differently if they had had greater confidence in the atomic bomb project. The first test of the product of this $2 billion project was not made, however, until July 16, the day before the Potsdam Conference began.

By August, Truman had two bombs that he could use against Japan. His predecessor would surely have used them if he had been in Truman's situation. Roosevelt had, after all, been chiefly responsible for the project and had regarded it as very important. He had been spurred along by fear that the Germans would develop the new weapon before the Americans did, and he had supported the policy of tight secrecy insisted upon by the Army, which controlled the project. While the British as well as the Americans were involved in it, the Russians were not, and Roosevelt had rejected suggestions from scientists in late 1944 that the Russians should be told about the bomb. By then, project leaders predicted that the first

Figure 25   The Potsdam Conference (*U.S. Army Photo*)

bomb would be ready by August 1 and a second would become available
before the end of 1945, and Roosevelt intended that they would be used.
Use would be in line with the way in which the United States fought the
war, which involved heavy reliance upon technology, and use would be in
harmony with the devastating fire bomb raids that were made before
Roosevelt's death.

The Truman administration knew that Japan was defeated but also
recognized the Japan was not ready to surrender on American terms.
Strategic bombing, which was very heavy during June and July, had
severely damaged Japan's industry and inflicted heavy losses on the
civilian population, and American submarines had blockaded Japan so
that the people could not get enough food. The administration recognized

that Japan's sea and air power were nearly destroyed and that a peace faction, which included the Emperor, had substantial political strength and was seeking to negotiate an end to the war. Washington also recognized that the peace faction had substantial opposition, which included the still strong Army, and that opposition to the demand for unconditional surrender was widespread. American leaders were determined to produce great changes within Japan, including the removal from power of wartime leaders, other than the Emperor, and the demilitarization, democratization, and liberalization of the nation, and to destroy the empire that had been developed over half a century, and Washington was convinced that only massive military force could produce these changes.

Following Japan's rejection on July 28 of a new surrender proposal, which repeated the unconditional principle, Truman decided that he must use the new weapon. Influenced by uncertainty concerning the bomb's effectiveness, the administration rejected suggestions from most scientists connected with the project for a demonstration in an uninhabited area, and the President decided to use the bomb without warning against population centers, just as the fire bombs had been used. The only alternative seemed to be a costly invasion, preceded by heavy bombing and bombardment and a strangling blockade and followed by extended and bloody fighting in Japan against a still-strong and zealous Army of 2 to 3 million men. The invasion, for which final plans had been made in the spring, was scheduled for November 1. Kyushu was to be the first target, and Honshu was to be attacked on March 1, 1946. Now the bomb seemed likely to make invasion unnecessary and also to make it unnecessary for Russia to enter the war. The bomb, not American or Russian ground forces, could accomplish the objective.

Two bombs, coupled with Russian entry into the war, produced an unexpectedly quick surrender. The first bomb, carried by a B-29 from the Marianas, obliterated Hiroshima on August 6, killing at least 70,000 people; Russia declared war on August 8 and quickly moved against the Japanese on the mainland, and a second bomb hit Nagasaki on August 9, taking the lives of 35,000 people. Conventional bombing continued throughout the period, and other atomic bombs were to be dropped as they became available. But on August 14, Japan accepted surrender terms that conformed to American objectives, left the Emperor on the throne, but subordinated him to the commander of the occupation forces.

The defeat of Japan made the United States the dominant influence in that important and productive, although seriously damaged, country. At Potsdam, American leaders had rejected a British suggestion that the Combined Chiefs of Staff should manage the war against Japan and had maintained American control of it, and they had also turned down

Figure 26   Nagasaki (*Wide World Photos*)

Moscow's request to participate in the occupation. Thus, American forces alone moved into this major Asian nation and gained an opportunity to shape its development.

 Victory also enlarged the American presence in Asia in other ways. The nation regained its position in the Philippines and acquired other Pacific islands, including Okinawa. The United States also moved onto the continent, occupying the southern half of Korea, previously a part of the Japanese empire.

 Victory did not, however, establish the United States as the dominant force in Asia. The Russians also made gains there, establishing positions in Manchuria and Sakhalin, and affairs in China were not moving in the direction that Washington desired. Russia as well as the United States now supported Chiang, but he was unable to establish control, and the country was moving toward civil war. And developments elsewhere in Asia conflicted with American anti-imperialism. After the fighting stopped, the British returned to Burma and Malaya; the Dutch returned to the East Indies and the French returned to Indochina. The United States had relaxed its pressure against Western imperialism after Truman came to power and was not in a position to promote trusteeships or independence. British forces, not American, had led the campaign to liberate Southeast Asia from the Japanese and had accepted the surrender of the Japanese troops there. Furthermore, many Washington officials had reservations about the leaders of the independence movements, such as Ho Chi Minh in Indochina, regarding them as too close to Moscow.

Thus, there were limits on American power in Asia. The United States did not have many troops on the continent at the end of the war, and it was linked with unpopular regimes, Chiang in China and the imperial powers in South and Southeast Asia.

Nevertheless, American power and influence had become very large in some very important parts of Asia, above all Japan. The situation in Europe was similar. The movement of American troops had made the United States a major influence in the most productive parts, including the highly industrialized Ruhr Valley, an area now occupied by American and British forces. In Europe also, however, there were limits on the American accomplishment.

There were even limits on American strength in Western Europe. Washington was far from satisfied with the regime that was now in control of France and was also troubled by political developments in Great Britain. Late in July, Churchill had been rejected by the British people, and the Labour party had been elected. That party's plans for the nationalization of basic industries alarmed many American leaders.

Russia and Eastern Europe were the most troubling parts of the world by the late summer of 1945. In those places, the limits on American power were most obvious. The successful testing of the atomic bomb had enlarged the administration's sense of power, and this development had seemed to some officials, including the President, to strengthen their hands in dealing with the Russians. It had encouraged them to hope that they could now persuade the Russians to change their behavior in Eastern Europe. Evidence of this hope has suggested to some historians that the bomb was used against Japan, not to influence the Japanese, but to demonstrate to the Russians how powerful the United States had become. No direct evidence has been presented in support of this interpretation, however, and the use of the bomb was not followed by a change in Russian behavior. The Russians continued to reconstruct Eastern Europe in ways that conflicted with American views.

The war had enlarged American power. Bigger than any earlier war, it was also more destructive as a consequence of technological developments, but the United States was not damaged by it as other nations were. It destroyed much of the strength of the defeated nations but also damaged most of the victors in serious ways. Thirty-five million people were killed. At least half of them were Russians, and the Russian losses included approximately 7 million members of the armed forces. The United States, on the other hand, lost less than 400,000 people, almost all of whom were in uniform. The war inflicted very heavy damage on almost all the major economies of the world, including Russia's, but the American economy was strengthened and enlarged. The main element of Russian power was now her army, which was the largest in the world, but the American Army was second only to the Russian force, and the American Navy was the world's largest. Furthermore, the United States had a monopoly on the new weapon of mass destruction and on the means of delivering it to remote targets.

Thus, although there were still limits on American power, it had been enlarged enormously by the war. Other nations, especially the Russians, still had power that enabled them to resist American pressure and shape their own futures, and the American Congress was not ready to support every proposal designed to influence developments in other parts of the world. The Congress was not ready, for example, to use American economic power in large-scale programs of economic assistance. The economy, however, was stronger than ever before, and so was the American military establishment.

This pattern of strength and limitations had enabled Truman to enjoy victories and suffer frustrations during his first four months in the White House. He had brought the war against Germany and Japan to an end on terms that American leaders desired; he had carried to completion the plans for the establishment of and American membership in the United Nations Organization, and he had enlarged the American presence in Europe and Asia. Yet, relations with the Soviet Union had deteriorated. Truman's accomplishments, and the nation's, while very large, were not as large as the President and other leaders hoped they would be. The world did not conform to American desires at every point.

SUGGESTIONS FOR ADDITIONAL READING

Most of the items already cited on diplomatic and military history during the war remain helpful here. On Truman's foreign policy, also see Herbert Feis, *Between War and Peace: The Potsdam Conference*, Princeton University Press, Princeton, N.J., 1960. Feis has also made a major contribution to the controversy over the dropping of the bomb: *The Atomic Bomb and the End of World War II*, Princeton University Press, Princeton, N.J., 1966. The most controversial book on this subject is by Gar Alperovitz, *Atomic Diplomacy: Hiroshima and Potsdam*, Simon & Schuster, New York, 1965. He argues that the desire to influence Russian behavior was the decisive influence. Other important items on this subject include Louis Morton, "The Decision to Use the Atomic Bomb," *Foreign Affairs*, vol. 25, pp. 334–353, 1957, and Richard G. Hewlett and Oscar E. Anderson, *The New*

World, 1938–1946, The Pennsylvania State University Press, University Park, 1962. The latter is also the major study of the development of the bomb.

For discussions of the controversies among historians over Truman's early foreign policy see, in addition to Divine's *Causes and Consequences of World War II*, Arthur M. Schlesinger, Jr., "Origins of the Cold War," *Foreign Affairs*, vol. 46, pp. 22–52, 1967; Christopher Lasch, "The Cold War, Revisited and Re-Visioned," *New York Times Magazine*, January 14, 1968, pp. 26–27, 44–59; Henry Pachter, "Revisionist Historians & the Cold War," *Dissent*, November–December 1968, pp. 505–518; and the relevant essays and commentaries in Kirkendall, ed., *The Truman Period as a Research Field* and the *Truman Period as a Research Field: A Re-examination, 1972*, University of Missouri Press, Columbia, 1973. I have discussed Truman's ideas somewhat more fully in "Truman and the Cold War," which appears in Gerard G. Steckler and Leo Donald Davis, eds., *Studies in Mediavalia and Americana: Essays in Honor of William Lyle Davis, S. J.*, Gonzaga University Press, Spokane, 1973.

Chapter 24

The Significance of the War

The Second World War was an event of giant significance in American history. It was a time of great change in the life of the American people. The war converted the nation into a global power interested in and capable of promoting major changes in many parts of the world and in the relations among nations. At the same time, the war promoted large changes in life inside the United States.

Some of the most important developments were made in the structure and performance of the American economic system. The structure did remain essentially what it had become during the 1930s, but the war promoted additional and substantial structural developments along lines that had emerged earlier. The most obvious was the enormous increase in the size and cost of the federal government and of its role in the economy. The war also stimulated the growth of business firms, especially those that had already become large before the 1940s. And labor organizations also grew in response to wartime conditions. Thus, the economy became even more highly collectivized. More than ever before, it was by 1945 dominated by the interplay among large public and private organizations. The most important were the federal agencies, the large corporations, and the labor unions.

These developments did not represent a sharp break with the past. They were a continuation of well-established themes. One aspect of the story did represent something quite new. This was the emergence of the military as a very important part of the economic system. It had been there before and had had ties with some business firms that supplied the goods it needed. But the military had been only a very small part of American life during the 1930s, and the complex composed of the military establishment and its suppliers had been only a minor part of the economic system. The complex took on great size during the war, and some Washington officials hoped that it would remain very important after the war.

Although the structural developments were important, the changes in the performance of the system were even more impressive. There were some defects in that performance. The system did not provide as much military production as the military leaders desired, and it experienced more inflation than leaders in the administration wanted. The list of successes, however, was even longer. Production levels were adequate for the accomplishment of a major task: the defeat of Italy, Germany, and Japan. Furthermore, there was much less inflation than the nation had experienced during World War I. And the production of consumer goods moved above the prewar level in spite of the great demands that the war placed upon the economy.

For the American people, the war was an economically stimulating rather than an economically destructive force. Wartime fiscal policy and the response of American business to it moved the economy out of the Depression, which had been reduced in size but had not been destroyed completely by the public and private policies of the 1930s. Employment was increased by nearly 40 percent, and unemployment ceased to be a problem. In this situation of rapid economic recovery and rapid economic growth, millions of people moved above the poverty line and millions moved into the middle classes.

For the American people, the war was a source and a period of economic progress, and one consequence was greater confidence in the economic system, There was concern about its performance in the future. Many feared that when wartime spending stopped, wartime shipments to other nations came to an end, and war plants no longer produced the materials of war, the Great Depression would return. Many Americans were convinced, however, that depression could be avoided and that the wartime experience had demonstrated that it need not return. The experience had strengthened confidence in fiscal policy. It had persuaded economists and others that if the federal government functioned wisely, the national economy could perform very successfully.

The war was also a highly significant period in the history of American race relations and a promoter of change in this area. For one group of people, the war brought intense suffering. These were the Japanese-Americans. For them, the war was not a period of progress.

For black Americans, however, the war stimulated a significant challenge to the system of Jim Crow that had been established long before and that remained in place at the beginning of the war. The defense plants and the armed forces provided blacks with new evidence of their second-class status in American society, and these experiences strengthened black determination to protest. The war did not destroy the resistance to change in this area. Most white Americans continued to resist proposals for change in race relations. Nevertheless, the wartime experiences did work in a variety of ways to increase concern among white Americans about race relations in the United States and to increase their interest in reforming this part of American life.

One can exaggerate the amount of change in this area. The developments did have important debts to the past, including the 1930s when important preparations were made. And the war did not destroy the Jim Crow system. Nevertheless, wartime experiences did strengthen the challenge to that system and did move the civil rights issue to a higher place on the American agenda.

The war also was very significant for American power in the world. The war expanded that power enormously. To a very large degree, the changes in the performance of the economy were responsible for this. The economy enabled the United States to develop the two major instruments that it used to affect the behavior of other nations. One was a massive program of economic assistance to America's allies. The other was a large, well-equipped American fighting force. By the end of the war, it was second to no other in destructive power.

The instruments that the United States developed during the war enabled the nation to operate with a high degree of success on both sides of the globe. The United States had not been able to do this in the past. Its operations had been quite limited during World War I, and its operations at the end of the 1930s and the beginning of the 1940s, while quite large, had been quite unsuccessful. Furthermore, the nation had remained predominantly unsuccessful in the early months after it had been drawn into the fighting.

During the war, however, the United States became a major promoter of change in the world. It contributed significantly to the destruction of the political regimes in Italy, Germany, and Japan and to the destruction of their empires and their ability to make war. American leaders refused to compromise with the leaders of those regimes, insisted upon total victory and unconditional surrender, and gained an opportunity to shape the futures of the defeated countries.

The United States also gained a chance to influence developments in some of the areas, such as Western Europe, that were liberated from control by Germany and other Axis powers. American military forces became a large influence in the liberated areas. American economic strength also contributed to American successes there. One of the consequences was the frustration of the parties of the left that also had ambitions in these areas.

In addition, the United States successfully promoted the establishment of a new international organization. To a very large degree, this was an American idea and an American interest. The promoters of this saw themselves as carrying on the work of Woodrow Wilson and as working to change the ways that nations conducted their relations with one another and to bring international affairs into harmony with American principles.

American leaders worked to change the conduct of international affairs, but they did not expect to discard all the old ways. They intended that the United States would remain very influential in Latin America, and they constructed an international organization that did not prevent the United States from acquiring territory of its own in the Pacific that could be used for bases. Administration leaders also planned to maintain a substantial military force, and they expected that the United States would be a major influence in the new international organization and would use it to create the kind of world that Americans desired.

The war enlarged American power enormously but did not give the United States an unlimited amount. The nation developed large instruments to influence international affairs, but it was also forced to depend upon allies for help. It was not able to do or accomplish precisely what it wished.

The limits on American power were obvious in China. Roosevelt had great hopes for its emergence as a strong democratic nation, but the United States could not give the Chinese much help in their war against the Japanese and could not convert the government of Chiang Kai-shek into an effective and enlightened regime. By the end of the war, the Chinese situation was moving in directions that Washington regarded as undesirable, even though the Japanese had lost their bid for control.

The United States had enough strength to contribute to the weakening of Western imperialism but not enough to bring about the destruction of it. American leaders, including Roosevelt, criticized it frequently, proposed international trusteeships as a substitute, and pressured the British on the imperial preference system, but American pressures and proposals were resisted by others, especially Churchill. Also, American leaders were restrained by their desires for cooperation with the British and by their fear of some of the revolutionary leaders in the colonial world. American influence as an anti-imperial force was also restricted by the movement of armies against the Japanese. Those movements did not make the United States the dominant power on the Asian mainland.

While it became very great, American power in Western Europe also had limits. The United States contributed significantly to the liberation of France, but the regime that replaced the Nazis was not fully satisfactory to American leaders. They worked closely with the British during the war but were distressed by the triumph of the left in British politics at the end of the war.

The limits on American power were especially apparent in Eastern Europe. While the war inflicted very severe damage on the Russian people, their armed forces, and their economy, it also created a large opportunity for Russia, and Stalin and his aides seized the opening created by the movement of armies in Eastern Europe and used the instruments that they had to shape political developments there. The United States tried to influence Russian behavior in the region but failed to accomplish this objective.

By the end of the war, the future was filled with uncertainties. It appeared that the nation now knew how to avoid a depression, but it was not certain that the United States would do so. Pressure for change in race relations seemed likely to persist, but the success that it would enjoy could not be predicted. The American people would surely continue to play a large role in the world, but just how large the role would be and just how it would be played awaited definition. They could operate chiefly within the international organization, or they could rely mainly on their own power. The nation could expect to continue to influence developments elsewhere, but victory at every point was not guaranteed.

The future was uncertain, as futures always are, but Americans knew that their recent past had been very significant. The Second World War had been a time of great changes for the United States. The war had produced many changes at home and had produced even more spectacular ones in the nation's relations with the rest of the world. The United States had experienced a great increase in its power, had shaped political developments in many places, and had modified the ways in which nations conducted their affairs. Yet, the war had not made the United States all-powerful. By late summer of 1945, the still-limited nature of American power was very obvious in Eastern Europe.

Conclusion

In the sixteen years since 1929, two major crises had hit American life and changed it significantly. The nation had not made a complete break with the past. Many old parts of American life, including the basic political and economic institutions, remained in place. American leaders had, in fact, deliberately preserved those institutions, protecting them against serious challenges at home and abroad, and the American people had resisted as well as demanded change. Furthermore, preparations for the changes, such as the enlargement of the federal government and of the nation's role in the world, had been made before the 1930s, indicating that they were not merely responses to the special conditions of the years after 1929.

Nevertheless, the United States in 1945 differed significantly from what it had been in 1929. Its economy was much more highly collectivized, and its role and power in the world were much larger and greater. The fast-moving, action-packed years had also made the economic system much more productive and altered class and race relations and

other important aspects of American life, including the status of the
military. Americans could still debate about their relations with one
another and with other people and about their institutions, but the debates
of the future would take place in a situation that had been influenced in
large ways by the years of crisis and change from 1929 to 1945.

Index